Experiences of
in Predominan
Institutions

Centered on the narratives from ethnically and racially diverse scholars of color with experience studying and working in predominantly White institutions in the United States, this volume offers critical reflection on common assumptions, policies, and practices which limit or preclude racial diversity and inclusion in various types of educational contexts and settings.

Scholars at different stages of their careers and from varied sociocultural backgrounds offer powerful critiques of contemporary experiences of disproportionality, mis/labelling, and exploitation, among others. Exploring both personal and professional repercussions of these lived inequalities, the candid insights of racialized challenges and imbalances are linked to the schooling experiences of minoritized K-12 learners and their families. This book proposes solutions to promote equitable and inclusive environments for faculty and scholars from racialized backgrounds in higher education with a specific focus on universities with education programs.

Students, scholars, and researchers across a broad number of fields including Educational Leadership, Ethnic Studies, Teacher Education, Higher Education may benefit from the discussions provided in this work.

Rachel Endo is Founding Dean and Professor in the School of Education at the University of Washington Tacoma. Her research interests are in the areas of critical and decolonizing approaches to multicultural education, the language and literacy practices of diverse populations, and urban teacher education. She holds a Ph.D. in Language and Literacy Education from the University of Illinois at Urbana-Champaign.

Routledge Research in Educational Equality and Diversity

Books in the series include:

Intersectional Pedagogy
Creative Education Practices for Gender and Peace Work
Gal Harmat

Schools as Queer Transformative Spaces
Global Narratives on Sexualities and Genders
Jón Ingvar Kjaran and Helen Sauntson

Promoting Academic Readiness for African American Males with Dyslexia
Implications for Preschool to Elementary School Teaching
Edited by Shawn Anthony Robinson & Corey Thompson

High Achieving African American Students and the College Choice Process
Applying Critical Race Theory
Thandeka K. Chapman, Frances Contreras, Eddie Comeaux, Eligio Martinez Jr. and Gloria M. Rodriguez

Community Participation with Schools in Developing Countries
Towards Equitable and Inclusive Basic Education for All
Edited by Mikiko Nishimura

Experiences of Racialization in Predominantly White Institutions
Critical Reflections on Inclusion in US Colleges and Schools of Education
Edited by Rachel Endo

For more information about this series, please visit: www.routledge.com/Routledge-Research-in-Educational-Equality-and-Diversity/book-series/RREED

Experiences of Racialization in Predominantly White Institutions

Critical Reflections on Inclusion in US Colleges and Schools of Education

Edited by Rachel Endo

Routledge
Taylor & Francis Group

NEW YORK AND LONDON

First published 2021
by Routledge
52 Vanderbilt Avenue, New York, NY 10017

and by Routledge
2 Park Square, Milton Park, Abingdon, Oxon, OX14 4RN

Routledge is an imprint of the Taylor & Francis Group, an informa business

© 2021 Taylor & Francis

Library of Congress Cataloging-in-Publication Data
Names: Endo, Rachel K., editor.
Title: Experiences of racialization in predominantly white institutions : critical reflections on inclusion in US colleges and schools of education / edited by Rachel Endo.
Description: Abingdon, Oxon ; New York, NY : Routledge, 2021. | Includes bibliographical references and index.
Identifiers: LCCN 2020015090 (print) | LCCN 2020015091 (ebook) | ISBN 9780367376987 (hardback) | ISBN 9780367544850 (paperback) | ISBN 9780429355639 (ebook)
Subjects: LCSH: Segregation in higher education—United States. | United States—Race relations. | Education, Higher—Social aspects—United States. | College teachers—United States—Attitudes. | Race discrimination—United States.
Classification: LCC LC212.72 .E87 2021 (print) | LCC LC212.72 (ebook) | DDC 378.73089/96073—dc23
LC record available at https://lccn.loc.gov/2020015090
LC ebook record available at https://lccn.loc.gov/2020015091

ISBN: 978-0-367-37698-7 (hbk)
ISBN: 978-0-367-54485-0 (pbk)
ISBN: 978-0-429-35563-9 (ebk)

Typeset in Sabon
by Apex CoVantage, LLC

Contents

    SANDRA L. GUZMAN FOSTER

7   Disproportionate Underrepresentation of Faculty of
    Color in Education: A Critical disAbility Studies in
    Education (dSE) Analysis   99
    HYUN UK KIM

8   From the Mekong River to the Merrimack River: One
    Lao American Refugee's Journey Through the Academy   109
    PHITSAMAY SYCHITKOKHONG UY

9   Still Searching: My Present Reality   120
    KEITHA-GAIL MARTIN-KERR

10 "You Need to Be More Social": Controlling Images of
    Black Women in Tenure Dossiers   130
    STEPHANIE L. BURRELL STORMS

11 Iconic Modernism and Gendered-Racialized Realities   139
    SHEILA W. STAMM

    Conclusion – From Relics of Racial Oppression to Sites
    of Authentic Inclusion: Challenges and Possibilities   152
    RACHEL ENDO

    References   160
    Index   175

Acknowledgments

After a five-year pregnancy, a beautiful baby (i.e., this book) has finally been birthed into this world. Foremost, I thank all of the authors for contributing to this project. Your brilliance, candid views, humor, loving ways, refusal, and wit will capture many hearts, minds, and souls across "the color line." Continue to share your experiences, knowledge, and wisdom with the world. Continue to insist on equity wherever you go. Also, special thanks to Sheila W. Stamm, my dear friend, mentor, and much-admired woman warrior, for generously allowing us to incorporate her beautiful artwork.

I am always grateful for the intellectual nourishment that my many mentors have offered me over the years. Foremost, I thank Violet Harris for being my North Star. I am deeply honored to know a scholar who embodies the highest level of brilliance and grace in all aspects of life. Other scholars I would like to thank for inspiring and supporting me over the years include Shireen Bingham, Veena Deo, Julia Garrett, the late John Langan, Kevin Kumashiro, Susan Naramore Maher, Gary Marshall, Fayneese Miller, Jody Neathery-Castro, Kent Ono, Yoon Pak, John Pyle, Mike Reynolds, Phil Smith, the late Peter Suzuki, among many others. I thank my intellectual community for keeping me sane over the years, particularly Diem-my Bui, Vichet Chhuon, Mary Ellerbe, Frank Hernandez, Mike Jones, the late Keshia Korman (Bless/Bliss you, heart), Sharon Lee, Shelley Lee, Timothy Lensmire, JB Mayo, Jr., James McShay, Ali Modarres, Naomi Taylor (and Julia and Willie), and Stanley Thangaraj. Special thanks to Bradley Cole for helping me with some last-minute work with this project.

The academy has Yellow Periled me time (and time) again. I often experience deep disaffection . . . until I remember how education scholars, like the contributors of this book, have positively transformed the lives and minds of hundreds of high-talent students. Finally, my extended and immediate families have been the key source of my life and livelihood. I also fondly remember and lovingly acknowledge my ancestors, as well as my relatives who passed away during my lifetime. I am grateful to everyone, alive and deceased, for uplifting me through some of the most trying times of my professional life, especially as I try to find my path as the "free and easy wanderer" – with and/or without the academy.

Author Biographies

Rachel Endo
University of Washington Tacoma
Rachel Endo is Founding Dean and Professor in the School of Education at the University of Washington Tacoma. Her research interests are in the areas of critical and decolonizing approaches to multicultural education, the language and literacy practices of diverse populations, and urban teacher education. She holds a Ph.D. in Language and Literacy Education from the University of Illinois at Urbana-Champaign.

Sandra L. Guzman Foster
University of the Incarnate Word
Sandra L. Guzman Foster is Associate Professor and The Sister Theophane Power Endowed Chair in Education at the University of the Incarnate Word. Her research interests are in the areas of critical multiculturalism, critical pedagogy, reflective practice, and urban education. She holds a Ph.D. in Educational Leadership and Policy Studies from Arizona State University.

Ezekiel Joubert III
California State University, Los Angeles
Ezekiel Joubert III is Assistant Professor in Educational Foundations at California State University, Los Angeles. He was previously an adjunct instructor at Hamline University and Metropolitan State University's Urban Teacher Program in Minnesota. His research interests are in the areas of the educational challenges and visions of Black rural communities, where he researches the ways that Black students and their families respond to and reimagine the contemporary educational structures that prevent equal access to quality education. He holds a Ph.D. in Education with an emphasis in Culture and Teaching from the University of Minnesota.

Hyun Uk Kim
Simmons College
Hyun Uk Kim is Associate Professor in Education at Simmons College. Her research interests are in the areas of autism across cross-cultural

contexts, critical disAbility studies, and equity-focused approaches to special education policy. She holds a Ph.D. in Psychological Studies in Education from the University of California, Los Angeles.

Alvin Logan, Jr.
Seattle Central College

Alvin Logan, Jr., is Director of Student Leadership at Seattle Central College. He also is a Lecturer in the School of Education at the University of Washington Tacoma. His research interests are in the areas of the experiences of Black males in higher education with a special focus on Black collegiate athletes. He holds a Ph.D. in Cultural Studies in Education from the University of Texas at Austin.

Brian D. Lozenski
Macalester College

Brian D. Lozenski is Assistant Professor of Multicultural and Urban Education at Macalester College in the Educational Studies Department. His research explores the intersections of critical participatory action research, Africana Studies, and cultural relevance, particularly in the education of youth of African descent. He holds a Ph.D. in Education with an emphasis in Culture and Teaching from the University of Minnesota.

L. Trenton S. Marsh
University of Central Florida

L. Trenton S. Marsh is Assistant Professor of Urban Education in the Department of Learning Sciences and Educational Research at the University of Central Florida. Prior, he was a postdoctoral fellow for the National Center for Institutional Diversity at the University of Michigan. His research interests include the conceptualization of student success, teacher-student interactions, the social context of education, and school choice with an emphasis on "no excuses" charter schools. He holds a Ph.D. from New York University's Steinhardt School in the Teaching and Learning Department with a concentration in Urban Education.

Keitha-Gail Martin-Kerr
Saint Paul College

Keitha-Gail Martin-Kerr is Associate Dean of Faculty and Staff Development at Saint Paul College. She also has taught courses in the areas of cultural diversity and elementary literacy at Hamline University and the University of Minnesota. Her research interests are in the areas of critical literacy, critical pedagogy, and the educational needs of families and learners from "non-traditional" families. She holds a Ph.D. in Education from the University of Minnesota.

Ferial Pearson
University of Nebraska at Omaha

Ferial Pearson is Assistant Professor in the Teacher Education Department at the University of Nebraska at Omaha. Her primary research interests are in the areas of culturally responsive teaching, socio-emotional learning, mindfulness, and kindness education, and the recruitment and retention of K-12 teachers of color. She holds an Ed.D. in Educational Leadership from the University of Nebraska at Omaha.

Sandra Rodríguez-Arroyo
University of Nebraska at Omaha

Sandra Rodríguez-Arroyo is Associate Professor in the Teacher Education Department at the University of Nebraska at Omaha. Her research interests are in the areas of educational opportunities for English Language Learners (ELLs), assets-based service-learning experiences, and Latina faculty members' *testimonios*. She holds a D.Ed. in Curriculum and Instruction with emphases in ESL and Applied Linguistics from Pennsylvania State University.

Sheila W. Stamm
American Intercontinental College

Sheila W. Stamm is Dean and Professor in the School of Education at American Intercontinental College. She is also President of S. Wright & Associates, which provides consulting support to academic leaders and faculty in higher education and community sectors. Her research interests are in the areas of innovative and interdisciplinary pedagogies, faculty career trajectories, and improving access and responsiveness to diverse learners across PK–20 education. She holds a Ph.D. in Curriculum and Instruction from North Carolina State University.

Stephanie L. Burrell Storms
Fairfield University

Stephanie L. Burrell Storms is Associate Dean and Associate Professor of Multicultural Education in the Graduate School of Education and Allied Professions at Fairfield University. Her research interests are in the areas of education for social justice, faculty development, and assessment and evaluation. She holds an Ed.D. in Social Justice Education from the University of Massachusetts, Amherst.

Phitsamay Sychitkokhong Uy
University of Massachusetts Lowell

Phitsamay Sychitkokhong Uy is Associate Professor in Education and Graduate Coordinator for Ph.D. Programs at the University of Massachusetts Lowell. Her research interests are in the areas of immigrant and refugee youth, Southeast Asian American communities, family and community engagement, and professional-development training. She holds an Ed.D. from the Harvard Graduate School of Education.

Figure 0.1 Window of Opportunity: Be bold, have courage, and take action for the greater good.

Credit: Sheila W. Stamm

A Note on Terminology
The Power of Language

Rachel Endo

"Language matters" (Endo, 2018a, p. 13), as labels and words have the power to both disempower or empower groups and individuals, particularly those who have historically been denied opportunities to narrate their own experiences. This section offers a brief overview of the common labels and terminology used throughout this book. Core labels and terms explained in this section have been standardized across each chapter for the sake of consistency. However, some contributors, to engage in the process of self-definition on their own terms, have elected to provide distinct definitions of certain sociocultural contexts and labels. Ultimately, despite efforts to use common frameworks and language in this book, the authors and I recognize two limitations and realities as follows: (1) language is not neutral, and (2) disagreements abound, even within a group, about how its members desire to identify their collective experiences and identities both outside and within their community or multiple communities.

Drawing from University of Houston's Division of Student Affairs and Enrollment Services guide on diversity-related terminology (n.d.), we offer the following broad definitions of diversity, equity, and inclusion that are applied across the chapters:

1. **Diversity:** the various characteristics of human identity inclusive of both invisible and visible forms of one's many social identities including age, dialect and language, disAbility, ethnicity and race, gender, LGBTQIA identity, nationality, political affiliation, and religion. Due to the stronghold of racial exclusion and segregation in colleges and schools of education and K-12 schools in the United States, diversity here will primarily refer to ethnic and racial identities. However, different forms and types of diversity are often referenced in each chapter based on the unique assemblage of each author's various social identities.
2. **Equity:** is not the same as equality. Within the context of an organization, **equality** is when leaders aspire to treat each person in a similar manner. Often, there is a core set of assumptions among those

who believe in equality that fairness and meritocracy are givens in US society, and thus, it is appropriate and desirable to treat and view all people as "the same" rather than as individuals who come from complex sociocultural contexts. In contrast, an equity lens acknowledges that certain groups and the individuals representing them have historically been denied access to equal opportunities and resources based on one or more of their social identities. Equity-focused actions and perspectives also acknowledge that there are ongoing and significant disparities and power differences among and between certain groups. Promoting equity is thus an intentional effort among an organization's leaders to provide all people with access to information, opportunities, and resources. If equity gaps exist, especially if they are pointed out by those who are disproportionately impacted by them, then intentional actions are taken by leaders to actively identify and reduce these disparities.

3. **Inclusion:** is the intentional act among people in an organization, particularly those in positions of authority and leadership, to create and sustain positive environments where all groups and individuals, particularly those who have been historically excluded and isolated in these spaces, feel respected, supported, valued, and welcomed. Inclusion is also a consistent effort to actively involve, solicit input from, and take feedback from persons from diverse backgrounds, as well as to intentionally include them in decision-making processes that will advance an organization's goals and mission.

Terms such as race, racialization, and racism are also defined within a particular context and specifically focus on US culture, history, and politics. In this book, the authors and I largely draw from the subfield of the sociology of race to contend that racial categories are human-made social constructs and not based on biological differences (Omi & Winant, 1994). Such a view may challenge many, as in the United States, there are ongoing associations linking one's disposition and intelligence to scientific views of racial difference (Webster, 1993). Furthermore, racial categories in the United States, particularly those along the Black-White or White-"non-White" binary, have significantly impacted different groups of people in terms of how ideas or policies are shaped, as well as how scarce resources are allocated in a capitalistic society (Feagin, 2013; Omi & Winant, 1994). It also must be reiterated that Whites, as the dominant group in the United States, have invented and used racial categories to justify the enslavement, genocide, mass incarceration, and segregation of groups that they have labeled as racially different (Feagin, 2013).

Similarly, racialization is a complex process where people, particularly those who are in positions of authority and power, assign different types of racial meaning to groups of people based on assumed or real differences (Omi & Winant, 1994; Webster, 1993). Racialization could include extreme examples of state-sanctioned racial profiling, such as when 120,000 Japanese Americans were incarcerated in the 1940s, based on false assumptions and claims that they were dangerous and disloyal foreigners. Racialization could also entail what could be seen as innocuous and positive generalizations about a group such as labeling Latinx individuals as family oriented and hardworking individuals (Sue, 2010). However, self-racialization could also be used by a subordinate group as a means for its members to demand recognition by mainstream social institutions and to engage in self-definition on their own terms (Espiritu, 1992). For example, the term Asian American did not exist until the 1960s, when activists from culturally, ethnically, and linguistically diverse backgrounds in the West Coast forged solidarities with each other and other racialized Americans to contest racist laws and practices that had historically excluded Asian-origin persons from citizenship and full participation in US society (Espiritu, 1992; Takaki, 1998). We thus recognize that racialized groups often coalesce around certain shared cultural knowledge, symbols, and traditions, as well as shared experiences with racial discrimination and exclusion.

Collectively, this project also uses the following definitions (Sue, 2010, pp. 7–8) as they relate to various types of racism:

1. **Individual racism:** intentional or unintentional actions by members of a dominant group (i.e., Whites) to discriminate, exclude, and/or harm a group of people or an individual from racialized backgrounds. An example is when a White staff member calls the campus safety department at her university whenever a Black male enters into the common area in her office suite, because she just has "a gut feeling" that Black men are dangerous and will physically harm her.
2. **Institutional racism:** when decisions are made by a group in power (i.e., Whites) to intentionally or unintentionally subordinate members of a marginalized racial group. This type of racism often allows a dominant group to financially, individually, and/or socially profit from exploiting and subordinating racialized bodies. Institutionally racist practices are further promulgated when an organization's leaders are unable and/or unwilling to address and tackle them. A common example of institutional racism in higher education is when a university's all-White executive leaders publicly state that they value diversity to attract enrollment among community members from historically underserved backgrounds, but in reality, the campus has a mostly White faculty, leadership, and staff and also has a poor track record supporting students who are from racialized backgrounds.

Any person from any background could exhibit biased behaviors toward another person. However, in the previous definitions of racism, it is vital to clarify that people who are White are the sole perpetrators of individually and institutionally racist acts because they, as a collective, hold the majority of perceived and real political and social power in the United States: "those with the greatest power, principally white Americans in the US case, have the greatest control over society-wide institutional memories, including those recorded by the media and in most history books, organizational histories, laws, textbooks, films, and public monuments" (Feagin, 2013, p. 17). As Matias (2013 further notes, Whites often claim to have benevolent or good intentions when confronted by racialized Americans about racist acts or policies created by them, their institutions, or other Whites. Yet, irrespective of one's intentions, racism is harmful to people who identify as racialized Americans as well as those who are White.

Unless presented in their original context or included using direct quotes, specific labels and terms commonly used in education such as "minority" and "non-White" are not used because they are outdated and problematic. For example, Tatum (1997) notes that as we do not refer to girls or women as "non-males" or "non-men," we similarly should not refer to persons who identify as African American or Black; American Indian, Indigenous, or Native American; Asian American and Pacific Islander; or Hispanic or Latinx under the rubric of "non-White." The pan-ethnic term Latinx is used to recognize the significance of gender-neutral and inclusive terminology. However, two contributors specifically identify as Latina; their ways of self-definition are retained in their chapters. Drawing from Benitez (2010), the term minoritized (e.g., minoritized group) may be used in place of "minority" to acknowledge "there is a history of structural and institutional actions" (p. 131) that have created disparate outcomes among various racialized populations. Similarly, the term racialized (e.g., racialized American) refers to persons who represent populations in the United States that have been subjected to racial exclusion, oppression, and violence. Thus, when referring to people who collectively do not identify as White, terms such as minoritized people, individuals from diverse backgrounds, persons from underrepresented or underserved populations, racialized Americans, individuals, and scholars, and so forth, are used. Also, the terms Indigenous and people of color are purposefully differentiated (rather than grouping everyone together under the latter category) to acknowledge the distinct political and territorial identities of Indigenous communities and tribal nations in the United States (Reese, 2011). Reference to the term BIPOC (Black, Indigenous, and People of Color) may also be used as an umbrella term to refer to persons from racialized backgrounds (The BIPOC Project, n.d.).

Certain labels and terms around abilities, citizenship, and identity also have racialized undertones. For example, it is still common in the United States for laypeople and scholars alike to use the stand-alone term American to automatically reference White Americans and not other racialized populations. In this volume, the racial labels of White or White American/s are explicitly used, as they acknowledge several realities including that persons who are White invented modern racial categories (Tatum, 1997). Whiteness is used to refer to the reality that most social institutions in the United States, including K-12 schools and universities, are primarily managed and occupied by White individuals, even if they do not associate themselves with a racial label (Feagin, 2013). Similarly, the term disAbility is intentionally used instead of "disability" to promote a strengths-based versus deficit approach to refer to persons who have various exceptionalities. Intentional efforts were made to avoid ableist language often appearing in equity-focused scholarship such as color-*blind*, falling on *deaf* ears, and the like. Efforts were also made to use people-first language where appropriate, although one limitation of this framework is how identity-neutral views may be unintentionally perpetuated in such references. Several authors thus centered and used certain sociocultural labels in naming the communities that they represent and their own identities. The variation in language use illuminates the complexities, multiple contexts, and nuances of identity development and social identities.

Finally, the contributors have all taught and/or worked in predominantly White programs, departments, or schools of education where racially coded jargon in K-12 education is commonly used in ways that may appear to be apolitical, neutral, and objective (Apple, 2014). However, in this collection, colonizing and deficit-based assumptions, language, and theories are avoided whenever possible. For example, common references to an "achievement gap" inappropriately centers a learner's underperformance out of context; instead, we use terms such as access, equity, and opportunity gaps (Milner, 2010). Even commonly used language in education around "best practices" are avoided or challenged, as these descriptors often are used in ways that not only normalize Whiteness (Hernandez & Endo, 2017) but legitimizes White-racial frames around what is often described as what is (or should be) best, desirable, and normal (Feagin, 2013). As the authors will articulate in their chapters, even within exclusively or predominantly White settings, there are many ways for scholars of color in education to express their ideas and knowledge in ways that both challenge and decenter dominant canons, epistemologies, and frameworks.

Optical Illusions

On Being Un/Desirable Bodies of Difference in Education

Rachel Endo

Re/Living Racialized Trauma

Daily, I reflect critically on my past and present professional experiences as a racialized body in the nearly all-White world of teacher education including now as a dean of a school of education. In this process of critical reflection, I am reminded of the sociocultural contexts of my K-12 years that were marked by everyday experiences of racial exclusion, mockery, and objectification. I was born, educated, and raised in a predominantly White community in the Midwest. Within this sociopolitical context, bodies of difference were hyper-visible and thus subjected to extreme forms of scrutiny and surveillance by White Americans. As a K-12 learner, I never had an Indigenous teacher or a teacher of color. The curriculum was almost exclusively taught from Eurocentric perspectives. Rare moments learning about diversity included being presented with distorted and problematic views such as when a White teacher asked our class to "dress up as different cultures" for an elementary-level lesson on world cultures. As an adolescent, I continued to be racialized in more problematic ways. Labeled by many White teachers as a "low kid" who they also saw as defiant and oppositional, I was tracked into remedial education in a segregated wing of my predominantly White high school. While known as one of the top high schools in the region at the time, those of us who were in self-contained classrooms were overwhelmingly racialized bodies.

I entered the field of education with high hopes of serving families and learners whose experiences largely reflected my own. As a K-12 learner who only saw an all-White teacher workforce, I aspired to be a bicultural role model for ethnically and racially diverse children and their families. Yet, in my undergraduate teacher-credential program at a public regional university, most of my classmates and professors were White. The official curriculum promoted White-framed theories of classroom management, diversity, and human development. In our education courses, we generally did not read works by authors from racialized backgrounds. When diversity was mentioned, we were mostly taught theories that depicted racialized Americans in highly deficit and essentializing terms. I was fortunate that as a doctoral student at a public research university, I was taught by a cadre of faculty of color and Indigenous faculty who helped me unlearn much of what I learned as a K-12 student and in my teacher-credential program. I also took coursework in ethnic studies, which provided frameworks to understand that what I had experienced in school was also common among millions of other racialized Americans. As I was nearing completion of my doctoral program, I was optimistic that once I found a faculty position as a teacher educator, my commitment to realizing racial equity would be fully embraced and supported by those around me.

I was in for a rude awakening. My first faculty position was in an all-White education department that was situated in a majority White campus setting. During my interview, the hiring manager, a White female, hired me on the spot, saying, "It's going to be *good* to have someone *like you* here who *is different* . . . you will be *really good* because we're trying to reach more *minorities*." After the interview, I researched the institution's history to learn more about its sociohistorical context. I discovered that I was only the second full-time faculty of color the campus had ever hired in its 80-year existence. I also learned from a White colleague that my hire was tied to a recent accreditation visit where external reviewers had censured the campus leadership for not actively recruiting and retaining a diverse faculty body.

My time at this institution was also rife with challenges that revolved around re/living racialized trauma in spaces of Whiteness. I was consistently disciplined, reprimanded, and scrutinized by White administrators and White students/teacher candidates. Each year, a few White teacher candidates complained to my supervisors. Their main grievance: I was not promoting the feel-good narrative of "education is good for all" that they were accustomed to hearing from in their other classes taught by White education faculty. Rather, in my courses, I asked teacher candidates to critically explore topics such as the history of US education as an assimilationist and colonial project, as well as contemporary issues in K-12 education around race-based disproportionality, tracking, and why the teacher workforce remains predominantly White. I also asked them to reflect critically on how their own schooling experiences and upbringings would shape their practices as future classroom teachers. Thus, what I thought I was initially hired to do, which was to bring diverse perspectives to a White-dominated enterprise and to serve as a bicultural role model for the very students/teacher candidates with whom the institution's White leaders claimed they wanted to serve, ended up being an optical illusion. As I was wrapping up my third year at this institution, I received a letter in the mail not even a month before the start of the new academic year stating that my contract was not going to be renewed.

As of the year 2020, I have been affiliated with five departments, colleges, and/or schools of education situated in White-dominated universities across the United States. I have served in a variety of roles including most recently as a dean of a school of education and a chair of a teacher-education department. In these racially exclusionary, isolated, and segregated settings that also aspire to or claim to represent models of equity and inclusion, I am usually among the few or the only racialized American present or represented. My visible racialized body of difference, coupled with my ideologies as a self-identified third world feminist (Sandoval, 1991) and identity as an ethnic studies scholar in education, unsettles spaces of Whiteness, especially in White-dominated institutions where racialized Americans are expected to be agreeable and subservient to Whites. Ultimately, the types of racialization I had confronted as a child and youth continue to trouble me today including being constantly disciplined, monitored, and scrutinized by colleagues, students, superiors, and subordinates, the majority who are White. Now, in all of my professional interactions in my varied roles as a leader, scholar, and teacher educator, I reflect critically on what it means to be an Asian American body in a nation-state long known for its anti-Asian sentiment involving the centuries-long accumulation of imperialistic views and racialized resentment (Chan, 1991; Hune, 2011; Takaki, 1998).

Project's Aims and Scope

My experiences with racialization in all-White or predominantly White schools of education are not idiosyncratic or isolated incidents. Rather, they reflect a contested history of racial exclusion and segregation in K-12 schools, teacher-preparation programs, and universities as interconnected social enterprises that impact racialized Americans in strikingly similar ways. This collaborative project centers on how 12 scholars of color in education who are currently or formerly affiliated with predominantly White programs, colleges, and schools of education across the United States have distinctly experienced racialization in these spaces of Whiteness. The authors are all education scholars at different stages of their careers including recent Ph.D. graduates, university staff members with instructional experience, adjunct faculty, full-time non-tenure-track faculty, tenure-track faculty, tenured faculty, and scholars in leadership positions. Diverse perspectives are represented including education scholars who identify as African American and Black, Asian/Asian American, Latina, and multiracial. Several authors chose to name and narrate salient parts of their intersecting identities such as disAbility, ethnicity, gender, LGBTQIA identity, nationality, religious/spiritual connections, transnational affiliations, and so forth. Many spoke about their ancestral and familial connections, as well as their own K-12 schooling experiences as racialized Americans if they were educated in the United States.

Some authors grew up in poverty and lived in racially segregated neighborhoods during the decades following federally designated integration efforts. Others are among the second and subsequent generations of affluent and middle-class families of color in the United States who have discovered that their socioeconomic status has not fully protected them from experiencing some of the more undesirable effects of racialization. The authors also identify as equity-focused education scholars who are deeply committed to advancing racial equity through their pedagogies, perspectives, and practices.

The experiences of racialized scholars in education programs are connected to a troubling legacy of racial oppression in the United States. Despite the various conditions that have kept the academy a racially exclusionary enterprise, the authors, through their mere and very presence in predominantly White colleges and schools of education, have paved the way for future generations to enter these spaces. Their accomplishments are particularly noteworthy because they have beat substantial odds in institutions and systems that continue to devalue children, communities, and families who are from similar backgrounds. For one, the contributors are all college graduates with advanced and terminal degrees from some of the nation's top education programs to their credit. Their accomplishments challenge common White-framed deficit narratives in education that people of color devalue education and struggle to excel academically because they lack the intellectual capacity or intrinsic motivation to exceed rigorous expectations. The majority of the authors (nine in total) were also former K-12 classroom teachers who helped facilitate culturally affirming and rigorous learning environments for children and youth from diverse backgrounds. Yet, despite their many personal and professional accomplishments, the authors have experienced various types of racialization in White-run education programs that echo longstanding views of racialized bodies in the United States as dangerous, deviant, and different. The authors narrate how their behaviors, physical appearance, and professionalism were constantly under attack, questioned, or scrutinized including by predominantly White aspiring or practicing K-12 teachers enrolled in their courses, as well as by some of their White faculty colleagues and White leaders. Taken together, the persistent racialization of scholars of color in US colleges and schools of education across rank, social identification, and status might suggest that many Whites who occupy these spaces are only interested in speaking about diversity, equity, and inclusion in theory but not implementing these principles in practice.

This book has the following intended audiences in mind. Foremost, racialized scholars who are currently or formerly affiliated with predominantly White education programs, as well as those who aspire to become education scholars in the future, will likely relate to the experiences and insights shared by one or more of the contributors. While the chapters primarily focus on critical incidents in the classroom, the authors also speak to racialized interactions that had occurred at community events, faculty meetings, lunchrooms/breakrooms, and through e-mail and other communication with their colleagues, students/teacher candidates, and supervisors. The authors thus offer several critical frameworks and perspectives regarding how education scholars from similar sociocultural contexts might negotiate various individual and institutional barriers, constraints, and realities. Second, this book may offer equity-focused insights to people in leadership positions including but not limited to department chairs/heads, academic deans, and tenured faculty who influence or make high-stakes personnel decisions. The previous individuals will likely learn new information and perspectives about how and why common practices occurring in their academic units and organizations that they may view as neutral, positive, or promoting diversity may be seen by members of minoritized groups as dehumanizing, offensive, and racially oppressive. Finally, those in senior leadership positions such as directors of human resources, provosts, and university chancellors or presidents, as well as leaders in other academic disciplines, may find compelling and relevant perspectives from the authors that they may be able to translate into their respective institutional contexts and settings as they grapple with their own equity-focused problems of practice.

Unequal Education and Racial Exclusion in the United States

Despite the common belief that formal education is the great equalizer in US society, issues of access, opportunities, and outcomes in one's educational prospects have long been determined by racialized identity, as well as by disAbility, gender, and other markers of difference. As Span, Robinson, and Villegas (2007) note, race-based disparities in education institutions, having been long ingrained in America's consciousness, are arguably the most challenging ones to dismantle. The authors provide a few core examples of how generations of African American, Chinese American, and Mexican American families were denied or restricted entry into mainstream schools due to Whites harboring extreme racial anxiety and hatred toward bodies of difference. While forced to attend racially segregated schools with fewer resources than in White communities, families and parents of color have long made demands to White-dominated courts and institutions that their children, like White children, should receive access to a high-quality education. Over the past several decades, generations of racialized Americans, such as the authors of this collection and their families, have been integrated into mainstream educational spaces. Yet, integration has not guaranteed equal or equitable opportunities in one's educational and employment pursuits.

A more comprehensive analysis of the current demographics of these institutions, from the overall K-12 teacher workforce to persons occupying US colleges and schools of education as key authority figures who are shaping the field, will frame how equity and representation gaps persist in a post-integration era. The most visible example of the demographic gap in education is evident through the K-12 workforce, as approximately three-quarters of all K-12 public-school teachers in the United States are White whereas fewer than one-half of all K-12 students are also White (Gregory, 2019). The overall lack of diverse adult role models has cumulative effects not only on how the learning environment is structured but also in terms of children's identity development, as young minds internalize explicit and implicit messages about other-self dynamics from teachers and other adults in their lives (Ladson-Billings, 2008; Milner, 2015). Similar to the composition of the K-12 workforce, most colleges and schools of education, in addition to the majority of universities where they are situated in the United States, are demographically imbalanced compared to the diverse student populations they aspire to or currently serve. Largely drawing from the pool of former practitioners in the K-12 enterprise who are overwhelmingly White (Myers, 2016), the composition of administrators and faculty in education programs are generally more demographically homogeneous than in the K-12 system or other non-education university programs (Milner, 2010). In addition to representing over three-quarters of all academic administrators and instructional faculty in higher education (Myers, n.d.), approximately nine-tenths of all personnel in departments, colleges, and schools of education in the United States are White (Gasman, Kim, & Nguyen, 2011; Milner, 2010). The severe underrepresentation of diverse faculty and leaders in these spaces have large-scale impacts ranging from how curricula are developed including whose perspectives are (or are not) represented in coursework and programs, how institutional policies are set, and most significantly, how future generations of classroom teachers and other school personnel are educated and professionally socialized into the profession (Hernandez & Endo, 2017).

Diversity, Equity, and Inclusion in Education Programs: From Compliance to Commitment

Over the past few decades, diversity initiatives in exclusively or predominantly White US colleges and schools of education have appeared in peculiar ways, highlighting multiple contradictions about how racialized bodies are inherently de/valued in these spaces. Most diversity efforts in US teacher-credential programs are generated by high-stakes mandates to fulfill compulsory accreditation requirements. For example, accrediting bodies such as CAEP or the Council for the Accreditation of Educator Preparation (formerly the National Council for the Accreditation of Teacher Education or NCATE) and state-level accrediting bodies require universities with teacher-credential programs to demonstrate how they prepare teacher candidates to effectively work with culturally, ethnically, linguistically, and racially diverse K-12 learners. CAEP also integrates various diversity criteria into several of its standards around, for instance, clinical placements, faculty qualifications, and recruitment goals (CAEP Handbook, 2018). Significantly, CAEP and other accreditation bodies represent how most White-framed education programs view diversity as an add-on (Banks & Banks, 2010) rather than, along with the core tenets of equity and inclusion, integral to all aspects of their curricular approaches, instructional methods, and intentionally integrated as core values aligned to individual behaviors that shape organizational outcomes. These accreditation standards further promote decontextualized views of culture and difference that primarily speak to mostly White audiences about the value of additive forms of diversity rather than a more nuanced understanding of why racial inequities and White dominance persist in these organizations. These standards also largely fail to address how color-neutral organizational practices and systems of racial oppression operate in educational institutions from K-12 through the level of teacher credentialing, and for the most part, do not hold programs accountable for their actual hiring/recruitment and retention practices. At best, some state departments of education in the United States such as in Minnesota and Washington require programs in good standing to describe their "good-faith efforts" related to recruitment practices without clear evidence of accountability if they do not meet specific targets (as efforts do not necessarily translate into outcomes). However, despite these challenges, CAEP and other accrediting bodies at least implicitly recognize that education programs with mostly White faculty and student/teacher candidate demographics cannot adequately represent the interests and needs of ethnically and racially diverse communities, families, and learners.

Predominantly, White colleges and schools of education in the United States are ultimately mirrors of our nation's contested and racialized past and present. Specifically, these sites are particular types of racial projects (Omi & Winant, 1994) where predominantly White micro-communities attempt to set certain expectations for how racialized bodies of differences should appear in these spaces. Often, a problematic assumption promoted at predominantly White US colleges and universities is that racialized Americans who do not "fit in" or "struggle to succeed" have these experiences because of mismatches between their cultural values and those of their White-dominated institutions, or more troublingly, based on assumptions that bodies of difference are unsuccessful because they are intellectually challenged, lazy, and undisciplined (Matias, 2013). However, a more accurate assessment may be troubling to many White scholars in professional education programs: the persistent mis/labeling of children who are Indigenous and of color by White teachers as academically challenged, disruptive, and emotionally disturbed (Blanchett, 2006; Howard, 2013) is nearly identical to the types of deficit thinking that many White administrators, faculty, and students/teacher candidates use to mis/interpret and mis/judge the competence, intelligence, and social worth of racialized scholars in predominantly White colleges and schools of education (Gutiérrez y Muhs, Niemann, González, & Harris, 2012; Holling, 2019).

In all, the incentives and motives for how and why programs, colleges, and schools of education recruit, retain, and support faculty and students/teacher candidates from various backgrounds require critical analyses that may challenge several core fundamental assumptions regarding why diversity matters. This project both challenges and decenters common White frameworks (Feagin, 2013) such as CAEP criteria and state-level accreditation standards that often drive how colleges and schools of education in the United States define and make/claim progress around efforts related to diversity, equity, and inclusion. However, this book does not focus heavily on recruitment strategies, as others have discussed ways to fulfill such goals (e.g., Carter, Pearson, & Shavlik, 1996; Cobb-Roberts & Agosto, 2011; Justice & Barker, 2007). Rather, this project focuses on broader issues related to race relations within colleges and schools of education in the United States as microcosms of other racially stratified organizations and social structures. The authors call attention to the multiple contexts of education including the reoccurring patterns of racial oppression that have disproportionately and negatively impacted individuals who identify as BIPOC. Readers are invited to reflect critically on the content of these narratives as direct and indirect connections to their own individual experiences as well as institutional contexts.

The Un/Intended Consequences of White Dominance in Education

Sleeter (2017) reminds us that the perpetual Whiteness in education, especially in teacher education, is problematic on multiple levels with high stakes and wide-ranging impacts. Under traditional models of shared governance in higher education, faculty and leaders of an academic unit wield significant power in shaping decisions that impact current and prospective students/teacher candidates. Faculty members generally decide which people to admit to their programs, a decision in education programs that directly impact the production of credentialed and licensed professionals who are allowed to enter the field. Faculty members further influence curricular decisions including deciding what is deemed as essential knowledge in an academic program. In professional credential and licensure programs such as in teacher education, the general absence of diverse perspectives may perpetuate culturally insensitive and distorted views of diverse communities and individuals, and in turn, may impact how practicing and pre-service professionals will react to certain people and situations. At many universities, faculty members also influence hiring, promotion, and tenure decisions (Gasman et al., 2011) that have a direct bearing on which types of people current and future students will (or will not) see in the university classroom as authority figures, mentors, and role models. Colleges and schools of education in the United States are thus political sites that, along with accrediting bodies and other professional organizations, influence how future generations of aspiring and current professionals such as classroom teachers, counselors, and school leaders are socialized to interpret and understand (or potentially misinterpret and misunderstand) the communities and people they serve.

It must also be recognized that most White-dominated academic units, particularly in education and allied fields, will likely remain demographically homogeneous for at least a generation, as tenure-track faculty hires are usually long-term institutional commitments spanning decades of employment. More universities are turning to contingent labor to fill instructional gaps to reduce expenses, and thus, opportunities for future tenure-track positions will likely remain scarce. These sites will therefore continue to perpetuate and replicate Whiteness and White-framed views of diversity (Feagin, 2013) until there is a demographic shift among faculty and leadership ranks, as well as significant attitudinal changes among existing individuals within these organizations. Nevertheless, institutional acknowledgment must be made that the hiring process itself is not neutral. Periodically hiring or including one or just a few racialized bodies may fulfill shallow diversity goals, but until measurable outcomes are realized in these spaces, predominantly White colleges and schools of education must find ways to advance opportunities and support racialized scholars who are already part of their communities. Part of providing a supportive space is acknowledging the importance of the various contextual factors that shape how racialized scholars in education enters a space that does not reflect their lived contexts and realities.

Modes of Inquiry

Cooke (2019) reminds us "in the power of naming things" (p. 226). The 12 authors of this collection were invited to narrate their lived experiences as racialized bodies who are or were formerly affiliated with predominantly White programs, colleges, or schools of education in the United States. Profiting from intersectional theories that complicate single-group approaches to understanding the complexities of social identities (Crenshaw, 1989; Landry, 2006), the authors recalled varying points in their personal and professional trajectories, from their early childhoods to their postsecondary training, as well as through their professional careers, that shifted their understanding of their identities as racialized scholars in education. Each author employed diverse autoethnographic or interpretive frameworks (e.g., Connelly, Phillion, & He, 2003; Crenshaw, 1989; Denzin, 1997; Denzin & Lincoln, 1998) to construct a distinct narrative profile. Beyond minor editing for clarification or to maintain consistency in the usage of certain terminology, each chapter reflects the author's original thoughts and words. Sharing and theorizing their experiences using creative modalities and various forms of data such as art, autoethnography, connections to popular culture, critical self-reflection, humor, poetry, and storytelling (Denzin, 1997) allowed the contributors to express themselves in ways that are not always possible through (or valued) in dominant scholarly venues. The diversity in narration, prose, and style of each entry reflects a rich range of experiences, insights, and perspectives.

Each contributor reflected critically on a variety of topics involving racialized incidents and moments in and out of the classroom. Several authors critically analyzed author-generated primary data sources including critical incidents or moments, course/teaching evaluations and tenure documents such as dossiers, and redacted exchanges with White administrators, colleagues, and students/teacher candidates to reflect on and synthesize common themes throughout their experiences as racialized scholars in education. Some contributors specifically chose to retell a critical incident or a series of similar moments with a unifying theme while others reflected on various connections between their personal and professional experiences. Many intentionally reflected on their ancestral and familial connections to frame their experiences as ones rooted in intergenerational memories, struggles, and triumphs. Some elected to share disturbing and traumatizing experiences that were triggered primarily by White Americans including colleagues and leaders, as well as White students/teacher candidates. Some authors also experienced blatant race-based bullying and harassment in the workplace. Others experienced more covert types of racialized insults and slights, both non-verbal and verbal, now commonly known in academic circles as racial microaggressions (Sue, 2010).

This collection also represents a diversity of ideological stances and ways of self-identifying. Some authors decided to not explicitly or implicitly disclose much about themselves beyond their racialized identities. They also do not represent their entire communities. For example, seven scholars who identify as Black contributed to this collection. They all speak to being racially typecast by Whites in strikingly similar ways that also echo derogatory racial tropes of persons who are Black. Yet, readers will note after reading each chapter that there is no one prescribed template for being a Black education scholar. Rather, Black education scholars hail from various ideological, political, and sociocultural contexts. Some cautiously enter the nearly all-White world of teacher education while others are comfortable disrupting these spaces through their radical pedagogies and practices. Second, this collection represents a range of healthy ideological disagreements about, for instance, the role of White allies in actualizing anti-racist work to the larger social responsibility of White-dominated education programs and institutions to take corrective action to remedy past and present wrongs. For example, some contributors offered pointed intellectual critiques of White allies and liberalism while others suggest that racialized bodies cannot survive without Whites and therefore should attempt to work for and with them within current structures to address longstanding inequities. These diverse perspectives offer an array of possibilities about topics for rich dialogues that may ensue around, for instance, the nature and scope of equity-focused conversations for academic leaders and faculty who aspire to create inclusive and welcoming environments.

Limitations

This project has a set of core limitations. For one, there is the issue of basic representation. Multiple efforts were made to invite a diverse range of racialized scholars to contribute to this volume including direct outreach to persons with varying intersecting identities. At first, there was a robust response to this call for papers with representation of 24 scholars across the "color line" with a solid balance of gendered and racialized perspectives, but many were unable to contribute to this final project for personal reasons. This final collection is thus admittedly incomplete because it specifically lacks contributions from male-identified Asian American and Latino scholars in education, as well as scholars who are Indigenous and Pacific Islander. This collection also only includes scholars who traditionally identify as cisgender female and male. The previous gaps also point to a larger sociopolitical reality: the enterprises of K-12 and teacher education continue to over/represent White-identified females (Gregory, 2019; Milner, 2010). Finally, while not an explicit limitation, to be acknowledged is this project does not specifically focus on moments of interracial conflicts and tensions among and between various racialized communities and individuals in these organizations. Indeed, education scholars who are BIPOC do not always get along, form alliances around common interests, or publicly support one another. However, the reality is that the authors are among just a small number of scholars of color in their academic units and/or universities whereby their primary challenges and interactions pertain to navigating spaces of Whiteness. Nevertheless, the 12 diverse identities and perspectives represented in this collection provide several useful insights about what conditions are necessary to meaningfully and positively transform US colleges and schools of education into potential sites, where the principles of diversity, equity, and inclusion are central rather than peripheral to their everyday operations and practices.

Roadmap

This collection is organized by position and rank starting with authors who have served as adjunct faculty and graduate teaching assistants. The narratives of those on the tenure-track and tenured associate professors follow. The final chapters are written by scholars of color serving in administrative roles including a program coordinator, associate deans, and a dean of education. Some contributors have served in multiple roles over their careers across institutional settings and types that made it difficult to categorize them into any clear-cut category such as tenured faculty. Moreover, some authors who are tenured faculty focused on moments earlier in their careers as pre-tenured faculty. The sequential ordering of the chapters by rank is thus somewhat arbitrary but perhaps more logical than organizing the sections by pan-ethnic groupings given the uneven representation of contributors across the board. The current ordering of the chapters also allows for cross-case comparisons regarding how earlier-career education scholars and those who have been in higher education for decades experience racialization differently and similarly in White-dominated spaces.

Regardless of one's rank and status, it should be recognized that the pursuit of naming one's own racialized truth is a courageous but potentially risky process, especially for scholars who do not have certain job benefits such as full-time employment or tenure. Even those who are in leadership positions and/or tenured may fear individual or institutional reprisal for exposing unflattering and unsettling truths about how they, and perhaps others like them, have been mis/treated in professional settings by their own colleagues, leaders, and supervisors. However, there are benefits of narrating one's own experiences. For many, writing without the fear of censorship allowed for an opportunity, and perhaps the only viable one, to make sense of their experiences and to reclaim rights to their own narratives. Others view this type of narration as a distinct form of soul care that encourages their creative ideas to converge, and ultimately, nourishes their minds after years of experiencing intellectual starvation in assimilationist and White-dominated environments. Finally, for others, narrating their journeys is part of a larger social responsibility to document what they have endured, and to candidly share with others who aspire to consider similar professional journeys what the costs and rewards are for entering spaces that historically were not created about, by, and for them.

1 "A Slippery Slope"

From Deficit-Based Vantage Points to Ignorance for White Pre-Service Teachers

Alvin Logan, Jr.

First-Day Introductions

"Hello everyone. My name is Alvin. I will be your instructor for the semester." This is generally how I begin my classes each term. Perhaps first-day-of-class introductions are clichéd to many White teacher educators, but they are sorely necessary for people like me. My verbal introduction paired well with my *incognito* attempt at learning how mostly White teacher candidates imagine who will teach them before class starts serves me well. I wear casual clothing on the first day of the term. Prior to the class starting, I sit among the students to ask them to share their thoughts about the upcoming class and the instructor. Over the years, the mostly White teacher candidates enrolled in my courses generally provide the same answer when I ask what racial background they think the instructor will be: "Probably White . . . *like the rest of them.*" Yet, when a mid-twenties Black male stood up in front of them, they appear confused. For example, etched in my mind to this very day was the perplexed look on a young White woman's face. I later learned she was from an affluent and mostly White community in Texas. I remember how she looked around the room in confusion after my welcome . . . and asked her classmates if this was "the right class." She then proceeded to check the room number on the door outside to ensure it matched the location printed on her course schedule.

It was amazing for me to witness her and other White teacher candidates' emotional reactions as they scrambled to compose their stereotypes about the intellectual ability and place of Black people in teacher education, especially those who are teacher educators. Those who become pre-service teachers, especially White women, generally are sympathetic toward the scripted struggles of students from minoritized backgrounds. Subsequently, the development of a White-savior complex (Matias, 2013) primed their propensity to both underestimate and essentialize the ability of racialized bodies, especially those who are Black. This toxic disposition locates White teacher candidates as consummate beings and their future students as empty receptacles needing a cultural auxiliary to deposit an "education" in and on their minds (Freire, 1993). As a Black teacher educator who watched this pattern develop through many young minds, I sought to understand the following: the extent to which the cross-cultural understanding of racially diverse students impacted the ontology and epistemology of White pre-service teachers.

My life as a Black student, and now as a Black educator, is filled with trying to understand (and undercut) deficit perspectives toward racialized bodies, particularly children and youth who are Black. I was raised in Denver, Colorado. I attended racially diverse public schools until I entered my secondary years, where I enrolled in a predominately White, all-boys, Catholic high school. The school was known in the community for producing high-achieving students. My parents sent me there because they wanted me to have the best chance to enter college and also prepare for the demands of a university education. Consequently, most of the "real education" I would receive in this space was in the hallways or in the multicultural office where the few Black students at this school used as our safe haven. It was outside of these spaces that the insidious stereotypes about Black students lived on including among the minds of many White teachers and the majority of White students. I quickly realized that I was *the proxy* for all Black people and our collective intellectual ability (both imagined and real). Thus, my identity as a young Black male was molded against the antithetical White male privilege that was the symbolic epitome of this prestigious school. In all, my Black male identity surfaced at the intersection of being an athlete, a student leader, and a critical thinker.

In my four years in this space, one realization was made clear: I was expected to be academically and intellectually inferior to my White peers. Seemingly, this positioning located any Black student who was intelligent as "acting White" (Ogbu, 2004), negating associations between Black identity and cerebral ability. This unsettling feeling radiated from the gaze of White teachers and the peppering of jokes by White classmates about my stereotypical lack of "academic ability" when juxtaposed to other White students. It was in these spaces where I first encountered White saviors who treated Black students like we were children who were in need of academic and cultural assistance to become like the rest of the White student body. Ultimately, Black youth were to be "saved" from our own plight by Whites. Luckily, our cohort of Black students and some amazing White teachers prevented much of the treatment from seeping into our subconscious and helped those of us who were Black to ultimately preserve our self-worth. Had it not been for the multicultural office staff, some of our football coaches, and several teachers, our intellectual place among other capable White students at this Catholic institution of learning would have been co-opted. Through those memories, I treaded a path to disprove timeless eugenic myths. Instead, I seek to educate future teachers how to recognize the tremendous wealth and sociopolitical struggles that people who are BIPOC represent in our schools and society.

Unfortunately, in my role as an instructor at a large predominantly White research university in the South, my passion was swiftly met by resistant White teacher candidates with adversarial results. For example, I taught a course titled "Sociocultural Influences on Learning" for a pre-service teacher-credential program. The course was designed to guide teacher candidates through the socio-historical relationship between schooling, interlocking forms of oppression, and the meaning (or many meanings) of education. The course was also cross-listed with the African American Studies Program; thus, there was a heavy emphasis on Black students and the education and experiences of African Americans. Initially, I led students through an understanding of race, gender, and sexual orientation in the US context, as well as interlocking forms of oppression (Collins, 2000; Crenshaw, 1989). We then applied these frameworks to understand the history of unequal schooling in the United States. Once we finished dissecting the relationship between schooling and racial segregation, we began to delve deeper into the foundations of Black education and the various equity issues that Black communities experience in contemporary contexts. The later class sessions became interesting during the campaign and subsequent election of President Donald J. Trump. His inflammatory rhetoric and emboldened defense of White-supremacist ideologies were reminiscent of the blatantly racist discourse prevalent before and during in the 1960s. My goal in unpacking this and similar types of rhetoric was to deescalate mostly White pre-service teachers' deficit understanding of Black students. Although I was mildly successful, this approach led way for the deflection of a deficit-based vantage point for understanding racialized bodies to White teacher candidates' embodiment of ignorance when confronted with their participation in everyday racism.

The Racial Contract Theory

Charles Mills (1997) artfully constructed a critique of color-neutral rhetoric in his seminal work titled *The Racial Contract*. His work details the omitted rights of racialized Americans and the impacts to how we discursively construct morality and humanity. It further details the moral, political, and social aspects of humanity that purposefully ignore racialized bodies to ultimately protect the privileged rights of White people. The contract outlines boundaries for those who are considered White, denoted as the White polity, as well as all others who are designated as subpersons. He defines subpersons as "humanoid entities who because of racial phenotype/genealogy/culture, are not fully human and therefore have a different and inferior schedule of rights and liberties applying to them" (Mills, 1997, p. 56). The White polity is headed primarily by

White males of European ancestry who serve as signatories to the creation and maintenance of exploitive treatment toward people they label as "non-White." The transnational White polity further privileges White people as "civilized" and juxtaposes BIPOC individuals as "savages" because of their supposed barbaric dispositions. The racial contract is proposed to be infinite due to its malleable boundaries and its signatories vowing to keep it place at all costs. The contract has a powerful impact on those in the White polity, as it garners a level of cultural superiority among its members. Mills further states that the racial contract is epistemological by "prescribing norms for cognition to which its signatories must adhere" (Mills, 1997, p. 11). The contract ultimately seeks to create and sustain sociopolitical power to subordinate individuals who are BIPOC worldwide.

In the context of teacher education, the racial contract frames the experiences of White pre-service teachers because it outlines their thought process toward their future students who they already view as racially different. As I have learned, White pre-service teachers tend to believe that for students who are from racialized backgrounds to become "academically successful," they must be like them (i.e., White). However, as I try to explain, the system of schooling in the United States is set up for those who understand or mirror hegemonic culture to succeed. More specifically, their epistemology, knowledge base, and scripting of "academic achievement" vis-à-vis racial identity aligns with the White polity, thus, manifesting in ideologically violent treatment toward racialized bodies. When White pre-teachers come into their education classes with a deficit-oriented positionality, they participate in the process of erasing the vast wealth that their future students will bring to their future classrooms.

One White female teacher candidate was persisting in denial as she combatted stories of the many wrongdoing against Mexican American families and students when we were reading Angela Valenzuela's rich ethnography titled *Subtractive Schooling: U.S.-Mexican Youth and the Politics of Caring* (1999). This White pre-service teacher was adamant that the author's account of White teachers treating Mexican American students as if they were not educable was acceptable and appropriate because, as she put it, "*Some students* just do not want to learn . . . so what else can you do?" This epistemological understanding pegs children from racialized backgrounds as outsiders or othered (Kumashiro, 2000). Once another is considered as the Other is the point of cerebral demarcation between official knowledge (Apple, 2014); that is, in this moment, a teacher's attempt at "building knowledge" to educate future students resorts to expelling Othered knowledge and values. Mills (1997) describes this process within the context of cultural genocide against Indigenous persons: "[T]he mission kills us from within . . . they impose upon us another religion, belittling the values we hold. This de-characterizes us to the point where we are ashamed to be Indians" (p. 88). The stripping of Indigenous spiritual practices by White settlers is similar to the Othering of students' cultural knowledge and values because it is a genocidal act that funnels students toward assimilation. That is, many White pre-service teachers are preparing for the goal of education for assimilation by centering their sociocultural knowledge as official and normative while dispelling all others. Yet, this entire process begins with deficit perspectives that spring into "a slippery slope" toward White ignorance. Now layering the impact of Trump on the mindset of many White pre-service teachers, it creates a context for dissonance between fighting to recognize Indigenous persons and people of color as equals against their perpetuation of deficit-oriented practices. In the next section, I will discuss "the slippery slope" between deficit-oriented positionalities and the willful ignorance of many White pre-service teachers.

From White Guilt, to White Saviors . . . to White Ignorance

Common cycles of emotional responses for White pre-service teachers seem to follow the pattern of White guilt when they learn about the foundation of racial inequality in US schools and society (Iyer, Leach, & Crosby, 2003; Steele, 1990). Their guilt then often transitions to what is known as the White-savior complex (Cole, 2012; Matias, 2013). White guilt is the feeling generated when White Americans actually recognize the advantages that White supremacy has afforded them, as well as how it has systematically disadvantaged groups like African Americans (Steele, 1990). This feeling of guilt has the ability to destabilize understandings of American success stories and debilitates European American and White American identity as pure and moral (Branscombe, 2011; Branscombe, Doosje, & McGarty, 2002). My White teacher candidates' own experiences with White guilt was invoked by my approach to deeper interdisciplinary analyses into the ramifications of slavery for enslaved Africans and their descendants in addition to Jim Crow laws. I was not shy about showing the gore and having them read explicit details of the gruesome institutions that perpetuated the mass enslavement of Black people. I purposefully presented an in-depth and uncensored history of White American terrorism, genocide, and disdain for Black people to situate White pre-service teachers' thoughts within the politics of omitted knowledge. Many White teacher candidates were disgusted by the actions of their ancestors. Consequently, they began to shift their epistemological stance from morally denouncing slavery to absolving their personal connection to their ancestors. However, they eventually became uncomfortable with their ties to what they saw as their immoral and racist ancestors (DiAngelo & Sensoy, 2014). The previous shift is important to note because it starkly connected them to the blatant abuse and hatred of Black people. As a Black male educator in front of a group of mostly

White pre-service teachers, I grappled with their emotional dissonance as it appeared to only fuel their guilt. I connected the horrors of slavery to inequities in US schooling through explaining the illegality of educating Black people. It was at this point that most White teacher candidates recognized the harm that inequitable and oppressive measures have had on Black America's schooling experience and the impacts to their literacy rates over generations. In these moments, they further recognized the dangerously foul methods that some White people have employed to frame White students as the norm and young Black people as needing *their knowledge* to become intelligent, learned, and literate. Though this frame of thinking, the White pre-service teachers' proposed approach shifted toward becoming assumed superheroes who were able to replenish deficits by showing Black youth and other marginalized youth the so-called right (i.e., White) way to learn.

The "I have to do something about this" attitude fueled by White guilt laid a perfect foundation for explicating the White-savior complex in this course. White saviors are portrayed through many popular films in the United States such as *Dangerous Minds*, *Finding Forrester*, and *Glory*, and even shows such as *Last Chance U*. Matias (2013) describes the ramifications of the White-savior mentality in teacher education:

> well-intentioned White women enter urban schools, ridden with gangs, promiscuity, and drugs, they themselves become victims of the of the illness of urbanity that plagues People of color and in doing so, they become White martyrs/messiahs for taking on the risk of contaminating their inherent purity.
>
> (p. 53)

White pre-service teachers generally embodied these presumed "good intentions" and misappropriated the historical bastardized schooling experiences of urban youth as portrayed in the popular media to plot their vengeful fight for their future students' dignity. The White pre-service teachers in my class started using deficit rhetoric that positioned them as uniquely poised and qualified to usher success to urban learners. As a critical teacher educator, I have made every attempt to quell this attitude by naming it and calling folks out on the problems with the White-savior complex. I often will tell my teacher candidates the following: "They should put on a cape because they are acting like a White savior." It became a dunce cap for aspiring White teachers who became infatuated with being the one White person who could "save" Indigenous students and students of color from what they viewed as their "abnormal" schooling troubles. However, I sought to empower them to be a key part of a larger quest to erase the race-based opportunity gap, but not through hollow practices. Resultantly, several White teacher candidates were more purposeful in avoiding what could be seen as White-savor language and subsequently shifted their focus from historical to contemporary schooling experiences. This shift is significant because it drew their thinking away from being White saviors to focusing on the ways by which today's schooling experiences are better *and* worse for students from marginalized backgrounds. In most cases, focusing on the positive provokes optimism. However, I witnessed many White teacher candidates becoming or choosing to remain ignorant as we started to explore the issues facing K-12 students today in a racialized society.

Imagine the cacophony of feelings that mold young White privileged minds to believe that people unlike them need help that only they could give, which motivates them because they think it will "even the count" for a genocidal history and ultimately alleviate their individual guilt. Many White teacher candidates could not even fathom that they would do more harm than good because they were attempting to educate racialized bodies through colonization, or in simple words, Whitewashing (Brown, 2003) the educational experiences of racially diverse students. White teacher candidates could name and denounce the wrongs of the past toward groups of racialized Americans, especially with respect to various forms of overt racism. However, when shifting our thinking to the current day, they generally lacked a critical lens to understand the subtle and hidden ways by which racism and various other forms of oppression persist. As the "in-your-face" racism shape shifted to mainly hiding inside our institutions' structures, our White teacher candidates still lack the tools to track what is not explicitly spelled out for them. As their instructor, I have labored to help them develop various tools to recognize the nuances of oppressive tactics. Consequently, through this approach, I was met by color-neutral rhetoric for what I presume to be a couple of reasons. First, when racism is institutionally situated, White teacher candidates were less likely to believe it impacts racialized Americans significantly more than what they have experienced. Second, they juxtaposed their supposed progressive ideology to President Trump's, since he was reminiscent of what they saw as old-time/overt racism. Their actions perpetuated willful White ignorance. When I use the term ignorant, I do not mean that White teacher candidates lacked knowledge; rather, I am pointing to their general disregard of critical thinking to enable them to continue walking the path of least resistance.

Many White pre-service teachers were also skeptical of new-age racism because to them, one could not easily find or see it. They would make statements such as "There are a lot of Black people at [this university] . . . so racism cannot be as bad as it was *back then*," or "I treat all people the same regardless of race." Many White teacher candidates claimed racial equality was prevalent because before the 1970s, this university did not allow Black people to enroll. When I taught for this university, the Black student population was approximately 4 percent of the total student body. That figure and the assumptions of progress were extremely problematic because White institutional leaders used it to ignore issues such as major tracking leading to disparate outcomes, funding disparities, and racial microaggressions that continue to impact the Black schooling experience including in higher education. Not only did many White teacher candidates take on the perspective of color-neutrality and racial progress, but during Trump's campaign, they shifted to completely *not* focusing on issues of race and racial identity. Interestingly, Trump's overt support for White supremacy has largely gone uncensored. I noticed that many White teacher candidates felt the need to take on a color-neutral orientation after hearing Trump speak. To them, it was simple: Trump is clearly perpetuating overt racism. If they instead treat people according to "their character" and not the amount of melanin in their skin, they are able to prove that racism does not exist among their generation. This back-and-forth regarding Trump's actions and ideologies happened often. The more we highlighted examples of racism, the further that many White teacher candidates dug into the feeling of separation from older Trump supporters. For a teacher educator of color, this became a twisted issue to deal with because I understood that they were distancing themselves from Trump, but I could not find a clear-cut way to address this phenomenon at each of the levels that it existed.

Effectively, White teacher candidates moved from a White-savior complex engulfing their ontology and epistemology to trying to "prove" that racism did not impact the majority of children and youth in our schools. This process placed the plight of Indigenous students and students of color on the auxiliary because it focused on White teacher candidates being official knowledge bearers in a supposedly equal society. Yet, thinking under that frame of reference demarcates the line between the White polity and those who are racialized bodies. To possess official knowledge means to be the benchmark to which everything is applied. In the history of education in the United States, that benchmark has been people who are White. Thus, the racial contract (Mills, 1997) is kept intact because White pre-service teachers often reify themselves as the norm. In their quest to save racialized Americans, they aspire to make these "colored bodies" as clones of their White selves. Additionally, through the scaffolding of color-neutral beliefs and ignorance toward institutional racism, the White polity sustains "the plight" of racialized Americans.

Trials and Tribulations

Teacher educators from racialized backgrounds and contexts often search for ways to increase the critical capacity of the work we do. We try to convince White teacher candidates that they have to do *something* (and several things) about the racism that still exists including the types that they themselves perpetuate. Understanding that this task is never complete and may yield resistance, I have retained some core pedagogical and course-design strategies to place the onus on White teacher candidates to labor in understanding oppression from different vantage points rather than making it my primary responsibility. Ultimately, I have attempted to approach teacher education differently than many White colleagues in my department and many other White-liberal teacher educators I have gotten to know over the years. I found that to increase the critical consciousness of teachers going into the workforce, one need not embody cookie-cutter thinking that is rampant in both K-12 and teacher education.

The following practices were useful in my journey toward the aforementioned goals that I would recommend to my younger self or another colleague looking to navigate working with White pre-service teachers. Pedagogically, I make connections and similarities that build empathy for pre-service teachers, especially the aspiring White teachers who seek to learn about different cultures and identities. I structure my syllabi to represent a process of thinking that builds bridges between the ideas of empathy and cross-cultural empathy/sympathy. To start the process, I draw in most White teacher candidates with introducing the notion of gender-based oppression by using articles that show gender inequity in career pay, educational pursuits, and wealth attainment (Sadker & Zittleman, 2005). The discussions around this topic are heavily dominated by the White women in my class, and in some respects, rightfully so because many have directly experienced gender-related disparities. My skillful coaxing toward foregrounding the voices of White women while discussing their oppression leads them to listen to and hear people of the oppressed class.

After creating buy-in from mostly White women, we move to the conversation to racial oppression, where the class is urged to listen to their colleagues who are from racialized backgrounds. I confront those who choose to subscribe to a color-neutral ideology. My use of, for example, Tim Wise's *Dear White America: Letter to a New Minority* (2012) and Peggy McIntosh's classic article "White Privilege: Unpacking the Invisible Knapsack" (1988), enables initial buy-in because White teacher candidates generally see White authors who speak about racial oppression as credible sources of information, perhaps more so than BIPOC scholars. However, I supersede those authors with reading passages from in-group narratives such as *Racism Without Racists* (Bonilla-Silva, 2010), *The Souls of Black Folk* (Du Bois & Marable, 2014), "*Why are all the Black Kids Sitting Together in the Cafeteria?" And Other Conversations about Race* (Tatum, 1997), and "From the Achievement Gap to the Education Debt: Understanding Achievement in US Schools" (Ladson-Billings, 2006). These are works that help transpose the zeal they had for gender equity to racial equity. The potent part of this strategy is highlighting the hypocrisy in being color-neutral but not gender-neutral, thus, providing the teacher educator with a recognized segue to call-in their teacher candidates by having them view contradictions in their belief systems and ideologies.

Another pedagogical approach that I use is incorporating films and other visual texts as opposed to just sharing our individual experiences. Naturally, personal stories are going to populate contentious as well as rich conversations. However, in my experience, the more personal a discussion gets, the more defensive White teacher candidates often become, especially when the topic of race is involved. Films thus give a great test case for teacher candidates to express their unfiltered thoughts, which minimize defensiveness to increase critical interaction and engagement. To give critical insight into different cultural representations of oppression, I employ films such as *Teach Us All*, *Precious Knowledge*, and *13th*. What makes the use of these films unique to discuss is they show the outcomes of oppressive measures, not just the everyday life of students in school settings. The films also incorporate interdisciplinary subject matters such as political science, sociology, psychology, history, economics, and business. As one example, my teacher candidates examined the topic of mass incarceration in terms of the total economic impact on Black and Brown communities through the lens of loss of wages from penal disenfranchisement. The previous analysis helped the class name and understand the impact of racial injustice, essentially leading them toward more critically reading the world (Freire, 1993) beyond words. This strategy also increased class engagement because we critiqued the film content based on what we read. Fundamentally, it created a conversation between scholars, artists, and students over the context of education and oppression.

Last, and most important, I encourage all teacher educators to help their teacher candidates challenge everything they know . . . and think they know. I foster a culture of critique where to prove oneself, one must learn to form an argument based on knowledge from credible sources. Throughout my courses, I reiterate three points. One, there are no universal truths. Two, nobody and nothing is perfect, and therefore, everyone and everything could be better. And finally, that there are countless ways to examine and solve problems. I engage with teacher candidates using the Socratic method to question everything they think is universally accepted. Consequently, many desire to research even the most citied information for themselves, and to draw independent conclusions about a particular topic. This practice is most helpful to engage with difficult topics, as we do not hold anything to be true, but instead, seek for truth (and in most cases, many truths) to be proved. I also encourage teacher educators to not be afraid to have their pre-service teachers both research and critique what and how we are teaching. The more opportunities that pre-service teachers have to practice being critical consumers of information, the more they will likely expand their intellectual toolkit to examine current issues that impact their current and future K-12 students.

In the end, I believe that teacher educators and teachers who are from racialized backgrounds ultimately serve in this profession to preserve our culture. That is, we want caring and exceptional teachers who will teach our children how to express their frustrations, joys, needs, and successes without penalty. This chapter serves as a building block for our future work, but it certainly is not a plateau of the work to be completed. As racism and other forms of oppression morph, so must we, as teacher educators, continue to fight against the racial contract (Mills, 1997). We cannot allow mostly White pre-service teachers to limit their epistemological understanding of social justice to comprehending the oppression trail that has been laid historically by not fixing the current methods used to reproduce inequities. Thereby, we must work to change the ideologies of our White pre-service teachers to reflect these practices: being inclusive, competent, and caring rather than being and playing the part of guilty and willfully ignorant White saviors.

2 (Re)discovering My Racialized Body

Critical Autoethnographic Connections

L. Trenton S. Marsh

Life as a Scholar of Color in Education: Autoethnographic Connections

As is true in ethnographic studies, the goal of my research as a scholar of color in education has been to develop a phenomenological understanding of various sites and actors within them through "deep immersion." Indeed, phenomenological research often leads to transformative effects and a "heightened perceptiveness, increased thoughtfulness and tact" (van Manen, 1990, p. 163). Thus, the implications of my dissertation research, which explored how one nationally recognized no-excuses charter school's philosophies about the construct of "academic success" informed the everyday practices of teachers and its implications on working-class students and their caregivers, also revealed a heightened (re)examination of my own identity. As a Black male scholar, I will explore why I, for so long, did not consider my racialized body within the context of researching other racialized bodies. I also reflect on what my newfound realization has meant for me as a Black education scholar in predominately White settings.

Where Do I Begin?

I have a deep-rooted familial link to public education. My sister is a kindergarten teacher. She followed the path of our mother, who earned her Master of Education degree and served as a reading specialist with the Cleveland Public Schools. My mother, in turn, was inspired by my grandmother (her mother), who also taught in the Cleveland Public School system for more than 40 years. In 1964, my paternal grandfather abandoned a successful career as a land-owning cotton farmer to pursue a Master of Arts in Educational Administration from the prestigious Teachers College at Columbia University. He would become a school principal and eventually the "Overseer" of many Black schools in rural Alabama. Possibly with the exception of my grandfather (although I am unsure of his opinion, as he passed away before I knew I wanted to pursue education as a profession), the educators in my family, like many educators within the United States, have been immersed in the master narrative concerning the education of Black children and youth. That is, their thinking has largely been that the primary reason for the "academic failure" and gaps (opportunity, achievement, and the like) among many Black children has an origin in so-called cultural deficits, meaning that they largely refuse to succeed because they have an oppositional culture that specifically devalues what they associate with Whiteness, or in this case, formal education (Ogbu, 2003).

However, I was also culpable in contributing to this larger deficit discourse until recently. From 2008–2012, I traveled throughout the United States to discuss my "turnaround success" of earning nearly a 1.0/4.0 grade-point average in high school to achieving a 4.0/4.0 at the collegiate level. I often urged the audience (typically low-income Black and Latino male students) to "stop being lethargic." I told these young men that they only had themselves to blame for their academic misfortunes, not their teachers, not their caregivers, and certainly not their schools. Even as I had an inclination that my relative socioeconomic advantages may have played a role in my "success" such that it provided me with regular exposure to programming and tutoring, I lacked the critical understanding to push against the dominant "pull yourself up by the bootstraps" narrative. Quite frankly, I lacked the courage to question the disproportionate and oppressive experiences of other Black males at my high school; that is, those who were counseled by White practitioners to enroll in less-rigorous courses and who may have endured more severe disciplinary infractions than I did. As Howard (2013) posits, "Black males are frequently thought of as a problem" by those around them (p. 55). With a review of my background established, the discussion shifts now to the framework of my racialized identity.

Becoming Black

In the psychology of nigrescence, also often referred to as the psychology of "becoming Black" or the process of self-actualization for Black Americans (Plummer, 1996), Cross, one of the seminal scholars of racial identity, developed a model to illustrate the complexity of Black identity (Cross, 1995). While Cross's work neglects to address the many factors that influence identity ranging from an individual's phenotype to sociocultural contexts, as I continue to develop my identity as a Black scholar, I am able to map out this framework almost like a legend on a map. I am able to map out specific aspects of my development and draw on the various racial-identity awareness gaps that I experienced as a youth and through my collegiate years.

Originally established in 1971, Cross outlined four stages that persons who are Black are said to undergo in the development of their racial identity. However, after considerable criticisms put forth by his peers, he addressed the shortages in his initial conceptualization over two decades later (Cross, 1995). In the following, after a brief description of each stage in the revised model, which includes miseducation and assimilation that precede the initial stage (pre-identity/pre-encounter) of the 1971 model, I will situate my development across these stages. The miseducation stage is the experience of being educated in the school system in the United States, in which the focus is principally on Western social-cultural-political history, and where the significance of Black/African history is not usually even considered (Awad, 2007). Such inaccurate portrayals of various nations within Africa, the continent itself, and the combined contributions that Africa and Black people in the diaspora have made to the world is largely unspoken. Blacks, as well as other groups, are often miseducated about the role of Africa and of Black people in the origin of Western civilization in K-12 schools and, as a result, often center and privilege Eurocentric perspectives as normative (Awad, 2007; Cokley, 2003). In the assimilation stage, Black individuals are more likely to see themselves as "American" as opposed to Black. Race is not a salient feature of identity for Blacks in the assimilation stage (Awad, 2007). The first stage of pre-encounter is described as a pre-discovery of one's racial identity. The individual will usually view the world in terms of a White frame of reference and concurrently devalue her/his Blackness (Plummer, 1996). In essence, the attitude is pro-White and anti-Black. At this stage, an individual lacks racial awareness and prefers to believe in a color-neutral society. The second stage of encounter is characterized by explorations of one's Black identity as a result of a critical incident or event due to race. The concluding result of this stage is that the individual gets steered toward the third stage or immersion-emersion; this marks the transition from the old to a new self-conception of Black identity. As a result of critical encounters with race and racism, these individuals immerse themselves in Black identity and culture. Blackness may present itself in many forms with such individuals. Some examples: one wearing ethnic hairstyles and clothing, associating primarily with Black people, and perhaps participating in Black-only organizations. Unquestionably, irrespective of the form, the individual becomes immersed in Black culture. The final stage is internalization. This stage depicts individuals' "comfort" in terms of their racial identity (Plummer, 1996, p. 170). An individual's identity in this stage would still give high salience to Blackness and also would not be consumed with hatred toward Whites. Instead, discord or "hatred" (Awad, 2007) turns into righteous anger toward institutions that continue to perpetuate racist and oppressive systems. In this stage, an individual is able to engage in cross-cultural discourse. Such individuals not only commit themselves to issues concerning Blacks but also engage in activities that help bring justice to other oppressed groups.

(Mis)Educated in Shaker Heights

Growing up in Shaker Heights, Ohio, I was convinced that simply "working hard" was the answer for many of the social ills that existed (and still exist) within US schools and society. Upon reflection, central to my argument for meritocracy was the belief in a color-neutral society, or what Cross termed as being situated in the pre-encounter stage of Black identity development (Awad, 2007). A color-neutral perspective assumes that major discrimination in the United States is a phenomenon of the past and the playing field has mostly been leveled among different sub-groups of Americans; therefore, if anyone is not successful, it is primarily a result of the person's own poor choices or lifestyle (Collins, 2005). I was socialized to believe in the myth of meritocracy. Here I was, the son of a Black physician, a proud man who was only one of his seven siblings who left the state of Alabama to pursue higher education. In adopting a color-neutral perspective, I never considered the behavioral outcomes of acculturation; for example, the difficulties of managing "everyday social encounters" if English is not a student's first language (Berry, Poortinga, Breugelmans, Chasiotis, & Sam, 2011, p. 315). I did not think about how a White teacher's implicit expectations could be adversely misaligned if a student's cultural repertoire was vastly different from the White dominant culture. Coming from a majority-White suburb, I never considered the role and the effects of poverty and social inequities on the lives of young people and the schools they attended.

Like most of suburbia in the United States, where many citizens are not considered to be "woke," I relied primarily on the White mainstream media to inform me about "the news." Upon critical reflection, the stereotypes concerning people of color, particularly specific constructions of Black masculinity, were prominent through these news sources. However, at the time, these images of Black males were not relatable to me. For instance, I recall in junior high school when the 1992 Los Angeles riots were occurring, and images of Rodney King were constantly on the television. At the time, Los Angeles seemed like a far-away land. Neither my family nor my school community encouraged any dialogue about what was happening to Black men writ large. We were supposedly safe, as here, we had no major disruptions to our everyday lives. Thus, we largely remained silent. Several months after the King verdict, I failed to make the connection with how he was brutalized to my racialized body being stopped one day by two White police officers as I walked home from a friend's house. Their queries of my whereabouts and current destination did not elicit any fear or apprehension in me. I simply pointed to my house, reciting the four-digit address that my mother embedded in my brain since I was a child. As I grew older and was able to drive, I was still unaware of how my racialized body was read in a White-supremacist society. In fact, when I had various incidents with law-enforcement authorities, like a superhero, it seemed that my social class came to the rescue. In high school, I recall getting pulled over by a local White male police officer for speeding through a yellow light. At the time, I was driving my mother's Mercedes-Benz. When the White officer approached me, I gave him my driver's license and confidently told him my reason for speeding as follows: "My family is going on vacation tomorrow. I had to rush to the orthodontist before they closed." I insisted that the officer could even call my mother to verify my account. The officer made the call on speakerphone and eventually let me go with a verbal warning. When I arrived home, I was reprimanded by my parents for the incident, but concerns about my race, our socioeconomic status, and the threat of law enforcement were not included in the conversation. However, much to my horror, I would experience the intersectionality of these three factors for the first time when I moved to Washington, DC (WDC) for college.

The Encounter: Being Black at a Predominantly White Institution

WDC was once referred to by locals as the "Chocolate City" because of large populations of African Americans since the 1960s. However, when I arrived to WDC as a college freshman in 1998, the demographics started to shift. There were certainly more White people in the upper-northwest part of WDC, which was also the home of my undergraduate institution, American University (AU). While my older roommate identified as Black, I recall being the only male of color in most of my classes. Then there were the occasional requests by my White professors to speak on behalf of all African American people. There was an assumption at AU from both White professors and White students that those like me who appeared to be Black and/or identified as an African American were from WDC, raised in lower socioeconomic households, or attended K-12 schools that lacked resources. That is, my time at AU became my encounter. Unlike Cross's framework, I did not experience one critical event; rather, it was the complete sociocultural context of AU that made me aware of my Blackness. For the most part, I fit in academically at AU as it related to academic achievement. I was also a student leader who held various positions during my four years. I seemed to fit in socially, hanging out with a predominantly White group of friends. Yet, there was an experience in class during my first year where something was happening that I could not quite put words to. *As a short matter of update, in 2017, the FBI was called in to investigate death threats to AU's student president, a Black female, after Trump's election. Also, after the election, bananas in nooses were found in trees. Perhaps if I had experienced these explicit forms of racist acts as a college student, I may have been able to clearly articulate what I was feeling as it relates to what is shared in the following sections.*

I recall reading about the concept "Driving While Black" for an anthropology course, which is a colloquial term for referencing the disproportionate racial profiling of Black Americans by law enforcement. It was the first time I ever heard about racial profiling. I also learned about the stark historical realities and fears of Black men driving at night through Prince George's County, Maryland, a county that borders the eastern portion of WDC. I read about the lessons most Black grandfathers, fathers, and uncles imparted to their grandsons, sons, and nephews when they were pulled over by the police such as, "Stay calm. Keep both of your hands on the steering wheel. Change the radio to classical music. Answer the officer politely." I only presume my father worked hard, thinking that our affluence would shield me from the special burdens and acculturation traditions that too many other African American males experienced inter-generationally. Instead of lessons on race, my father gave me a booster-identification card, which I used to refer to my friends as the "Get out of jail free" card. This card came about because my father donated generously to the Fraternal Order of Police of Ohio. He received identification cards from the organization indicating that he supported the local chapter. Previously, I had watched my father show this card and his business card, in addition to his driver's license and registration, when he was once pulled over by a White police officer. In hindsight, he did not offer this card to my sisters or my mother; however, he was insistent that I, like him, carry one. Perhaps this was a more color-neutral lesson from my father of how to engage with police while driving Black and especially as a young Black male. Let us now fast forward another decade as I continued with my racial-identity journey.

Immersion-Emersion: A Critical Discovery

I moved to New York City (NYC) to start a doctoral program concentrating in urban education under the mentorship of one of the most critically acclaimed scholars in the field, Pedro Noguera. Most people may assume that attending a university in such a diverse location such as NYC would automatically mean that the classrooms would be demographically similar. However, I was the only Black male in the incoming Teaching and Learning Program cohort of eight students in total. During my five years at the Steinhardt School of Culture, Education, and Human Development (also known as Steinhardt), I was the only Black male doctoral student in all of my classes.

Yet, when I arrived in NYC, I initially thought that not having colleagues who looked like me did not really matter. Let me quickly situate my disposition. Before attending NYU, I was a managing business consultant with IBM Corporation for over eight years, where I was often the only Black person in the entire room. I was certainly the only Black male in these settings. I led international teams, engaged executive leadership, and was selected for various honors, all without having many colleagues or leaders who mirrored my identity as a Black male. Thus, I thought I could handle graduate school on my own; that I could push through by faith/prayer and a strong work ethic but without a community of other peers in my program to support me. However, Steinhardt was different, as I was entirely out of my comfort zone. During my first year, I often felt isolated in the classroom. Since my trajectory to the doctoral program was unconventional after years of balancing volunteer work with youth organizations and maintaining a corporate career, I prayed to the Lord about my life's purpose. He revealed that anytime I was serving youth and working in education, it never would feel like "work" but instead would feel like my true calling. In the summer of 2012, I decided to walk by my faith and pursue a scholarly journey.

However, it seemed that one classmate, a White female, challenged my very presence at NYU. While I cannot recall a singular encounter to be able to type verbatim the discourse between us, I always felt that I had to be on the defensive whenever I engaged with her. I recall intentionally avoiding classes or any projects that she was aligned to or with. Perhaps because I was the only person in many of my classes and cohort who was not formally trained as an educator, she felt obliged to reject my ideas. Or perhaps because my teaching and learning experiences were "limited" to parochial schools, mentorship, and out-of-school programs, I felt inadequate to justify my passion for leaving a corporate position to enroll in a doctoral program and condemn my White peer's privileges. I did not know enough about the core theories, philosophies, and ideologies in the field of education. I did not have the technical jargon or understanding to articulate my positions in class. During my first year, I recall literally pleading to the Lord in prayer to equip me to have "scholarly speak." That is, I wanted to sound a certain way, or like most of my White classmates. At the time, I did not understand that my desire would perpetuate the centering of Whiteness in education. I later decided to relinquish this prayer; I simply trusted the voice that the Lord birthed into me.

I began to gain additional confidence toward the close of my first year as I engaged more with the various entities at the Metropolitan Center for Urban Education and the Transformation of Schools, the center that Noguera led and where I would call home (and my employer) as a graduate research assistant. The Metro Center, as it is affectionately known at NYU, furthered my research of marginalized and vulnerable communities, particularly Black and Latinx students and their families. At the Metro Center, I found scholars and practitioners, many of whom also identified as persons of color, working side by side. They were all explicitly interested in the assets and strengths (rather than the deficits) of Black and Latino male bodies. I first learned about the disproportionate overrepresentation of African American and Latino boys in special education, as well as the uneven disciplinary outcomes that these students overwhelmingly experience in the state of New York. I also learned how culturally relevant pedagogy could help correct these disparities.

Yet, there was still something missing. While the Metro Center served as a place of refuge, due to its sheer size and my student role, I was hesitant to publicly share my day-to-day struggles and apprehensions. As someone who identifies as a follower of Jesus, I understood the importance of "casting my cares unto the Lord" (1 Peter 5:7 New International Version), but I also needed to engage with others. I needed to forge relationships with individuals who looked like me and who could relate to this journey. I was fortunate to be introduced to the Research, Advocacy, Collaboration, Empowerment Mentoring (or the RACE Mentoring) from a postdoctoral fellow at NYU The RACE Mentoring is a virtual mentoring program co-founded by Donna Y. Ford at Vanderbilt University, Michelle Trotman Scott at the University of West Georgia, and Malik S. Henfield at the University of San Francisco. The aims of the group are threefold: (1) provide mentoring to faculty and doctoral/graduate students of color, (2) increase the representation of faculty of color on campuses and within the tenure-track, and (3) promote collaboration among academics in all educational settings.

Virtually through this space, I was able to vent about the various racial microaggressions that I experienced in class. I was able to receive immediate support and suggestions from other scholars who were either on the same journey or had similar experiences before during their doctoral journeys. Simultaneously, the group offered opportunities for collaboration with other scholars of color on publications. From the second and third years in my doctoral journey, it was the mix and exposure of the Metro Center and the RACE Mentoring where I really became aware of the notion of being a racialized person. As an education researcher, I also began to think about how a White teacher's implicit or explicit expectations could be adversely misaligned if a Black student's cultural frame is vastly different from the dominant White culture and norms that are often expected in the mainstream classroom. For instance, I began to consider broader and bolder policy approaches to educational inequities beyond schools and teachers. For example, I was encouraged to engage with youth as research-participants, using their voices as leaders to explore the root causes, consequences, and potential solutions of various educational inequities. I also had the opportunity to work with student-teachers at the pre-service level, helping them become advocates for their K-12 students through a curriculum that interrogated the dominant culture and embraced a pedagogy that humanized and honored the many assets that children and youth bring to various classrooms.

Yet again, something was still missing in my life. As I was evolving as a Black male scholar and building my research foci, I forgot about one of my most important assignments, which was my marriage. I recall listening to a senior male scholar of color at a national conference who publicly shared that while he had critical acclaim as a researcher, he struggled to balance his work life with his home life with his wife and four children. Privately, another prominent Black male scholar shared a similar dilemma. I knew that like them, I wanted to touch the lives of young people in an authentic and caring way, but I did not want to live in contradiction if my own home lacked the adequate attention, love, and care. Soon thereafter, my wife and I engaged with the marriage ministry at our local church. Every other week, we connected with other couples, discussing scriptures and sermons, and openly shared as a group how we wrestled and triumphed in our young marriages. I was in a safe space to take off my academic hat and just be a husband. Learning how to be a better husband, particularly the ability to press in through prayer and faith, echoing humility, being vulnerable, admitting mistakes, listening to different perspectives, and striving to be more selfless has been at the core of marriage and now permeates my narrative as an emerging scholar.

Internationalization

The final years of my degree led me to continue to become "more woke" about my racialized body. There was the murder of Mike Brown. Then Eric Garner. Then Tamir Rice. During the data collection, analysis, and writing of my dissertation study, it became apparent that unarmed Black male bodies were being killed by mostly White police officers, often without warrant or cause. How would my dissertation site, a no-excuses charter school servicing predominantly Black and Brown students, handle these concurrent injustices? How would the students, all students of color, interpret these tragic deaths of Black males? I was dismayed to learn that the deaths of these Black men were not usually discussed in classrooms, yet entire lessons were dedicated to the terrorist incident in Paris or the nightclub shooting in Orlando. I am not suggesting that one tragedy should outweigh another, but to remain silent, or in the case of this particular school, to simply not speak about police brutality as it impacts Black males, is extremely problematic, especially when the school serves a significant number of Black male students. However, this also is a school that insinuates the mis/belief that the most "well-behaved" Black student is, in fact, the most successful student who is supposedly immune from harm.

Significantly, the school's racialized silence reminded me of field notes that I collected in December 2015 when a White teacher seemed surprised that a Black male student introduced the topic of race in their class discussion:

> I quietly walked into Ms. Davis' eighth-grade science lab. The Tufts University advisory was present. As I entered, a student was snapping her fingers, as a sign of agreement to the video's pronouncement

that "drink a glass of red wine every day will help you live a long life." As I positioned myself in the back of the room (as I do for all classes), I was able to read the title of the video: *Prudential Insurance Company* presents, "How to live a long life." The cartoon was being streamed from the front of the classroom on the teacher's laptop. According to Ms. Davis, the video is based on a *Prudential Insurance* study that identified daily "real life" occurrences that were studied and correlated to living a longer life. As the class watched, the video continued with a series of different daily activities to preserve life, or as it was pronounced, "You'll live longer if . . ." as a cartoon image morphed into the participation of each said activity. "Getting along with your mother," "flossing your teeth," "if your name starts with A," "if you live in the country," "if you're a married person," "if you have at least four children," "if you have a pet," "if you eat a bit of dark chocolate every day," and a few others.

There was one reference to race, "if you're Hispanic," to which the cartoon image said, "Hola." As I watched, I noted the cartoon image involves a fair-skinned White woman or a fair-skinned White man. The fair-skinned man was attributed to three activities: (1) "you live longer if you have a Mediterranean diet"; (2) "enjoy gardening" as the cartoon man planted a full forest; (3) "you live longer if you live on a mountain."

To me, the cartoon caricatures looked White. For instance, for the activity, "If your name starts with an "A," the video showed a picture of a tall, slender White woman named "Ana" with long brown hair. As the video zoomed in to the woman's driver's license photo, we are able to get a close up on her face. She has a narrow nose and very thin lips (as opposed to full lips that are usually ascribed with women of African and Latina descent).

As the video ended, Ms. Davis, a White woman also with long brown hair like the cartoon caricature "Ana" asked the class, "So what does this mean?" A student named Sydney, a Black boy with an evenly picked-out Afro, raised his hand. He was the only student who had a hand raised. With little participation from students, Ms. Davis modified her question and asked about a specific account of the video. So, "What does this mean about flossing?" she asked. Sydney never lowered his hand and was called on. "[The video means] that if you are *White*, you are going to live longer," he offered. Several students burst out in laughter, others had puzzled looks, and some even had blank stares. Ms. Davis, too, looked perplexed by his racialized comment.

"Ooookay, it *may* show White people live longer," Ms. Davis responded, as she hurriedly moved the class past Sydney's response. I imagined however that Sydney was addressing Ms. Davis' original query: What does this video mean? Perhaps she does not know how to address the fact that only fair-skinned, Whitish looking people were displayed in the video about living longer. It could be that Ms. Davis is completely uncomfortable talking about race and doesn't know how to have this conversation. Since Ms. Davis identifies as a White American woman, the video may seem like a normative depiction of life, of her unconscious privilege. Before the class moved on, Sydney eagerly raised his hand and was called on again. He wanted to share additional context to his original response about White people living longer. "I was thinking about the White girl who had the letter 'A' for her first name [Ana]. I was thinking about stereotypes."

At Sydney's school, he has heard from the adults there that choices made as early as an eighth-grader mattered for his life, perhaps at a greater magnitude than a young White female (as depicted on the *Prudential Insurance* video) who lives in another more affluent community. His mostly White teachers constantly made statements reminding his classmates about the importance of, for instance, "following instructions," "being mature," being "resilient," and not "making excuses for failure" despite one's circumstances that may have prevented access to opportunities and resources. School rules (e.g., sitting in *STEP*, which stood for: *S*it up (and fold your hands), *T*rack teacher, *E*ager to ask and answer questions, and *P*roper respect) were constantly reinforced as well. He was constantly told to avoid falling into any stereotypical traps that could consume the lives of Black males in the United States. But sadly, as he has witnessed through the news media, Black boys and men could even be killed without falling into these so-called predetermined traps: Alton Sterling, Philando Castile, Terence Crutcher, and Keith Lamont Scott (among many more) were some of the many unarmed Black men killed by mostly White law-enforcement officials in the year 2016 alone.

Yet, the White-looking girl in the commercial, as Sydney eloquently reflected, did not have to live in this racialized society. Her articulated path would be different from his and others like him. The White girl in the video did not have to go to a no-excuses urban charter school because her traditional neighborhood school was not in a low-income urban environment. Individuals with darker melanin were not displayed in the *Prudential Insurance* video, which was concerning in a school context where nearly all students were of color and situated in a community with nearly identical demographics. Sydney's critical reflections were indeed timely and appropriate, as I wrote in my fieldnotes, but I was doubtful that Sydney's classmates or Ms. Davis understood their significance. Was it possible that Ms. Davis was uncomfortable talking about race? Or just did not know how to have these types of critical conversations? Nevertheless, her lack of awareness and understanding, and ultimately her silence in the classroom, did nothing to ease Sydney's racialized reality as a Black male.

I was comfortable being in a school with all students of color as a Black male scholar who was interested in the middle-school experiences of Sydney and others like him. However, I also acknowledge that my educational experiences were very different from the students I was engaged in with my dissertation study. Starting in the fifth grade, students in Shaker Heights begin to develop autonomy outside of their homeroom teachers. I recall being in a mathematics class for gifted students. I could exit my homeroom freely without asking for my teacher's permission and walk unescorted to a classroom down the hall. Inside the classrooms, movements were not regulated. There were no digital timers with countdowns, or a constant articulation by our teachers about college or being mature high-school students. I never heard reference to needing to be "college-ready," which is the term I often heard in my research sites. There was no talk about "changing the world" outside of the occasional schoolwide recycling programs. Teachers allowed us to be kids. As a larger homeroom, when we walked in the hallways, we had to organize ourselves in straight lines, but this requirement was not regulated with any attack on our character, and certainly, not with physical force or verbal tirades of a teacher or another adult in the building. There were no painted lines on the linoleum floors that we were required to walk on or between. Students were, for the most part, able to wear whatever they wished with some discretion. Jewelry and nail polish were allowed, as well as shirts with one's favorite sports team or cartoons. Some of my classmates wore mohawks while others experimented with various hues of hair dye.

In the seventh grade, my and other classmates' autonomy and freedom continued to increase. Similar to the university setting, we were able to choose our own classes based on our interests and the common Ohio state courses that were required for promotion. Here, there were no mandatory straight lines like what we experienced in the fifth and sixth grades. Homeroom was just a place in the morning where we could call home, but we really never returned to it. Since my public school was not co-located with another school, we did not have to eat lunch in silence in our homeroom; rather, we were able to speak and eat freely with our friends in a large open cafeteria. This level of freedom and individual choice continued through my years in high school. Throughout my public schooling in Shaker Heights, I never had to endure the more regimented spaces that emphasize rules and behavioral control like the schools that I am often researching, or the schools that are only serving impoverished and working-class neighborhoods (Anyon, 1980).

I recognize that my family's class status and the educational environment that I was socialized in helped offset the social construction of how White Americans often view Black males growing up in America. Yet, had it not been for other aspects of my social privileges (e.g., attending a socioeconomically integrated school, living in a zip code with affluent residents, no religious markers such as a turban, English as my primary language, having US citizenship, growing up with two married parents, and so forth), I may have shared educational spaces, lived experiences, institutional labels, cultural deficits, teacher perceptions, and consequently, the life trajectories that many young Black male participants of my research already had laid out for them. While my racialized insider position as a scholar provides me with certain advantages in the field, I only hope that my more privileged position as an American from more affluent means does not block my ability to see certain racialized interactions as either favorable or unfavorable for the students because they are so uncommon to my experiences. I continuously discover and accept, as a researcher, and particularly as ethnographers often do, that meanings could become clearer after leaving the research site.

Possibilities

In what follows, I will separate my ideas by different points of campus engagement when I was a doctoral student at a predominantly White institution, a key time when I both learned about and thought about my racialized body. I believe these implications would have wide-ranging impacts for a variety of persons including students and new faculty.

1. **Create a Specific Welcome Orientation:** while it may be an institutional tradition to have all faculty and staff welcome incoming doctoral students, what would have been even more powerful is an event where faculty and staff who are Indigenous and of color specifically were invited to engage with students from similar backgrounds. Such would be an ideal space for emerging scholars to benefit from seeing mirrors and role models, and also, for having a space to engage with others without worrying about code-switching or putting on yet another mask. This type of event would also illustrate that the university may genuinely be interested in our intellectual growth and our positive socio-emotional development.

2. **Engagement With University Life:** from serving on several research teams, to participating in the planning committee for the sixtieth anniversary of *Brown vs. Board*, to writing a federal grant, being situated in a research center or a unit that is focused on the challenges and issues facing marginalized and vulnerable populations were important for the rediscovery of my racialized body. Thus, universities need to build and sustain specific opportunities for engagement to create spaces for these types of collaboration. These engagement opportunities would also ideally be counted toward positively toward performance or tenure requirements in some way.

3. **"Grad Dinners":** was a monthly offering sponsored by the Center for Multicultural Education and Programs that allowed diverse graduate students to engage in informal conversations with faculty from

racialized backgrounds across schools and departments about their journeys and experiences in navigating academia and other professional arenas.

4. **Everyday Zone Training:** also sponsored by the Center for Multicultural Education and Programs, there were three zones of foci: Justice, Dream, and Disability. I participated in the "Dream Zone" training, as I was unfamiliar with the issues and challenges facing undocumented communities. A series of training sessions, the first looked at immigration transnationally, the second part looked at the issues faced by undocumented students in NYC and specifically my PWI, exploring ways in which students could express solidarity with undocumented members of our community who were undocumented.

5. **Mentorship:** the Research, Advocacy, Collaboration, Empowerment (RACE) Mentoring virtual group provided a much-needed space to reflect on my everyday experiences as a scholar in training at a predominantly White university (I reference its mission and purpose earlier in this essay). All participants are invited by existing members. Everyone is expected to contribute to the aims of the group, whether that is commenting on a question, uploading an article, sharing a job announcement, and the like.

Final Thoughts

As a Black male who has only studied (for undergraduate, master's, and doctoral degrees) at predominantly White institutions, and now as someone who is working at a predominantly White setting, the first word that comes to mind when thinking about how to cope, survive, and thrive as a racialized body is building community. Creating a space, or what I have referred to in the past as a haven or refuge from the everyday traumas at these institutions, is important. As an undergraduate scholar, though I was not totally "woke" to my racialized experiences, I was part of the Ronald E. McNair Scholars program, where I could be with other students like me in a supportive space together. As the only business major in my cohort and usually the only Black male in my business classes, the McNair Scholars community created a space for me to regularly see other racially diverse scholars who were also interested in research-oriented careers.

Then there was The George Washington University. As I entered the university's defunct chapter of the Black Graduate Students Association (BGSA) that had four members, I was asked to take over the presidency. Recalling the importance of having a community on campus. We went from four members when I started to 140 members when I graduated. As a community, we were able to hold forums and push for demands to contest policies and practices that were not in the best interest of our constituents. For instance, in 2003, the *Black Enterprise Magazine* listed

GWU as one of the top-25 schools for Black students. After polling many Black undergraduate and graduate students about their thoughts of GWU's ranking, the executive board determined that in reality, very few Black students agreed with the rankings. After contacting the magazine directly, we were informed that students were not contacted but, rather, the opinions of recruitment and development officers were central to making this determination. The BGSA then demanded a forum. Inviting every dean and the university president (who sent the provost instead), we held a forum that was designed to address resolutions from Black students about how the university could consider our perspectives. While the event inadvertently created the space for certain units to glorify their numbers and the well-intentioned claims of diversity at the university-level, there was no genuine progress on how to incorporate Black students' voices in the ranking methodology, even if the magazine was geared toward Black parents who might consider sending their children to GWU. Despite these challenges, as an organization, we found room for celebration, as the event put the university on notice that Black graduate students were capable of mobilization and would not sit silently on the sidelines to allow them to make certain claims that were not true.

At the doctoral level, building community at various levels still was the most relevant and significant factor in my life. As highlighted previously, the communities I have been part of have addressed my multiple identities. I now needed a community that supported my transition of being a person of color at a predominantly White university at the undergraduate level to another institutional context. I needed a community to help me anchor my research and scholarly knowledge. I needed a community to help me become a better husband. There is an underlying issue of representation at play. There are so few Black males in higher education, which may explain some of the isolating experiences I encountered as a student in addition to the racialized stereotypes including the exchanges with the White female student at NYU. These experiences suggest the reality that since there are so few Black males in the academy, that administrators, scholars, and perhaps even students hold very limiting views of what "Black male success" (i.e., the William "Bill" Cosby model of assimilation and respectability) looks like within the context of higher education that can be detrimental to aspiring Black male scholars who disrupt (or for some outright reject) these expectations. Consequently, regardless of whether emerging scholars choose to "color" within, just outside, or radically beyond "the lines," higher education institutions need to affirm multiple types of Black male scholars. As we continue to discover and build our authentic voices and narratives about our lived experiences, whether racialized, stereotyped, marginalized or not, Black male scholars should be able to engage within an institution that allows us to retain our true selves in public, as well as supports our ability to challenge inequities at the institutional, local, and national levels.

3 Life After Death

Beyond the Epistemologies of Black Education Struggle in Teacher Preparation and Toward a Pedagogy of Black Educational Life

Ezekiel Joubert III

Forethought

I hesitated to have class on the Monday after the grand jury announced that Officer Jeronimo Yanez would be acquitted of all charges related to the death of Philando Castile in Falcon Heights, Minnesota (a suburb within the Saint Paul limits). In July 2016, we had all become witnesses to his death and haunted by the screams, tears, and the blood captured by Diamond Reynolds's (his fiancée's) Facebook live-video post. Coincidentally, at the time, I was teaching in proximity to where he had been gunned down on a car ride home in front of his four-year-old daughter who was sitting in the back seat. If we would have listened more carefully, we might have heard the seven shots and their cries as we exited the classroom. With the intention to explore the trauma faced by the surrounding communities and specifically his daughter, I nervously asked my class of mostly White pre-service teachers in a course I teach titled "Educational Psychology" to consider the socio-psychological effects that racial violence may have on teachers and students who relive the afterlives of slavery, lynching, mass incarceration, and the brutal public deaths of unarmed Black men and boys by the state. I proposed that we should reflect critically on the possible effects of re-storying racial violence. In particular, we should have reflected critically on the effects on Castile's toddler, the children he served as a nutrition supervisor at a Saint Paul elementary school, and school-age children in general. Several of the predominantly White female teacher candidates in my class, many from affluent and middle-class backgrounds, provided me with puzzled glances that implied, "What does your question have to do with . . . *teaching?*" Yet . . . I waited, hoping someone would speculate or maybe even *feel* what I had proposed we explore, in order to consider racial violence a pedagogical and curricular concern for all educators including those who are White. Instead, they rejected my idea with silence, or the ultimate refusal to engage in the matters of Black life and death.

Nevertheless, after class, two White teacher candidates representing a group of their White peers confronted me about concerns regarding my "classroom expectations." The story of racial violence was concealed quickly and consumed by their need to make their discomfort, anxiety, and beliefs relevant and visible. When I asked, with care on my face and pain in my body, which of my "classroom expectations" were unclear to them, they were mum and unable to elucidate further. As a Black male scholar in the world of teacher preparation, I often experience suspicious White teacher candidates who weaponize their concerns about my "classroom expectations" as a foil for asking whether my anti-racist, anti-capitalist, and critical pedagogies would prevent me from being fair, democratic, and understanding to their "well-intentioned," ignorant, and/or innocent thoughts and practices related to race/ism and power. In culling over this moment, I have generated many questions on the matters of life, death, and teacher preparation for teacher educators who are in these programs to "save" racialized bodies. For example, how do we understand Black life and death in teacher education? How does the engagement of Black life and death in teacher-preparation classrooms act as a social instrument for resolving moral dilemmas in the US schools? How does this engagement impact the ability of racialized scholars to teach about *and* for racial justice? How are does this engagement afford scholars from racialized backgrounds (and the mostly White pre-service teachers we teach) with the tools to name, reflect, and act on the ways in which we are implicated in (and understand) the educational structures and logics that construct and impose racial ideology as well as the violence and oppression that it depends on?

Critical educational scholars (e.g., K.D. Brown & A.L. Brown, 2010, 2012; Berry & Stovall, 2013; Dillard, 2006; Dumas, 2016) have described and interpreted the ways in which the material and discursive lives of Black people force us to examine the unsettling and bleak realities of racial violence and oppression in our society and schools. Unfortunately, these realities act as social instrumentality for several Whites Americans to resolve many of the moral dilemmas between their democratic beliefs and anti-democratic practices (Ellison, 1953), and between the cherished democratic belief that we are all created equally against the toleration of heinous acts of the unholy trinity including the dispossession, displacement, and disenfranchisement of Black people in the United States and throughout the diaspora (Marable, 2004). Much of the educational research and teacher-education curricula about and for Black people (but usually not by us) largely focus on issues such as the astonishing effects of social violence, racial difference, urban schools and communities, poverty, and terrorism within the premise that knowledge of these topics will redress the centuries of inequality in our society and schools. However, research and practices used in pre-service classrooms too often form an image and understanding of Black people that are bound by immanent violence, suffering, and death (Dillard, 2006). This racial script is internalized, normalized, and mobilized by White pre-service teachers and White-dominated teacher-preparation programs in the responses and in the treatment of racialized scholars (Johnson & Bryan, 2017; Matias, 2013). In a sense, my Black male body is seen by Whites as the "Negro giant trussed up like Gulliver" (note: this metaphor is used by Ellison (1953) to describe the ways by which stereotypes about Black people are constituted). My Black body thus constructs the stage for White future classroom teachers, the majority who are never or are rarely in proximity to Black bodies, to associate (my) Blackness with inhumanity, disorder, and other conditions of social death. As a move to understand the matters of Black life and death in the world of teacher preparation, I have developed a pedagogy of Black educational life as a corrective and reparative tool for teaching and engaging in research as a scholar of color in the mostly White world of teacher preparation.

This chapter conceptualizes my pedagogy of Black educational life as a method for articulating and disrupting the ways by which racial knowledge about Black struggle and oppression is mobilized in relation to racialized scholars in teacher preparation. We aim to rupture and resist the partiality of these stories; the enactment of dehumanizing pedagogies and policies; and the construction of educational structures that reproduce distorted constructs of race, class, gender, and sexual orientation. For these purposes, we could better attend to the ways that the Black body is treated in educational spaces, while also developing a humanizing praxis for our predominantly White teacher candidates from affluent and middle-class backgrounds, many who also claim a desire to teach for *and* toward social justice. I have learned that White teacher candidates are generally unaware of how they abstract racialized bodies for their own personal growth and understanding. Therefore, I propose that racial-justice discourses and approaches in teacher education adopt frames that embrace the fullness of Black life – struggle, resistance, and future.

Methodologically, I consider autoethnography, specifically an "auto-ethnography of reconciliation," to reflect and build on my feelings and readings of the world (McClellan, 2012, p. 89). The author defines this type of autoethnography as one that centers the complexities of lived experiences in order to systematically examine the personal. My writing focuses on the self to examine my teaching in relation to teacher educators like me who are trying to reconcile with our teaching, racial violence, and the positioning of dominant knowledges in teacher preparation. Hence, this level of critical reflection provides a glimpse into the ways I reckon with (and also attend to) the role of race and being in the classroom.

In what follows, I consider how the racial knowledge, from what Wynter (1994) coins as "no humans involved" through which K.D. Brown (2013) further describes as "framing discourses," impacts knowledge production in teacher education. I make the case that the knowledge embedded and produced in teacher education frames Black lives and people in imminent struggle, which manufactures White consciousness to recognize and deny the matters of Black life and death. I also explore the metaphor of "enclosure" and how it impacts the responses to and treatment of my body-soul, which becomes an additional curriculum text for mostly White teacher candidates (Milner, 2015). Thereafter, I will outline how my pedagogy of Black educational life counters the violence of abstraction (Hartman, 2008; Sharpe, 2016), as well as disrupts social redress through the consumption of minoritized bodies (Hong, 2018). Finally, I conclude with a summation of my thoughts and a proposition that scholars who are BIPOC in teacher preparation seek "[t]he renunciation of actual being for historical being; the preservation of the ontological totality" (Robinson, 1983, p. 168) to envision our lives and teaching beyond the boundaries of imminent violence and death, and thus, toward the possible.

Teaching With "No Humans Involved:" How Framing Discourses Impact the Epistemologies of the Black Educational Struggle in Teacher Education

In 1994, the acquittal of the policemen involved in the Rodney King case generated frustration and outrage among historically disaffected Black communities across the nation. Wynter (1994) reveals that many of the public officials in the Los Angeles judicial system repetitively used the acronym NHI (no humans allowed) to refer to the cases involving the violation of young and unemployed urban Black males and their rights. She proposes that the impacts of the Civil Rights movements in the 1960s and affirmative-action programs (and thus, the incorporation of the Black middle class in the American project of democracy and capitalism) allowed for the jobless category to emerge in which unemployed Black males like King bore the burden of being "deviant" in status and theory. As our society improved the conditions for some African Americans, the price paid by Black males who could did not "fit the mold" (of Whiteness) were, with respect to state apparatuses such as the judiciary system, increasingly and routinely enclosed by the logics of the prison-industrial complex. She argues that the classificatory logics wherein mostly White scholars determine how Black people and their intelligence are "evolutionary" lower than White people are connected to the ways by which "knowledge" is ordered and common disciplinary paradigms are constructed.

Critical scholars in education (e.g., Dumas, 2016; Giroux, 2009; Sojoyner, 2016; Vaught, 2017) add that Black bodies are managed and conceived by the neoliberal economy and the US government to maintain and re-establish social hierarchies, particularly ones that are racialized.

These systems have retained the legacies, logics, and practices of White supremacy, patriarchy, and other oppressive political systems that often result in the removal and/or enclosure of Black bodies. In fact, Black K-12 students are more likely to have repressive educational experiences compared to White students including those that involve school arrests and surveillance through metal detectors, tracking systems, zero-tolerance policies, and interactions with the military, to name a few (Saltman, 2016). In light of the aforementioned challenges, teacher preparation has become "ground zero" for purchasing and consuming these forms of knowledge, and thus, teacher educators and other members of these programs largely participate in constructing tools and methods in which these systems either endure or change.

K.D. Brown (2013) posits that the sociocultural knowledge of the "social, cultural, economic, political, and historical knowledge that informs how societies and schools operate" (p. 232) in educational research, policies, and popular discourses frame Black students as "trouble, troubling, or troubled" (p. 318). She further argues that these discourses, "regardless of their intent . . . exist within and help to reinscribe an already limiting notion of human constituted by historically contingent, Western epistemic notions of humanity" (p. 318). These dehumanizing discourses about Black bodies, students, schools, and communities enclose and position them as low-income, "at risk" for academic failure, unmotivated, disruptive, and dangerous to Whites. As an intervention, framing discourses challenges the operationalization of these forms of knowledge in teacher preparation.

Unfortunately, as a scholar of color in teacher education, I find myself in the midst of these discourses and approaches: as a perpetrator and a casualty; also, as a carrier of troubling news in a troubled body. When I trace how these frames produce and order racial knowledge in my classroom, I often find myself fettered to the perennial question posed by Du Bois as follows: "How does it feel to be a problem?" (Du Bois & Marable, 2014, p. 4). In other words, as it has become customary for me to feel in psychological and physiological ways, I often reflect on the following: one, how Black bodies are abstracted and often reduced to "achievement-gap" data or culturally specific behaviors, and two, how White practicing or pre-service teachers largely consume Black bodies as social tools for making sense of (and confronting) issues/struggles related to cultural/racial differences, democracy, and power. Thus, the racial knowledge that mostly White pre-service teachers obtain, through White-framed curricula and textbooks, are mostly attached to racial stereotypes instead of the material realities of racialized subjects (Vaught, 2017).

Thus, Wynter's (1994) notion of "no humans involved" informs the curriculum, which could be defined as a set of knowledges learned at a given time (Eisner, 1994) or the official knowledge that is seen as "worth knowing" (Berry & Stovall, 2013; Pinar, 2012). These understandings essentially order the ways by which race and racialization are proliferated in teacher-preparation classrooms. In contemporary teacher-education programs, the official curriculum, which is conflated by framing discourses, aims to meet the various sociocultural and sometimes the political needs of various learners (K. D. Brown, 2013). These knowledge forms permeate through program requirements and syllabi to encourage multiculturally just philosophies and approaches to teaching. However, if what Woodson (1990) proposes that the dominant curriculum serves to *misrepresent* other knowledges about race and racialization, then one could argue that the institutionalization of social/racial justice-oriented curricula in teacher preparation reproduces a manufactured consciousness in which White teacher candidates will likely experience cognitive dissonance due to our society's reproduction of the disavowal . . . of the threat of (racial) death. That is, "we recognize it superficially so that we can deny it more profoundly on the deeper registers that constitute our ontological and political being" (JanMohamed, 2015, n.p.)

The aforementioned cognitive dissonance is evident in several of my White teacher candidates' internal struggles, along with notions that they cannot (and will not) take any responsibility for the impossible-to-believe and violent acts manufactured and perpetrated around the globe and in their communities by a people they "love to death." In many cases, they turn away from humanity and *"the humans involved"* in grappling with ideology and culture. They instead consume and surface other non-material ideas that will make up their future teaching practices. However, it is important to dismantle and disrupt the ideologies that reproduce White-supremacist/racist logics. That is, there is a need to dismantle a culture that promotes violence, as well as the usual ahistorical and narrow positioning of dominant knowledges framed in the discourses about Black bodies that construct a crisis narrative (Lozenski, 2017) in which White teacher candidates largely learn to embody "a concern" for Black struggles in education while simultaneously mobilizing strategies that make Black educational experiences a site of enclosure.

Black Teacher Educators as Curriculum Texts

In the previous section, I aimed to story how common framing discourses impact teacher preparation in ways that abstract and reduce Black bodies to the logics of "no humans involved" (Wynter, 1994), which is in large part due to the White fixation and gaze on the assumed Black educational struggle. Here, I argue that Black teacher educators, who often embody and teach these discourses and material realities, are used as social instruments, both metaphorically and physically, as curriculum texts wherein their White colleagues and students become more "socially aware" of injustice, as Milner (2015) suggests:

> Teachers' race, ethnicity, sexual orientation, and gender, among other identity markers, shape what they teach and even how they enact a curriculum. Their very being, their experiences, and the ways in which they interact with their students and the curriculum are curricular in nature. Students [of color] "read" teachers and engage in an iterative process of knowing and coming to know that is shaped by the social environment.
>
> (p. 2)

The framework of Black teachers as curriculum texts (Milner, 2015) proposes that Black teachers embody the core approaches and principles in Ladson-Billings's (2006, 2008) notion of culturally relevant pedagogy. This framework helps me understand why I am concerned with the story of Black life/death, and how I embody those epistemologies in my own pedagogy. However, if we assume that Black teachers embody experiences that help racialized learners understand social contradictions and conditions, then how might White teacher candidates respond to me and what I embody?

For instance, during the 2016 US presidential election, one White female teacher candidate in my class asked me the following: "*How does it feel* to be the only Black male in this class? Do you feel safe?" I found her observation to be a critical one. I felt as though I embodied racially and socially just pedagogies in ways that helped her develop a sociopolitical consciousness about underrepresentation. Then she suggested that it would be normal for me to feel unsafe because under such regimes of blatant racism, which she had witnessed the day after the election as a substitute teacher (specifically, she had witnessed a White elementary student tell a classmate that President Trump was going to send the family back to their home country by force). With cloudy eyes, she looked at me as if I was going to suffer premature death or racial violence upon exiting the classroom. In actuality, her response reflected the potential inhumanity that the Black body retains. This all has made me think about how Black teacher educators, as curriculum texts (Milner, 2015), repeatedly "hand over" our bodies to our White teacher candidates to build, for example, what they see as culturally relevant pedagogies. This all is not without experiencing a blockade of erasure and estrangement on our end. For one, where I find myself grappling with the fact that my body is mis/read as if it is in danger and vulnerable, and thus, an essential tool for White-liberal teacher candidates to feel as though they need to "save" not only Black children, but me as well. Matias (2013) argues that this White-savior mentality is dangerous because it really is more about them (i.e., White teacher candidates) equating their pain and trauma with the oppressed members of society who have experienced racial terror and violence directly over generations. This mentality also allows White future teachers to retool their ignorance and innocence. Therefore, I propose these processes, at least for Black teacher educators, should happen in the form of enclosure.

Enclosed by Framing Discourses in Teacher Preparation: Those Who Struggle Need "Structure"

Black teacher educators play a significant role in transforming White and White-washed visions of education. We spotlight (and also understand through firsthand experiences) the many challenges that Black people experience with educational systems, teachers, and curricula of various types. I propose that critical education scholars who are interested in the labor and lives of Black teacher educators should consider not how we are excluded from the project of capitalists' democratic education but rather focus on how we are (or should be) included in the process intentionally. In this view, the inquiries about our lives and livelihood could be used to demonstrate the effects of larger educational structural arrangements. I now turn here to the notions of educational enclosure (Sojoyner, 2016) to think through how Black bodies have been racialized in ways that allow for the dispossession of our knowledge and physical bodies. Sojoyner (2016) argues that in the contexts of post-industrial schooling, in particular in the language of urban schooling, the formation of the prison is the dominant model of forced enclosure in the (educational) lives of Black people. This enclosure makes (my) Blackness a target for surveillance and policing. Browne (2015) suggests that Blackness is a key site in which a system of surveillance is enacted, narrated, and practiced; teacher-preparation programs are not exempt spaces. In the following, I demonstrate how the framing discourses and Wynter's (1994) logics of "no humans involved" not only abstract Black educational life and uses Black bodies as social instruments, but they also impact and shape the responses to and treatment of my Black body in teacher-preparation classrooms by White teacher candidates, which largely limits my freedom to achieve actual being through a form of enclosure. White teacher candidates often embody tacit policing techniques and bind my life (and Black children's lives) to narratives and the conditions of social death.

To illuminate, I have regularly had experiences in my courses when I historicize, racialize, and thus challenge disciplinary norms in K-12 education. In particular, I bring up the notion that common practices of classroom management promoted in the literature on culturally responsive teaching could potentially cause harm to children from racialized backgrounds because they reproduce techniques and a systems of management from the plantation, factory, and neoliberal management strategies that limit collective critical learning and the ability for children of color to "just be" (Casey, Lozenski, & McManimon, 2013). The earlier framing is in direct opposition to what mostly White pre-service teachers have experienced in their own schooling, and also, what they learn in their other education courses taught primarily by White education faculty whose values, consciously or not, are embodied in these oppressive practices. In one case, a young White male teacher candidate towered over me (for reference, I am considered to be below average in height for a Black male). He was clearly distraught by my storying of an eight-year-old Black girl who had been isolated, alienated, and defined as "bad" by her peers, confronted in what I thought to be clear example of how programs such as the *Responsive Classroom* may unintentionally punish children from racialized backgrounds and thus shape other types of problematic racial knowledge in classrooms. During the class break, he walked up to me, without fear or hesitation, to tell me that he aimed to be the "best classroom manager" because "struggling" students of color need "structure" in order to succeed. As the semester went on, I noticed how he would constantly dismiss and devalue statements that would encourage the class to think about the ways by which our pedagogies often surveil and discipline racialized bodies. Once, I even heard him encourage his other White classmates to disagree with me because I was apparently turning "classroom norms" into "political issues."

In my view, his desire to gain control over my pedagogy and my Black body was a form of enclosure informed by a curriculum of fear (Nguyen, 2016) and violence (Cridland-Hughes & King, 2015). Here, my Black body was storied as a problem, dangerous to democracy and capitalism, and undisciplined in nature. While his actions could be defined as racial microaggressions (Sue, 2010), I suggest instead that they are essentially representative of good ol' fashioned White-supremacist reactions to Black bodies. Whether intentional or not, these types of reactions elevate an incarcerable logic and system that perpetuates the enclosure of Black and other racialized bodies.

The White teacher's general yearning to discipline racialized bodies is also about controlling racial knowledge, which signals a systemic delusion about the matters of life and death that systematically blur the lines between political and natural deaths (JanMohamed, 2015). In education, the disavowal of racial violence toward racialized bodies happens in a similar way. The combination of recognition and denial constructs a curriculum of tragedy (Berry & Stovall, 2013), which bounds Black subjectivity to racial violence, death, criminality, and other troubling societal ills. This curriculum makes the subject of the Black body hyper-visible without ever acknowledging the danger of it being seen. Thus, as my Black body interacts and engages with/in these logics, it forms layers of enclosure that remove my history and my knowledge from these spaces.

Since my Black body is surrounded by and attached to narratives of racial death, it is further mobilized to restrict the production of counter-knowledges and methods that humanize Black oppression. My responses in these moments become essential to disrupt the practice and rhetoric of Black social death performed in White-dominated school environments. I have made efforts to create incommensurability when describing Black educational struggles such as reflecting on "underachievement" and the formation of micro-prisons in the K-12 schools. I insist on using pedagogies that embrace my relationship to subjects such as Philando Castile, Trayvon Martin, Michael Brown, and other young Black males who were slain because the state and others continue to view our bodies through the logics of "no humans involved" (Wynter, 1994). However, it is painful to have to rehash this pain with White folks who only desire to redress these issues through my/our bodies instead of a systematic analysis of White-supremacist racism, or critical reflection of approaches that both frame Blackness in a constant and inevitable struggle. Thus, I aim to develop pedagogies that reveal forms of enclosure and move toward exploring teaching in ways that engage our actual being versus the historical/stereotypical being.

Toward a Pedagogy of Black Educational Life in Teacher Education

> In the treatment of the child the worlds foreshadows its own future and faith. All words and all thinking lead to the child – to vast immortality and wide sweep of infinite possibilities which the child represents.
>
> (Du Bois, 1916, n.p.)

I began with the story of brother Philando to reflect and describe a moment where I aimed to shift the notions of Black struggle, oppression, and troubles to instead think about the ways in which we might preserve the immortality of Black life. My pedagogical approach was to engage in questions about the living (i.e., his daughter and fiancée, school community, and the Black community at large) to redirect our methods of teaching and philosophies toward not only the topic of slow and fast racial terror (Dyson, 2015) but also to the spectacle of Black death and institutionalized structural racism, as well as Black resistance and Black futures. As I learned, my Blackness and my Black body became a social instrument in which mostly White pre-service teachers aimed to resolve their emotions, politics, and ideologies regarding race and power. Here, many White future teachers combined a crisis narrative and il/logic that made Black people subhuman subjects, and thus, their reactions and responses to Black struggle are ones of control and management.

I have developed pedagogical strategies and approaches that go beyond the epistemologies of Black suffering because our methods and tools for working through the damaging effects and encounters within the oppressive systems reproduced in educational structures have made us into "academic coroners." That is, we learn to perform educational triage, enabling us to diminish and dismiss oppressed communities' agency and visions for society (Woods, 2002, p. 63). Hence, in my teaching, I seek to disrupt these modes of being and knowing by centering the life-after-death knowledges, the knowledges of self-determination, and radical visions of futurity in order to develop critical pedagogies that center Black educational life instead of Black education imminent suffering and death.

To demonstrate, I aim to achieve what I outlined earlier through an inquiry of how I envision my work with the curriculum and my "classroom expectations." Beginning with the Du Bois quote at the beginning of this section, which is placed at the top of all of my course syllabi, I signal the goals and approaches of my pedagogy of Black educational life that demand us to think deeply about infinite possibility, imagination, and agency that our pre-service teachers embody and possess. In fact, I ask them to reflect on the meaning of this quote before we talk about the goals of the course. I have learned that many of us (and they too) struggle to see the light at the end of the tunnel when speaking about race and power in education. However, Du Bois's radical theorizing resists how we imagine the knowledges used to speak about oppressed children from racialized backgrounds in repressive school systems. Namely, I witness my White teacher candidates' attempt to name and trouble how they remove Black life from their analyses of children and communities from racialized backgrounds. In fact, many White teacher candidates have begun to embrace the notion that engaging in resistance and supporting communities in their analyses of racial violence will disrupt dominant consciousness by shifting their teaching to focus on actual life.

By the same token, the movement toward Black educational life orientates my body in dialogue with theirs instead of against it. I noticed a shift in the responses to my body when it calls for us to act against, for example, deficit ideologies, dominant epistemologies, and racialization. Before, my body would become the tool in which they would work out social and political contradictions. Now, many of my White pre-service teacher candidates place their own bodies and minds in a dialogical space in order to examine how the educational structures dispossess, as well as how dominant curricula misrepresent many people's experiences. We make the process of learning collaborative. Here, they are more open to creating critical questions and analyses that pertain to (and ascertain) the differences between natural and political life and death.

While this pedagogy aims to counter the violence of abstraction and refuses to redress social issues through the knowledges of Black suffering, I understand that there are limits to this method. For one, I recognize that focusing on Black educational life could fall into the multicultural trap of "celebrating" Black people's historical accomplishments, which is relatively easy for White teacher candidates to consume. Second, tracing schools in the United States as sites of social suffering for Black people (Dumas, 2014) often produces a sense of defeat, demoralization, and confusion among White teacher candidates. Given these points, a pedagogy of Black education life must engage routine praxis, a reflection of theory, and actions (Freire, 1993) in order to ensure a constant reflection on the ways the Black body is imagined and structured in educational spaces.

Afterthought: The Souls of Black Teacher Educators

When I was a youth, I went to church every Sunday. I went not because I was religious, but because I was enamored with the radical imagining of Black life that was taken up in that space. In songs like "Living Testimony" by the Williams Brothers (Williams, 1996) that I learned as a youth, it was clear that the Black figure struggled . . . but lived regardless. I have always carried this tune in my mind because once I became a classroom teacher, I realized that sometimes we are *the only ones* who believe we are alive and thus will live. Now as a teacher educator, the epistemologies of Black struggle cannot be one produced and consumed by White-dominated institutions that are only interested in "restructuring" the schools that our children, brothers, and sisters attend. Instead, we must consider the politics of our teaching in ways that engage in and with *the possible*. This means we must actively engage in the escape from enclosure to ensure living testimonies of Black educational life/future are always present in our pedagogies and our bodies.

4 Even if Our Voices Shake

Refusing to Be and Teach "Inside of the Lines"

Ferial Pearson and Sandra Rodríguez-Arroyo

Why Do We Stay?

> Leave safety behind. Put your body on the line. Stand before the people you fear and speak your mind – even if your voice shakes. When you least expect it, someone may actually listen to what you have to say. Well-aimed slingshots can topple giants
>
> (Maggie Kuhn, n.d., n.p.)

On a blustery, snowy morning in February in Nebraska on our way to our university, we each drove slowly and carefully (while swearing in a combined five languages); we were sure we were going to die a slippery and icy death far away from our homes. When we finally got to our meeting place, we asked each other, "So . . . *why* do we stay here? This African and Puerto Rican were not meant to live and drive in this weather!" Beyond the challenging winters in Nebraska, this chapter seeks to explore the larger question of "Why do we stay?" at our university?

There are actually many reasons for us *not* to stay. One of the most significant ones is the consistent pain we feel when we are constantly accused by several White teacher candidates of bias due to our personal identities, which is something our White colleagues, even those who identify as racially progressive, will never have to experience. Since we are people of color, we are expected by our White administrators and White colleagues to teach the most controversial and difficult topics that put us at risk psychologically, financially, and even physically. For us, the political is quite personal. We cannot separate our personal, professional, and communal identities that are inextricably braided together. Delgado Bernal (2008) describes this perspective as a *trenza* (or braid) as follows: "When we are able to weave our personal, professional, and communal identities, we are often stronger and more complete. . . . At the same time, weaving together these and many other identities is fraught with complexity, tensions and obstacles" (p. 135). This *trenza* phenomenon is unique to our experience as women of color who are viewed as outsiders in the majority culture with which we are situated: racially segregated,

White, Midwestern, politically conservative, and suburban. Here, most White people describe themselves as "Nebraska Nice" and never have had to negotiate their racial identities privately or publicly (let alone personally or professionally) because they generally live and work in "a bubble" where everyone around them is just like them.

As women of color, we have no choice but to constantly question our motives and perspectives against Whiteness. We must constantly grapple with whether certain thoughts should be spoken or censored (or even silenced) to protect our mostly White colleagues' and teacher candidates' sensitivities. We also are concerned about other racialized Americans being harshly judged by Whites due to our behaviors and words. The gendered experiences we may marginally share with other White women in our professions are interwoven with different experiences that we have as women of color. The professional space we occupy is thus at the intersection of gendered and racial/ethnic identities, which present unique challenges and opportunities for us as teacher educators. Therefore, the concept of identity intersectionality Crenshaw (1989) plays a significant role in how we live our lives and work as women of color because it explains how the various aspects of humanity such as class, race, sexual orientation, disAbility, and gender do not exist separately from each other but rather are interwoven in complex ways. Rather than thinking of identity as a collection of separate elements, intersectionality allows us to better understand the various elements that are interlocked together and exist as a whole and that cannot exist without each other. Our experiences are important to tell from those intersectional spaces as we consider the unique gifts and curses that occur where our gendered and racialized realities are joined in our lives and educational spaces.

Testimonios and the Importance of Speaking Our Truth

Through centering our narratives and *testimonios* in oral and written forms, women of color scholars in the field like us "embrace the use of counter-stories and other methodological and pedagogical approaches that view the community and family knowledge of communities of color as a strength" (Delgado Bernal, 2002, p. 121). It is in this process of sharing our *testimonios* that we grow as a community of scholars and gain the strength to not only continue our journeys but also not lose our identity in academia. Cervantes-Soon (2012) emphasizes the value of:

> *Testimonios* as a pedagogical practice fosters humanizing knowledge stemming from students' and teachers' own narratives of survival and resistance and promotes theory that offers both a language of critique and a language of hope through the reclamation, transformation, and emancipation of their own lives and communities.
>
> (p. 387)

If we do not share our *testimonios*, we cannot move forward. We need to be conscious that our experiences go beyond our individual contexts. They are part of a larger system of oppression in academia and beyond these walls. Moreover, we aim to embrace our political identities as critical agents who reclaim the rights of all marginalized groups. Through sharing our *testimonios*, we also recognize that we are not alone in our experiences. As women of color, we have each other and our cultural roots to sustain our journeys to hopefully become a stronger presence in academia. Our resilience is part of the answer to why we stay and also a reason we are *able* to survive as women of color in these historically and predominantly White spaces in teacher education despite the daily struggles we encounter. It is also vital to directly name these struggles to tackle them.

Our Educational Spaces

Every month, we have two meetings with our colleagues in a department of teacher education. When we look around, what we see is as follows: 23 White females, one White male, three Black males, one Black female, one mixed-race female, one Latina/White female, and one Latina. We are the mixed-race and the Latina females in this department. There is not much hope that the demographics of our department will change anytime soon. We also spend time in meetings in the community and the local K-12 schools for our teacher candidates' practicum experiences. We always find ourselves being asked by mostly White community members and school personnel to identify ourselves, whether it is racially, ethnically, or "where" we grew up. We realized quickly that it takes a lot of time to truly explain the various parts of our identities. We often get the dreaded question by a curious White American: "*What* are you?" In the sections that follow, we try to answer the complex question of: "*Who* are we?"

Ferial

I grew up in Kenya. I am of African and Indian descent. While I am conversationally fluent in six languages and grew up speaking English with a British accent, I somehow now have a Midwestern American English accent, which changes back whenever I visit my family in Kenya. I have brown skin, extremely curly dark hair, and what many White Americans would view as ambiguously "ethnic" features. I also wear colorful "foreign-looking" clothing and jewelry. I was raised Muslim and am still practicing the faith, although I do not wear a *hijab*. I also identify as Queer. All of these contradictions mean that few White Americans in my Midwestern community likely know what to make of me, as I do not fit into any identity "boxes" that they may have in their minds (unlike Sandra, who fits very clearly defined sets of "boxes"). Therefore, I am often considered to be a "diverse" person and am often asked to fill in gaps by Whites that no one else seems to fill. When asked by someone "what" I am, I always have trouble answering that question, as I am still negotiating my identities. How I identify is very different from the way I am perceived in the United States. I lived half of my life in Kenya and half my life in America. Who I am changes based on every single context in my life. I also do not always get to choose which part of my identity comes to the forefront in any given scenario. The question itself is also uncomfortable, as I sometimes get the feeling that the mostly White people asking (colleagues and students alike) are trying to decide, based on my answer, whether or not I am qualified to be in their space. As a former high-school English teacher, I often was asked by my mostly White students on the first day of school if I was their substitute teacher. Once, a White parent even tried to get me fired from my position, refusing to believe I was "qualified" to teach English in the United States because of my physical appearance. I often have wondered the following: "Would these things have happened to me if I had been a White woman?"

Sandra

Even though I have been living in the United States for the past 17 years, I will always describe myself as Puerto Rican or *boricua*. I have lost some of my "brown" color after so many years living in the cold weather, but I have not lost my Puerto Rican accent (and I am proud of it). Throughout my career, I have discovered that being bilingual and Puerto Rican automatically makes me, in the eyes of several White people, an expert on all things related to language and Latinx culture. Having "an accent" in my field also gives me "street cred," as I was also a former English Language Learner (ELL). Even though becoming an ESL and bilingual education teacher educator was my choice, I do not consider myself knowledgeable on all language learning and teaching topics. However, as the sole faculty member in my field in our department, I am expected by most of my White colleagues to fit into this clearly defined "expert" box. For the past several years, I have been the only self-identified Puerto Rican/Latina education faculty and the only Spanish speaker in my building. Sometimes, I wonder what would have happened if instead of ESL and bilingual education, I would have chosen to be a teacher educator of mathematics education. Would my "accent" still be considered an asset? Would my White colleagues and White teacher candidates view me as an expert in mathematics education?

How Are We Different?

Our physical appearance as women of color, as well as our ideologies as critical educators, dictate where and how we are expected to work in our predominantly White college of education. Such expectations manifest in two different ways because of our perceived and real identities. We are consistently the only racialized bodies in every meeting, but we also are treated differently because of our identities. Sandra's racialized identity gets brought up every single day. It is very clear that she is Puerto Rican. She is constantly asked to represent all Latinx people at the university and in the community. Ferial is a well-known public speaker. Her work on the "Secret Kindness Agents" has had several positive impacts at the national and international levels. She is also a published author and has had numerous speaking engagements. Our White colleagues generally acknowledge Ferial's public persona at our meetings when her work is shared, but many of her other identities (especially her cultural and religious ones) are curiously forgotten and erased. Being both visible and invisible by our colleagues, the majority of whom are White, brings multiple emotions to the surface.

What Makes Us Similar?

Every time we talk, we find that we have something else in common that no one else around us is able to relate to. The other day, we discovered that we have what Sandra calls a *"Panadol* Connection." That day, we were ecstatic! Unless Sandra talks to another Puerto Rican, nobody knows what it is. However, Ferial knew what Panadol was; she knew that instead of Tylenol, we should take *Panadol*. It is moments like this that we know we have a connection beyond the one that we will ever have with our White colleagues. When we are at meetings and White people make offensive comments, or when they single us out whenever there is a "new diversity" initiative, we are able to look at each other while trying not to show how perturbed we are to them. Seeing each other at meetings and outside of work (sharing our families, food, and chai) has saved us. We are the ones who support each other as our way of surviving, but it is rather difficult for most of our White colleagues to understand what we are doing and why.

Even though we have become sisters and have developed our support system, we are exhausted. We share some experiences, but we wish there were more people with our specific backgrounds in our college of education and university rather than mostly White folks. We need more people like us to connect with our experience and who do not question why we do what we do. We also need colleagues who will allow us to be our unmuted and full selves.

Interaction with White Peers: Tokenization and Microaggressions

It is extremely validating for us to learn that there are names and theories for the experiences we are going through. We are not alone in our experiences or exaggerating their impact on our well-being. Two experiences that women of color like us find themselves immersed in are tokenization and microaggressions (Sue, 2010). We are no different here, as we are living in a highly segregated Midwestern city in a blood-red state. Since we truly are in the minority in a department and college that is predominantly White, many of our encounters with tokenization and microaggression happen when interacting with our White peers and higher-ups.

Harvard University professor Chester M. Pierce coined the theory of microaggression in 1970 to describe the insults and dismissals that he regularly witnessed "non-Black people" (mostly Whites) inflicting on people who are Black. Three years later, in 1973, MIT Ombud Mary Rowe expanded the term to include similar aggressions directed at women of all backgrounds including White females, those with different abilities, religions, and other socially marginalized groups. She named this phenomenon as types of "micro-inequities" to define aggressions experienced by people who are perceived as "non-traditional" in any context (Rowe, 1990). Rowe's work led one of the nation's first harassment policies at MIT. Eventually, microaggression (e.g., Sue, 2010) became an umbrella term that covers the casual but extremely harmful degradation of any socially marginalized group such as people living in poverty, people with disAbilities, people from minority faiths, and members of the LGBTQIA community.

There is a Fusion Comedy video that compares microaggressions to mosquito bites. If someone gets one bit once in a while, it is easy to brush off. However, if one is bitten multiple times a day, the person spends a great deal of cognitive energy thinking about the bites and being reminded of them. When one has multiple and intersecting historically underrepresented identities, each of which comes with its own set of microaggressions, the amount of cognitive energy that is spent processing these experiences really impacts a person in a significant and often negative way. Interestingly, many of these microaggressions supposedly come from places of "good intentions" (Sue, 2010). While the intent behind an act is valuable to consider, the *impact* of it to the person on the receiving end of such aggressions matters more. For example, when I (Sandra) am told by my White peers that my "English is good" or that I am "eloquent/articulate/well-spoken," my initial reaction is to assume that these remarks are coming from a place of kindness. However, the larger implication or message to me (and others like me) is that speaking English well is not expected for immigrants or Latinx persons, and thus, is an anomaly that must be pointed out. Unfortunately, remarks about my English by mostly White Americans occur on multiple occasions. As a result, each time these types of incidents occur, I feel "Othered" and not a part of this community. I do not feel normal. The negative impact is that these types of microaggressions amplify my feelings of alienation. We ultimately feel like guests in our department: the token people of color on display like mascots but disregarded as experts in fields outside of those regarding the topics of diversity and social justice. In the following sections are some examples of moments where we have been tokenized and experienced blatant types of microaggressions.

We Are "On Display" at the Multicultural Food Court

A couple of years ago, a White colleague invited us to participate in a cultural fair at a local elementary school located within a predominantly White neighborhood. We were asked to have tables with artifacts from our native countries. The children were going to pass by the tables with their passports. We were to "stamp" their cards after they stopped by. Sandra took some of her Puerto Rican symbols (flag, *coquí*, books, map, and so forth) and stood beside her table. Ferial displayed the Kenyan flag, some art pieces from homemade of soapstone and ebony, and a few of her dresses that represented both her Kenyan and Indian cultures. We could clearly see each other from where we were located and as our first visitors passed us by. We both looked like we were ready to leave. The White children and the adults we met had no clue about our countries. They offered to buy our personal artifacts, complained that we were not offering food, and then asked strange questions that did not show that they were genuinely interested in learning more about us as individuals. Some of these White people did not even make eye contact with us as they handed us their "passports" to be stamped. As we walked out of the school building, we were mad. We were part of a White "cultural display." There was no real learning for the mostly White adults or children. That day was the last time we both said "Yes" to participating in any type of "cultural fair." If food-court multiculturalism was all White Americans were interested in learning about us, and if that was the only representation of us that was useful to them, then it is no longer worth our dignity or further effort (Soltero, 2011). We were tokenized at this "educational" event. It was demeaning.

Ferial's Racialized Body Under the White Gaze

I have areas of expertise and years of experience in specific areas, but I am expected to fill in gaps by several White American colleagues because of the way I look and sound. For example, a White coworker once complained that my way of dressing was not "professional." Other White people often question my ethnicity, asking me things such as if I am *sure* that I am actually from Kenya. I taught at a local high school for over a decade, but I was never allowed to teach in my content area, which is in English and language arts. I was always assigned to teach the "diversity" courses. In my years teaching in the K-12 setting, my identity as a person of color meant to my White colleagues that I had "diversity expertise," while my professional training as an English teacher was erased.

When I was first hired at my current university as an instructional coach, I had 12 years of teaching in local public schools under my belt, a graduate degree in the area of curriculum and instruction, and several local as well as national awards for my work in schools and the community. Helping to create a one-of-a-kind pre-service instructional coaching program was a refreshing challenge, a chance for me to grow, and a chance to learn what it was like at the higher education. I was excited to get to the next step in my career despite taking a large pay cut.

My idealistic enthusiasm deflated like an old balloon only one day in my new role. A White colleague first congratulated me on my hire. The person then "joked" to me: "Well, I guess they have to fill a quota, huh?" At those words and in the moment, every single accomplishment I had earned disappeared from my consciousness. I felt about an inch tall. The imposter's syndrome manifested itself and only continued to worsen for the next few weeks. I kept thinking about what that White colleague had said. It made me second-guess every single idea I had for building this program. Especially because I was in charge of coaching in the area of social studies, which I had never taught, as opposed to English, which I had. Within moments, I did not trust myself or my competence anymore.

However, I soon resolved to work twice as hard as anyone else to prove to this White person that I was worth being hired for the position. I started a Student Diversity Organization, served on the College Diversity Committee, wrote new curricula, accepted heavier loads than I was supposed to, and said yes to every opportunity that presented itself. I did all of this while also taking doctoral classes, sitting on three community boards, co-directing camps for youth, and being a wife and mother of two children. When the then-NCATE (now CAEP) Legacy Accreditation Team came to review our program, I was asked to participate in several focus groups. I was happy to share all of the work we had been doing with the various programs and committees in our college. I noticed during the site visit that each group I was part of had a "diversity" focus, but I did not mind (at the time) because I was able to speak to what the team wanted to know. However, when a White administrator came by our office, what he asked stunned me, and made me feel like all my work was for nothing when he said the following: "Yes, but did the team *see* you?" He then listed several other faculty of color; he then voiced "concern" that they had been out of the building that day, so it was important that the team actually *see* my racialized body. My actual work did not even register as significant to him.

While Sandra's work pertains to her experiences as a former ELL, because of my Midwestern American dialect, my White colleagues often forget that English is not my first language either. I am often complimented by Whites for being "well-spoken" and "articulate" or for having "pretty" clothing and jewelry, but never for the quality of my work. Aside from their reductive labeling of my racialized body, the other nuances of me in terms of my culture, languages, faith, and country of origin are completely invisible to them. For example, at a meeting with White colleagues about a Table Talk for faculty and staff on being culturally responsive to Muslim students, a White colleague said we should "check with a Muslim student" about whether our poster was offensive in any way, completely ignoring the fact that I, a bonafide Muslim, was sitting right next to her. This same colleague often seeks my help in figuring out whether everything else under the sun is "diverse" enough or not offensive to "diverse populations."

The only time my faith has come up is when I spoke at a rally after President Trump's Muslim Ban. A reporter asked me that if I believed that all refugees should be allowed here, and what I thought should be done about terrorism in the United States. My answer to him, which was aired on the evening news, was that gun control was the solution, since terrorism in the United States has been mostly committed by White men with access to guns. The very next day, I was counseled by the White leadership at my institution to never use the phrase "White men with guns" in public ever again, as I might have "offended" my White colleagues, bosses, and quite probably my White students as well. I was never given comfort or asked how the Muslim Ban would directly affect my family or me during that conversation, although it was addressed later when I talked about traveling home and whether I would be allowed back in. Moreover, my dietary needs as a Muslim are consistently ignored at catered meetings, even though my department chair has tried many times to get the caterers to at least label foods. Christmas is also a big deal in our department while Ramadan and Eid are completely ignored.

Unlike Sandra, whose heritage is always painfully on display, people know I am from "somewhere else" . . . but they are not sure exactly where. When the hurricane in Puerto Rico happened, Sandra felt hypervisible on our campus and was overwhelmed by people asking what they could do to help. They were constantly checking on her parent's address so they could send care packages. They wanted to find out if the power had been restored and frequently asked her how her parents were doing. In contrast, when terrorists attacked and held under a multi-day siege a mall in my hometown, killing dozens of people and wounding almost 200 more, I was a mess, not knowing who in my community was alive or dead. Not one colleague asked about the event or my family.. Not one person checked in with me. The same thing happened when my hometown was going through a lot of election violence and my nephew had to skip school for a few days because it was too dangerous. Crickets.

Sandra's Racialized Body Under the White Gaze

I like naming my experiences. I will call this one *Refried Beans and Chicken-Tortilla Soup*. I am getting tired of explaining that I am not Mexican; I am Puerto Rican.

I have nothing against my Mexican friends, but it would be nice if people, especially White folks, could recognize the differences. As one cringe-worthy example, a White colleague once suggested that I could bring chicken-tortilla soup to an event. When I clarified that I actually did not know how to make it because I am not Mexican, she said, "*I know . . . you can always search for the recipe on the Internet.*" I am not quite sure if this was true or if she actually realized that she had not given me a good suggestion. On another occasion, I was asked by a White colleague to bring refried beans for a Mexican-themed fundraiser. Once again, I expressed that I did not know how to prepare this dish. The person also suggested that I should look up the recipe on the Internet. If these people would take the time to get to know me, they would have realized that I rarely cook with recipes. That is, I do not know how to follow recipes, as it is not the way my mother taught me how to cook. She taught me how to cook by feeling and tasting the food; to enjoy the process of cooking and never be afraid of quantities. However, my White colleagues had not taken the time to learn those beyond the surface elements of culture (Hall, 1976).

This next experience comes out of my constant frustration with requests by White people for "help." I call this cluster of experiences *Am I the only Spanish Speaker in this Building?* I am mad! I get another e-mail from a White person asking me to "help" with something in Spanish or Latinx-related. Last semester, it was another White faculty with whom I have never even exchanged words with who requested that I be a guest speaker in her class to talk about Latinx people and physical activity. What do I know about this topic? In her words, I did not even have to talk about physical activity; I could "just speak about the Latinx culture, family structure/dynamics, etc." I said no because I taught at the same time of her class. However, I did not like this request, as I wondered to myself yet again:

> Why do I have to be the expert on all things Latinx? How could I talk about the Latinx culture in general? I am Puerto Rican, but I cannot even describe Puerto Ricans one way. Culture is a dynamic and complex concept and talking about the Latino culture in general means reinforcing stereotypes.

The latest request came from another White faculty in my building who needed me to listen to a phone message on her voicemail that was left for her in Spanish. As I was not in the building at the time, I said "No," but she contacted me again, asking if not only I could listen to a message, but if I could also make an initial phone call to Latinx families for her research study. This is a moment when I exploded and screamed, "Am I the only Spanish speaker in this building?" I knew that the answer was yes I was, but this fact does not give my White peers the right to ask for "my services" and for free. They should pay someone else for these translation services. I had to walk around and think through how to respond to this e-mail. Interestingly, one of my White female colleagues noticed that I was upset. She asked me what was wrong. I told her. She was very understanding. She suggested I should tell this colleague that I was too busy with my practicum students to help her with this request. I followed her advice and tried to be as polite as possible in my response. What I really wanted to say was "My time is valuable. I am not paid to be a language interpreter for you."

I receive these types of requests for translation help through e-mail, phone, and in-person all too frequently. These requests still make me angry. Everybody in my college knows I am Puerto Rican and that I also speak Spanish. I am very proud of my heritage and I do not hide it, but it is exhausting to always field requests asking me to help translate documents from Spanish to English, answer questions about Puerto Rico, or be the representative of all Latinx people in education at my institution. These are impossible tasks that have taken a toll on me. For example, after the news that Hurricane Maria hit Puerto Rico, I spent countless hours answering messages from people I barely knew. Perhaps I was the only Puerto Rican they knew? I appreciated their concerns, but it was overwhelming. I just wanted to hide and wait for my mother to call me, saying everyone was fine. Sometimes, I just want to be invisible. I do not want my language and my culture to be on display all the time.

Classroom Interactions and Course Evaluations

Many women of color scholars describe their experiences receiving course/teaching evaluations where mostly White students either questioned their expertise or described them as instructors who made them emotional (Gutiérrez y Muhs et al., 2012, p. 218). Whenever we read our evaluations and reflect upon our interactions with teacher candidates, we both often find ourselves asking this question: "Would they have done/ said that if I had been a White professor?" Our wonderings pertain to both positive as well as negative experiences. The irony is that many of the negative comments are part of the evaluations for graduate-level courses that have a "diversity" focus and the majority of the students who take these courses are practicing White teachers.

Ferial

In early December 2015, Republican presidential front-runner Donald J. Trump called for a "total and complete" ban on all Muslims entering the United States. He proposed barring followers of the world's fastest-growing religion into our land because he considers Muslim people to have roots in ideologies of hatred and violence. The following summer, 2016, I was teaching a course titled "Multicultural Literature for

Children and Youth," which was also during a time where the presidential campaign in the United States was going strong. Trump continued to make Islamophobic and xenophobic remarks. I took the opportunity to connect what was happening politically to the need for multicultural literature in K-12 classrooms. Students and I talked about how the lack of windows and doorways into underrepresented cultures and demographics in literature for children and young adults has several negative impacts including the dehumanization of entire groups of people, which then makes it easier for bigotry to go unchallenged. If Trump had developed empathy for immigrants and Muslims by reading books by and about those perspectives growing up, perhaps he would not harbor such bigoted views. I genuinely felt as though all of the students in the class were in agreement with the value of multicultural literature. While I am both a Muslim and an immigrant, and therefore, personally affected by Trump's comments, I was careful to make sure my comments were completely tied to our curriculum and objectives for the class. However, when I got the course evaluations back, I read the following comment with surprise:

> The instructor needs to keep in mind that not all teachers are liberals and democrats. While lecturing on certain topics, the instructor made offensive comments about Donald Trump, who is running for president on the republican side. If she is going to bash one side of the party, she needs to bash the other side as well.
>
> As a teacher, she needs to keep an open mind that everyone has different political views. She needs to look at both sides and keep her ideas neutral when talking to the class as a whole. I found her comments against my political party very offensive and upsetting. I am a strong Republican and am a strong believer in Donald Trump.

I felt as though I had been punched in the gut when I read this comment. I wondered if I had not been an immigrant and a Muslim, as well as a woman of color, if this student would have felt personally targeted and also felt so moved to make such a comment on a course evaluation. For a specific course assignment, a White student wrote that the activity we did to uncover hidden biases made him feel "attacked as a White straight male" and that he was a "hardcore supporter of Trump." Again, I wondered if this strong reaction was a function of who his instructor is (or is not). Another student in the course evaluations described me as being "overly dramatic," which is a function of my culture and personality. The emotions that arise when we read these comments must feel different than if we were White American teacher educators. Indeed, I cannot check my identities at the door when I teach. Like my White colleagues, my experiences make me the educator I am today. It is just that their experiences, as White teacher educators, are considered the "norm" and therefore not "controversial" or "political" like mine.

Sandra

> Do not teach from only a Puerto Rican female point-of-view. I felt as if I was taking a class about Puerto Rico and the current events that were taking place there. It also would have been nice to work with students and learn about things outside of the Latino neighborhood and Latino culture. I don't work with a large population of Latino students and didn't feel like we discussed any other cultures.

I cried the day I read the quoted comment on one of my course evaluations for my summer 2016 course titled "Language, Culture, and Power." I could not believe a student in a professional teacher-credential program could attack my culture. It was almost midnight that day, but I texted Ferial to share the comment. She responded right away. She knew exactly what to say to build me up again. Yet, time and time again, these types of comments show up on my course evaluations, reminding me that even though I am considered the ESL and language expert at my institution, my culture is still seen as foreign and undesirable in the White Midwest. Indeed, many of my White teacher candidates just cannot avoid mentioning my accent. Recently, I shared with a new group of graduate students in my "Language, Culture, and Power" course the comment quoted earlier. They all appeared to be in shock, but when I read the course evaluations at the end of the term, someone wrote the following: "Sometimes she doesn't enunciate clearly enough for me to understand her, but that wasn't a huge problem as I usually figured it out eventually. She is NOT too Puerto Rican!" After weeks of being in class and discussing how issues on language, culture, and power are connected, this person still wanted to make a point that my accent was a problem (but not my culture as if I were to be thankful for this assessment).

Whenever I read my course evaluations, I am reminded of this quote from a Puerto Rican woman scholar: "it is *my* action-my entering the space of instruction as a Puerto Rican woman conscious of the contradictions of what place, language, class, and race mean in the United States-that is affirmative" (Fiol-Matta, 1996, p. 73). Even though the comments on my course/teaching evaluations often hurt me, I cannot leave my Puerto Rican identity at the door. I should not even be asked by any teacher candidate to avoid teaching from a "Puerto Rican female point-of-view." Why do I have to do this? Have White professors ever been asked by their White students to not teach from "a White lens?" I simply refuse to leave my Puerto Rican identity at the door; it enters with me in my classroom.

Interactions With Students of Color: Emotional and
Invisible Labor . . . With Hope

Many scholars, especially women of color in academia, are well aware of how our emotional labor with our students takes a toll on our physical, emotional, and psychological well-being (Hua, 2018). Both of us know of this emotional and invisible labor:

> The hands-on attention that many minority professors willingly provide is an unheralded linchpin in institutional efforts to create an inclusive learning environment and to keep students enrolled. That invisible labor reflects what has been described as cultural taxation: the pressure faculty members of color feel to serve as role models, mentors, even surrogate parents to minority students, and to meet every institutional need for ethnic representation.
>
> (June, 2015, n.p.)

This pressure to be role models, mentors, and surrogate parents has become a significant part of our personal, professional, and communal lives. Every year, we see that our college's teacher-education program is becoming more linguistically and culturally diverse. We are thus doing everything in our power to keep BIPOC teacher candidates enrolled in our programs.

Ferial

Much of the emotional and invisible labor for me comes from three distinct places. The first is being a listening ear to students from racialized backgrounds, as well as students who identify as Queer and Trans at our university. Students tend to gravitate toward faculty who appear to understand their lived experiences, so my multiple intersections as a Queer, immigrant, and Muslim woman of color means that students who come from any of those identities often look to me for help with issues of bias or bigotry that they face on-campus and off-campus. They also often seek validation in their feelings when they experience all-out "isms."

The second place is consulting for mostly White faculty who frequently ask me to look at their syllabi, books, images, articles, PowerPoints, handouts, and a myriad of other classroom resources to see if they are, for instance: offensive, appropriate, authentic, diverse enough, or just to ask for general feedback about whether they are doing right by the "diversity thing." It is frustrating that these White faculty rarely come to the many community offerings about learning all of these topics on their own, but they never hesitate to exploit my time and energy to take short-cuts. I am learning to deflect those requests and make gentle suggestions to them about where else they might learn how to manage their learning . . . on their own.

The final place where my energy and labor goes to is all of the diversity initiatives in which all persons in the department, college, and university are expected to participate. I am placed on every bias/diversity/multicultural committee there is. Why do I do all of this? Why do I stay in this place where most of the emotional and invisible labor is placed disproportionately on a few individuals? It is because the work is needed. When I hear students tell me that the reason they have stayed on to finish their degrees and become teachers and role models to children is because I was there for them, I understand the power of representation. *You cannot be what you cannot see.* I have yet to meet someone with my identities with a doctorate in education working in teacher education, and I am still searching. In my work, I try to be the mentor and person I needed when I was younger. The work that I do for my White colleagues, while exhausting, is important in ensuring that our students do not have damaging experiences in the classroom.

Sandra

Why do I want to stay working (and living at a place) that historically and still is predominantly White and oppressive? My answer is as follows: I do not think my work here is done. One morning, I woke up early to talk to a Latino student who was struggling to make it to his high-school graduation. I was asked by his ESL teacher to stop by and talk with him. As she reasoned, maybe (just maybe) talking to me could encourage and inspire him. As I listened to him, I felt how tired he was. He had very long days, as he took his siblings to school, worked with the ESL teacher before school, went to his classes during the school day, then worked until 11:00 p.m., and afterward, tried to get his homework done. He told me he was up until at least 3:00 a.m. trying to get it all done. He worked at a restaurant. On weekends, he was also working. He really wanted to be an engineer, but he was just tired. I encouraged him to keep trying. It seemed that he already had a plan to not work, stay closer to school, let his mother borrow his car so she could take his siblings to school, and so forth. I left the school really hoping that he did everything in his power to get closer to his dream. The ESL teacher was thankful that I came; I also knew this young man listened to me. I left the school feeling needed. I also knew that coming out to mentor a young student was not part of my job duties, but I had to do it. Later on, his ESL teacher let me know that he had finished high school, which made me extremely proud.

On another occasion, I had a Latina student stop by my office to consult with me: if she should also get a Spanish minor. I said, "Of course." However, her academic adviser was trying to dissuade her from taking this option, as it meant not following the "recommended" plan of study. We ended up talking for more than an hour. We both shared how much our parents had to sacrifice for us. How much they wanted a college education for us; for us to do better than they did. We cried, we laughed, and we embraced. It was the type of conversation that made me feel more Latina than ever.

One time, someone asked me what was different about being a Latina professor. I do want to return home to Puerto Rico, but I do not feel the same urgency anymore. Believe it or not, I am fine staying here. It is something I never thought I would feel, but I do now. However, I am concerned that this commitment continues to take a toll on my personal and professional life.

Interactions With the Self: The Inner Voice(s)

Every day is also a struggle for us not to feel and internalize the imposter syndrome. The imposter syndrome refers to "successful women who, despite reaching significant intellectual milestones ranging from advanced degrees to professional awards, cannot internalize their success or convince themselves they deserve it" (Kaplan, 2009, p. 468). Being teacher educators who are also women of color, we teach not only undergraduate and graduate students but also groups of faculty, K-12 teachers, and community members. Often before, during, and after these talks and/or workshops, we second-guess ourselves. We often ask ourselves questions such as the following: "Should we do this? Am I/we prepared to talk to this group? How should I/we respond if we get push back from White majority audiences?" When someone in the audience, usually a White person, makes offensive comments, we feel like we should respond, but we often cannot find words to say right away. We often ask ourselves, "Why didn't I say anything?" Our work is exhausting and a constant struggle, but we keep showing up anyway.

Ferial

I serve on the Diversity Committee for our college. Every year for the past couple of years, we have put together a workshop for the entire college, which includes several different departments. The workshop occurs right after our first-semester meeting to make it easier for people to stay afterward. Last time, at the conclusion of the college meeting when I was invited up to facilitate our workshop, and when I was mid-sentence introducing the agenda, half of the room stood up . . . and started to walk out the door. I was already shaken because right before the meeting, two other committee members bowed out of facilitating the workshop and asked me to do their parts. Since these people are senior to me with more power in many aspects, I, of course, said I would do it for them. However, I felt taken for granted. Having most people leave while I was still speaking my first introductory sentence just compounded my shakiness. My inner dialogue was about wondering if I should really be in this space, whether I was the right person to facilitate this workshop, and whether my work and contributions were really valued. Moreover, there was a tremendous amount of psychological risk for me, as a young woman of color who was a month away from graduating with my doctorate from this college, to stand in front of a room of mostly White colleagues who have had their doctorates and worked here for years. I lost confidence in myself for weeks after this meeting. All of this served to silence me in many situations. I now tend to mute my real self. I keep my thoughts hidden from others. I do not usually say what needs to be said. It both hurts me and robs our students of a voice in rooms where they and people like them are absent. It takes an enormous amount of energy to recover from macroaggressions and microaggressions such as these. We need that energy to move forward and do the things our White colleagues do every day to advance their careers and individual happiness.

Sandra

One summer, I had the experience of talking to a group of over 80 mostly White teachers, university professors, graduate students, and staff who were attending a weeklong seminar to learn about service-learning pedagogy. The topic was "diversity." Another Brown person who had done this presentation by herself several times and I stood in front of this mostly White audience who, until now, seemed nice to us. I had already heard some words and expressions that made me concern. For example, I heard in the audience: "Help! I'll take my students to this neighborhood so they can experience diversity. They need to learn about *those people*." As I stood in front of the same audience I had spoken to the day before about community partnerships, I noticed this time was much different, as I was physically trembling. I gave them instructions to complete the White Privilege survey. I could see that many White people tensed up as they read through the survey. There was an uncomfortable silence. Even though someone told me that this group was pretty quiet the next day, this type of silence was markedly different. It was intimidating. I later learned that one of the three African American teachers present that day had refused to answer the survey. I guess they had done this exercise before and knew that it would put a spotlight on how teachers like them are not part of a privileged group. The silence was broken when some of the teachers completed their surveys. One White teacher asked me about Question 7, which read as follows: "I can be sure that my children will be given curricular materials that testify to the existence of their race." I decided to explain it to him through the microphone. My decision made him appear a bit uncomfortable, although I was glad I did what I did.

When I asked the audience the question of who is ordinarily represented in our textbooks, some mentioned White children/people. Fortunately, some teachers in the audience were critically aware of these issues of White privilege and power.

When I explained a cultural-engagement model and other examples, I could not stop myself from saying the following. Many times, we as teachers feel uncomfortable talking about diversity, but what should we do? Suddenly, I heard myself giving them this answer: "*Learn.*" I emphasized it so much, almost screaming it out, that the word "learn" became an order and not a suggestion. I must admit that I felt initially like I needed to apologize to the group for raising my voice, but I chose not to. I went on and gave the example of how bad it turns out when we try to teach something we do not know much about and then fail in the delivery. However, as and if we learn about a topic, we tend to teach it better with more practice.

The next day, I shared with the seminar's planning team how I was feeling. Everybody assured me that I did not show how scared I was. They shared that I transmitted passion to the audience and that I should definitely not apologize for what I said and how I said it. However, one person asked me how they could help make it a better experience so I would not be afraid. I must admit that I had not thought about my own comfort. Maybe if I had a White person presenting with me, the audience would have listened. However, that situation would be like me not finding my voice. The next day, someone from that meeting sends me a picture with the following quote: "Always speak the truth even if your voice shakes." Therefore, even with what I was feeling, I knew at that moment the following: "I have to continue speaking all of my truths, even if my voice and/or body shakes."

Coping

There are constant psychological risks and pain we experience in our work. From everyday microaggressions, to the invisible labor of our work, the constant self-doubt has taken a toll on both of us as teacher educators who are also women of color. We constantly remind ourselves that we need to be careful and not neglect our own self-care, but we are not very good at doing so, although we keep trying. Ferial has become better at saying "No" and delegating requests that she gets from White faculty members. Sandra is not afraid to use her voice to agitate for change. Our advice to each other, and others like us, is the following: try not to let anger overwhelm you. Instead, focus on staying true to yourself and your passions. Remember, the most important thing is to do what is best for our students. They are the ones who give us hope and who will carry on our work. We will continue to speak . . . even as our voices shake.

Final Thoughts: Finding Our Voices . . . Even When They Want to Silence Us

We know that as women of color scholars and teacher educators, writing this chapter is a risk. Sandra understands that as a tenured professor, she is more protected than Ferial. However, Sandra has been sharing her experiences even before she earned tenure. We firmly believe that the actual experiences of scholars from racialized backgrounds in predominantly White US colleges and schools of education cannot and should not be silenced. Our ability to empathize with and truly understand each other's intersectional experiences has allowed us to provide support to each other. If we were not in this space together, we would not still be here as individuals. We stay here for each other, we stay here for our students, and we stay here for the greater good. We also know the power of (and need for) representation and mentors for our students and the imperative of having multiple perspectives at the tables where decision-making happens. We are proudly part of the slow and often painful process of decolonizing these White spaces to create more equitable conditions for historically underrepresented groups.

5 From Consumption to Refusal

A Four-Part Exploration of the Dilemmas of Black Education Scholars and Radical Knowledge

Brian D. Lozenski

The Classroom as Stage of Racialized Consumption

This chapter is meant to conjure critical hope (Camangian, 2015; Duncan-Andrade, 2009) in my educational context, and moreover, perhaps provide catalytic fodder for other racialized scholars in education grappling with (and existing in) a contradiction. Weaving autobiographical anecdotes across three metaphors of *the stage*, *the distance*, and *the train*, I attempt to write myself into a space of pedagogical refusal. In a lecture at my college, one of my activist-intellectual heroes, Angela Davis, boldly told the audience the following: "Perpetual questioning is the nature of revolution." Keeping this assertion in mind, I work through a four-part tracing of my educational journey, exploring how US colleges and universities increasingly participate in the consumption and accumulation of liberatory knowledge systems to benefit populations of students who do not come from the communities who have inherited and maintained these systems. I also turn to Tuck and Yang (2014a, 2014b) and Harney's and Moten's (2013) explorations of refusal as a stance, which has the potential to reposition faculty who are from racialized backgrounds. I share my experience as a Black professor teaching liberatory studies in education to predominantly White students at a small liberal arts college in the hope that I am able to formulate the questions needed to propel me to a different place of thought and action. In this essay, I theorize how *the stage* of the classroom is a site of racialized consumption. Drawing from Mazrui's (1986) framing of colonial extraction on the African continent, I then illustrate how critical scholars become *the trains* in that we carry knowledge from our dispossessed home communities and deliver it to our institutions. *The distance* travelled between these community and university spaces are constituted by contradiction. I end with an examination of whether or not *the refusal* of this positioning is possible.

Throughout this essay, I draw from la paperson's (2017) framing of the first, second, and third university spaces. Building from Mimura's (2009) work in cinema studies, la paperson situates colleges and universities through their relationship to the maintenance of settler colonization in the United States as follows: "The first-world university is the academic-industrial complex, meaning, these institutions are "characterized by an ultimate commitment to brand expansion and accumulation of patent, publication, and prestige" (p. 36). He juxtaposes these to the second-world universities, or liberal arts colleges, which is where my work resides in that I seek to potentially "offer meaningful challenges to the academic-industrial complex and could be said to be a democratic and participatory academy" (p. 36). Yet, as I describe later, the second-world university often struggles to realize its full potential. Residing within the first and second-world universities are third-world universities. These are "assemblages" (e.g., spaces, programs, organizations, and so forth), which are fundamentally "decolonial projects" that "equip students with the skills toward the applied practice of decolonization" (p. 36). la paperson argues that each of these universities is found within the others in that "Each mode appropriates or contains within itself elements of the other two. There is a third university in every first and second university, and vice versa" (p. 37). Much of this chapter is about my search for the third university and its elusiveness when confronted with the realities of the ways in which it is deemed a fugitive space.

Part I: The Stage

In 2004, comedian Dave Chappelle was at the height of his career, riding the immense popularity of his hilarious sketch-comedy series *Chappelle's Show*. The program was edgy, complex, and raucous. It brilliantly blended insightful social critique, often focused on race with juvenile slapstick wrapped in the cultural blanket of hip-hop. Chappelle drew from the best of the Black male comedic legacy: the clever, justice-fused fire of Dick Gregory, the brutal honesty of Richard Pryor, and the sharp-cutting tongue of Paul Mooney who even appeared several times on the show. At the time, as a middle-school teacher of mathematics and a hip-hop artist in my mid-twenties, I was mesmerized, as Chappelle had mass appeal. His name rang out in Black communities. He had cross-racial cache among a generation of hip-hop-oriented young adults. The show was admittedly heteropatriarchal, but still, it seemed to be broad enough in its social critique that the vast majority of justice-minded folks I knew still enjoyed it, despite several of its deeply problematic aspects. The first two seasons of the show received wide critical acclaim. Then, in the middle of filming season three, Chappelle vanished.

There was dubious speculation as to what happened, where he went, and why he left. I remember hearing rumors that Chappelle was in drug rehab in Africa, or that he was on a *hajj* to Mecca. It turned out that Chappelle quit the show abruptly, turning down tens of millions of dollars for a myriad of reasons. He did spend some time in South Africa on what he referred to as a spiritual retreat (Ahad, 2015). Chappelle's recounting of producing comedy for a particular audience (his friends), while also being consumed by a totalizing audience (Whiteness), is illustrative of the paradox in which so many racialized Americans find themselves in. I describe Chappelle's competing audiences as "friends" and "Whiteness" to complicate the reductive notion that audiences could be reduced to phenotypically based identity groups (Green & Linders, 2016; Particelli, 2016). Here, friends are Chappelle's ideological confidants, his people, his White co-writer, and the comedic tradition that produced him. Whiteness is an orientation to the social and natural world that manifests itself through (dis)possession of land, labor, and humanity (la paperson, 2017; Mills, 1997). Through the lens of Whiteness, each of these is understood as property to be claimed, possessed, and accumulated (Harris, 1993; Lipsitz, 2006). As a producer of Black comedic knowledge, Chappelle, and the traditions from which he was constructed through, were nourishing incommensurable entities; one (friends), a reciprocal community of support, but the other (Whiteness), a cannibalizing beast. Each needed his knowledge. Both grew stronger from it.

As a faculty of color at a prestigious liberal arts college in the United States, I am far removed from Chappelle's comedic stage. Yet, I do exist on a "stage" of my own in some sort: the classroom. I enact a dialogic pedagogy that draws from the collective thought of my students in response to critical texts, so I rarely lecture or perform in the traditional sense. Still, the "stage" persists in the ways by which students receive my instruction, and moreover, in the ways that I synthesize and actualize curricula. Like the comedic stage, there is a consumptive aspect to any classroom context, making it a contact zone where nuanced ideas, as well as cultural attitudes and practices, come into play. Consequently, I also experience the competing audiences of friends and Whiteness. Teaching at a predominantly White institution in an interdisciplinary social-science department in a program in educational studies means that the vast majority of my students are socially positioned as White. The majority of my students are White because of institutional influences; that is, student demographics on college campuses are not by any means coincidental or purely based on "merit" and other factors of achievement. Rather, people in formal and informal positions of power on this campus decide who will populate our classrooms. The historical accumulations of these taken-for-granted assumptions about who is or is not "college-ready," for example, means that most people at my campus and in other universities do not question the ultimate outcome: the composition of most college classrooms. Nevertheless, my institution is notably progressive, which I mostly see as a good thing.

Moreover, I typically do not have to deal with the horror stories reported by many of my colleagues across the country who often experience belligerence, pushback, and even aggressive attacks from mostly White students who are ideologically opposed to their progressive or transcendent desires for racial, gender, sexual, linguistic, or other forms of justice. I am an openly radical Black scholar. My courses are explicitly political in nature and highly antagonistic of supremacist ideologies. My students, for the most part, eat it up. We read radical Black scholars like W.E.B. Du Bois and Derrick Bell, Queer feminists of color like Gloria Anzaldúa, Audre Lorde, and Bettina Love, and we critique the hell out of settler-colonial models of education with Indigenous scholars such as Eve Tuck and Linda Tuhiwai Smith. At this point, one may be thinking, "What does Brian's experience teaching radical educational theory have to do with the cannibalizing ways Chappelle's comedy was consumed by Whiteness?" I would argue there are quite a few parallels.

The fact that there are many ideological "friends" among my students is beside the point because the foundation of my educational philosophy is to interrogate the ideological frameworks that we all take for granted. I use critical theory produced by people like the scholars I have mentioned. Like Chappelle's comedic roots, my work is also situated in a particular intellectual tradition that grew out of the experiences of enslaved Africans and their descendants here in the United States. My scholarship is also highly experiential because I have commitments to produce actionable work outside of my campus in the local communities of which I am part. The duality of "friends" and "Whiteness" confronts me daily in the classroom because I teach people who primarily *are not* of the communities that birthed and nurtured these knowledge systems. In this way, Whiteness does not look like a man laughing too long at Chappelle's joke. It looks like White students consuming Black knowledge systems for their material benefit with no verifiable promise that it will benefit dispossessed Black communities.

There is also a more abstract consumption of these knowledge systems in the form of White liberalism. la paperson (2017) argues the following: "the second world (liberal arts) university 'liberates' through liberalism" (p. 37), meaning that it seeks to "challenge and provoke the critical consciousness of its students toward self-actualization" (p. 36). Yet, it ultimately fails to manifest this transformational potential due to its elevation and distinction from the work of radical movement-building and agitation of the material structures in which it sits. In effect, liberalism often critiques ideas without transforming communities, realities, or systems. I fear that through the consumption of Black radical educational theory, my White students will largely believe themselves to be "educated about" but not necessarily complicit in the liberation of oppressed communities, which is an inextricable demand of these intellectual traditions.

Part II: The Distance

In my own life, my university experience has dramatically shaped who I am and how I came to the work that I do. Like many of my colleagues who identify as BIPOC, ethnic studies saved my life. I came to Cornell University as an undergraduate student in 1995. I was drawn to the Africana Studies and Research Center (ASRC), as I had been dispossessed of the knowledge of my ancestors, both ancient and contemporary, through my K-12 schooling. The ASRC provided me with a transfusion of the lifeblood I needed to (re)locate my position and purpose in this world. This was the first time I was allowed to see my history outside of a Eurocentric paradigm. I began to understand my heritage not as a marginal history, but epistemologically and ontologically constructed on its own terms. My perception of reality was jolted, deconstructed, and reconstructed with that of many of my peers. While the ASRC was central to my undergraduate life, I quickly realized that the insurgent knowledge that it was producing (Brown, 2014) was seen as a threat by the university and that the Center was constantly fighting for its life and autonomy (Baker, 2011). Its inception, resulting from the first armed building takeover in the United States by students, situated it as not of the university but rather juxtaposed to the rest of Cornell University. The ASRC at Cornell University was created in response to the demands of Black students during the 1969 Willard Straight Hall Takeover (Baker, 2011). The student takeover gained notoriety as the first armed building occupation in US history on a college campus. Initially, students were unarmed, but firearms were procured after a White fraternity tried to forcibly enter the building and physically attack the protesters. The distance between the ASRC and Cornell University historically and today is still culturally, politically, and ideologically vast. It is this distance that academics from racialized backgrounds must often travail in our short walks between buildings on campus or quick trips to community centers a few miles away from our offices.

After teaching at the secondary level for a decade, I made my way back to the university to pursue my doctoral degree. This time around, I was armed with the knowledge that I was to be consumed and used by the university for their purposes of publicizing surface-level diversity. For example, as a doctoral student of color in a predominantly White program, I was featured in three separate profiles used for public relations by the university. I would like to believe that my work was that exceptional to have warranted my picture being broadly featured, but in reality, the university would have promoted other students from racialized backgrounds . . . *if* there were more in the program. The anticipation of this exploitation pushed me to seek out spaces where I could emotionally heal and maintain some sense of stability outside of the harsh environment of the university classroom. Again, I sought out spaces that centralized the knowledge systems I came to value like the ASRC. As a doctoral student, I centered my scholarship on illuminating and working to end the dispossession of youth of color, specifically Black youth, of their heritage knowledge systems in the K-12 schools (Cushing-Leubner & Lozenski, in press). To accomplish this likely impossible feat, I partnered with a family literacy center called the Network for the Development of Children of African Descent (NdCAD).

NdCAD (n.d.) is a community-based organization in Saint Paul, Minnesota; its mission is to "make cultural connections across communities of African descent" (n.p.) in the Twin Cities. The organization employs multiple programmatic strategies including a reading program for children in grades K-8 to embed literacy in cultural knowledge and to promote healthy identity development. NdCAD also runs a literacy advocacy series for parents who are looking to understand the cognitive aspects of their children's literacy practices. It also offers them strategies on how to navigate the mainstream schooling structures that tend to work against holistic conceptions of literacy. My work with NdCAD involved creating a program for high-school youth to engage in participatory action research (Caraballo, Lozenski, Lyiscott, & Morrell, 2017; Mirra, Garcia, & Morrell, 2015) through the lens of African knowledge systems (Lozenski & Ford, 2014; Lozenski, 2017; Mazama, 2003). The Uhuru Youth Scholars program (Uhuru) encourages youth of African descent to explore how knowledge could be constructed outside of the Eurocentric paradigms that they usually witness in their traditional high schools. Together, the youth and I laugh, read Du Bois, Freire, hooks, and Alexander, traversed the city with cameras looking for people to interview, presented at conferences, ate, and met with other youth researchers, and laughed some more.

The pedagogical distance between my work with Uhuru and in the academy is constituted by the relationship of my students to the curricular traditions from which we draw upon. The curricular texts that I use in Uhuru and in the courses that I teach on Black intellectualism in education are similar. The ways by which students in each of these contexts interact with these texts is dramatically different. To be fair, there is a significant difference between the educational purpose of Uhuru and educational studies for White students at liberal arts colleges. Uhuru is designed to be reciprocally self-actualizing and catalytic as an agent for intrapersonal, school, or neighborhood transformation. The latter element could be accessed but is not demanded at the liberal arts college. My mostly White undergraduate students are under no curricular expectation to engage in a political struggle beyond abstraction, which speaks directly to la paperson's (2017) critique of the second-world university. As a scholar of color standing in these particular knowledge systems, I am caught between these purposes. It is the manifestation of the fear of being consumed by Whiteness in the form of liberalism.

There is another layer to this distance between the community and the academy that lies in the affordances of these spaces for their inhabitants. I am reminded of Konadu's (2017) review of Rickford's (2016) *We are an African People*, which explores the history and work of independent pan-Africanist schools in the 1960s and 1970s. The Uhuru Youth Scholars program was fashioned in the image of many of these schools. Despite his overall praise for Rickford's work, Konadu (2017) notes a fundamental flaw, arguing the following about independent black educational institutions (IBEIs):

> They were theoretically and practically ill-equipped to do something many were not designed to do. . . . Their target was not the masses nor 'broad social transformation.' We might criticize these institutions as insular and utopian, but they were analogous to Maroon communities in the U.S. South.
>
> (n.p.)

Konadu clearly articulates the metaphorical distance I describe earlier through the goals and desires of marron-age. If we understand Uhuru as more of a maroon community (a fugitive collective) rather than a space within the first or second university, then a different set of metrics must be applied in terms of how we analyze it. The distance between Uhuru and the academy, then, is represented in a transcendent understanding of teaching and learning to live in fugitivity. Patel (2016) writes:

> Learning is, at its core, a fundamentally fugitive act, underscored with deeper fugitivity in societies where the dangerous, agentic act of learning is constricted with punishing precision. Learning as fugitivity exists as dialectic to the stratifying cultures of formal education that insist on contingent possibilities for well-being for some and unmitigated safety for others.
>
> (p. 397)

Uhuru must sift through the first or second university, looking for its well-being. But this well-being exists only in the third university. Its very existence is contingent upon it not being seen as dangerous to the broader goals of the first and second universities (la paperson, 2017). At the same time, the students in my traditional college courses exist with unfettered safety, even as we explore "dangerous" texts. Because Uhuru is in flux, it is sometimes difficult for even me to find. Since Uhuru's creation in 2011, it has been connected to three separate postsecondary institutions. There have also been some years where it has not been in operation due to a lack of funding or because I have not had the necessary time to coordinate it effectively. Nevertheless, Uhuru still reshapes (and must reshape) itself at many turns. The distance, then, is often amorphous, with Uhuru constantly shifting to maintain its survival. And I, a college professor, being pulled to the college classroom, am rarely in flux and rarely am "at risk" for direct harm. We could do whatever we want in there, and as part of the second university, it is rarely dangerous. It maintains a normalized and mostly White classroom.

Part III: The Train

In Mazrui's (1986) foundational series *The Africans: A Triple Heritage*, he uses the train as a metaphor to describe the colonial extraction of African resources for the benefit of European and Western nations. He shows imagery of trains careening across expansive landscapes (in Liberia) carrying what looks like dirt. He explains in the series how "the train is symbolic of the African condition. . . . The foreigners come. They take. And they depart, often bequeathing decay rather than development" (n.p.). The stark irony of the figurative and literal metaphor of the train as a manifestation of African resources being used to perpetuate and make the extraction more efficient is not lost on the viewer. This metaphor, when shifted to the context of the academy, paints a disturbing picture. The extractive practice of the university within colonial societies (Smith, 1999; Tuck, 2009) depends on the mining of resources (i.e., knowledge systems) from colonized communities to be processed by the university for their benefit. In this secondary metaphor, racialized scholars, especially those in predominantly White education programs, become the trains used to carry precious knowledge from their communities to the academy. As scholars from racialized backgrounds, we are often born and shaped by the very communities that have been historically marginalized by postsecondary institutions in the United States and elsewhere. Our ancestral communities have nurtured us with the knowledges of survival, cultural pride, and ingenuity amidst a dearth of access to material wealth. As children, we were sent into schooling systems that sought to strip much of this knowledge from us and repackage us in the model of our colonizers where our minds are replete with colonial thinking. Many of us resist this repackaging, yet our success in these schooling systems is very much contingent on our ability to either disguise our resistance or acquiesce to the colonial desires. Ultimately, we are expected to bury our cultural heritage into the depths of our subconscious. The few of us who succeed in these structures, then, are positioned as leaders of our native communities. Our assumed or real success stories are used to rationalize the entire process of cultural stripping, which was Woodson's (1990) major critique in his timeless text *The Mis-Education of the Negro*, that the most "educated" Black Americans are usually the least useful to the liberation of their communities. In other words, schooling is a form of extraction of embodied resources that will be repurposed and rendered useless to the community that made the sacrifice for us.

Some of us go into business, technology, managerial positions in the service industry, law, entertainment, or other fields. Some of us go into the academy; we are told by our mentors that we deal in thought, philosophy, and the preparation of a younger generation to take their roles as societal leaders. A subset of academics who are from racialized backgrounds take up critical dispositions and use their position at colleges to expose coloniality, as well as oppression based on race, gender, sexuality, and class. We reach into the depths of ourselves and our communities to unearth the knowledge systems that already taught us these things. We bring these knowledges into our work through our pedagogy and activism on campus, trying to assemble third universities. All the while, the first or second universities tout our existence as a testament to their efforts for and progress as it relates to promoting, for instance, "diversity." Like Whiteness needs Chappelle's comedic tradition, the university needs ours. We are the trains produced by our communities but manufactured through educational structures where several core players actually despise the knowledges we embody. We are repurposed for colonial benefit and sent back into our communities to extract more knowledge, more of the metaphorical iron, copper, bauxite, titanium, gold, and diamonds that our communities will never see in their manufactured "finality."

My experiences also fit this troubling paradigm. Unbeknownst to me, I began my career in education as a child in Philadelphia. Both of my parents were music teachers with the School District of Philadelphia. In my childhood photo albums, I am sometimes shown sitting in a classroom or auditorium at Overbrook High School while my parents are rehearsing with the orchestra or conducting a performance. One picture is of me at four-year-old peeking over my father's picket sign when there was a 50-day teachers' strike in 1981. My induction into our family business of education was often in observance of my parents' activities outside of the classroom. They would lead fieldtrips to cultural events and run summer camps for musicians. They often would drive their students home after a performance so these young people did not have to ride the bus or subway carrying their large instruments. We were sometimes invited to celebrations such as attending birthdays and weddings. Based on what I saw my parents modeling, I thought being a teacher meant being engaged with the community. I was shocked to discover that for so many teachers, most of them White, these kinds of interactions were deemed as "inappropriate" and "unprofessional."

I was dismayed when entering the field of education as a pre-service teacher when warned by mostly White university faculty against "getting too close to your students" outside of school, and moreover, that it was "unprofessional" to be part of the lives of the children and their families. I found this warning impossible to heed. In my first teaching job at Strawberry Mansion High School in North Philadelphia, I immediately got to know all of my students through their out-of-school lives. I taught mathematics, but when I discovered I had students who were seniors and interested in nursing, I linked them with a program at a local medical school for high-school youth interested in the medical field. The program took place in the evening, and thus, I drove my students to and from our school, the medical school, and their homes. I dropped them off one by one and greeted their parents along the way. When tutoring my students after school, I would also give them rides home. When asked by my colleagues if I was worried about being seen as "unprofessional," I would reply, "No." I knew the students' families. I called and spoke to their mothers about their children, so these were not my concerns.

At Strawberry Mansion, I taught all Black students, which was not a coincidence but rather a consequence of history. All of my students lived near the school. At the time, Philadelphia was (and it still is) a highly segregated city. When I look at my nearly all-White college classroom today, I recognize that like my segregated high-school classroom, it is a consequence of the history of racial accumulations in the United States. When I think about how I moved from teaching mathematics at an all-Black high school to teaching radical educational theory to a vast majority of White students, the metaphor of the train becomes more obvious. Like many educators of color who demonstrated some success working with students of color, I was cherry-picked to move out of the K-12 classroom. During my eighth years of classroom teaching, I was asked by other colleagues when I would become a principal or a district coach. I finally took the pathway of graduate school to become a teacher educator based on the logic that I could effect more change by teaching teachers rather than by teaching youth directly. At that point, I was still naïve to the ways I was becoming manufactured and extracted from the community that built me and gave me the knowledge of how to teach (and nurture) the youth in my community in North Philadelphia. Today, I am useful to liberal Whiteness as a benefit to those who have been historically determined to have access to my community's knowledge. Trains do not have the luxury of wild deviations. They travel gradually and consistently over pre-determined pathways, only able to change tracks when a switch is thrown . . . and then, only moving slightly to another predetermined path.

Part IV: The Refusal

In his classic text titled *Black Marxism: The Making of the Black Radical Tradition*, acclaimed historian Robinson (1983) argues that any exploration of the experiences of the enslaved in the Americas absent an analysis of resistance is woefully incomplete:

> Fugitives (from enslavement) drew the attention of Hernan Cortes as early as 1523 and the first general uprising in Nueva Espana is

thought to have occurred in 1537. . . . Once freed by their own wits, they returned to plague the Spanish colonists, appropriating food, clothes, arms, tools, and even religious artifacts . . . the Spanish would refer to these 'fugitives' as *cimarrones*. (The English would incorporate the term into their own language as 'maroons.'

(p. 130)

He further describes how maroon communities in Brazil, Jamaica, and the Gullah Islands of North America help us realize a different starting point for understanding resistive Black life amidst circumstances that are incommensurate with human life. Marronage is constructed dialectically as both self-determining and fugitive. Harney and Moten (2013) further encourage us to understand fugitivity as a stance to be taken up when we see ourselves working against structures that necessitate the colonial order. They describe the "undercommons" of the university as fugitive spaces, as maroon spaces where we refuse to succumb to the way things are. This refusal could exist as particular enactments that might dislodge us from how we are constructed by liberal Whiteness.

Chappelle sought out this space away from the comedic stage. By walking away from *Chappelle's Show*, he engaged in an act of refusal. Refusal as a stance has both material and psychological implications. Chappelle's refusal was grounded in not wanting to dishonor his Black comedic knowledge system by feeding Whiteness what it desires. As a subversive actor, Chappelle's comedy was intended to disrupt mainstream narratives of racial constructs and ideologies. Once he began to understand that this theory of change was not producing its intended result, he refused to participate. Yet, refusing to participate is not the only form of refusal one could take to exert their agency.

Tuck and Yang (2014a) argue that refusal is ultimately a humanizing act. They apply refusal to social-scientific research in marginalized, particularly Indigenous communities:

Refusals are not subtractive, but are theoretically generative (Simpson, 2007, p. 78), expansive. Refusal is not just a 'no,' but a redirection to ideas otherwise unacknowledged or unquestioned. Unlike a settler colonial configuration of knowledge that is petulantly exasperated and resentful of limits, a methodology of refusal regards limits on knowledge as productive, as indeed a good thing.

(p. 239)

Such a methodological framing is located within liberatory and resistive epistemologies of the subaltern. Refusal understands accumulation as a construct of supremacy and exploitation, whether it is the accumulation of land, capital, natural resources, labor, or knowledge. Modern university systems attempt to accumulate the latter: knowledge. Refusal does not accept the severing of knowledge systems from the bodies that pump, circulate, and actualize the abstractions of theory. Those who engage in refusal see this severing as the work of colleges and universities that seek the accumulation of knowledge for its potential to convert to material wealth for the institution through prestige, faculty labor, and the publicity of ideals such as "diversity" and "justice."

Tuck and Yang situate their exploration of refusal within three axioms of social-scientific research as follows: "(I) The subaltern can speak, but is only invited to speak to her/our pain; (II) there are some forms of knowledge that the academy doesn't deserve; and (III) research may not be the intervention that is needed" (p. 224). Here, I focus on the second axiom, although I hesitate to argue that there are some forms of knowledge that the academy does not deserve. There is a long and rich tradition of colleges and universities as breeding grounds for revolutionary political thought that does produce material benefit for historically repressed and exploited communities. For instance, the Student Non-Violent Coordinating Committee (SNCC) was born on the campuses of Shaw University and Howard University during the Civil Rights era (Carmichael & Thelwell, 2003). College campuses such as San Francisco State University, the University of California Berkeley, Cornell University, and the University of Minnesota were some of the first places where BIPOC students demanded and then realized radical ethnic studies programs with political missions that flew in the face of the academy's traditional (spoken but not practiced) agnosticism regarding political participation. Today, many language-revitalization programs, attempting to resist the colonial erasure of Indigenous languages, are being facilitated by university faculty who are skillfully leveraging institutional resources to run these programs (Hermes, Bang, & Marin, 2012). My earlier story regarding how the ASRC saved my life is another example. Again, as la paperson (2017) reminds us, these liberatory projects are not the fundamental purpose of academic institutions but rather are assemblages that exist in the machinery as people work to redirect capital and energy toward the creation of the third university. The examples I have provided, like the ASRC, are juxtaposed to the university and not of it. Thus, they are inherently contingent and surveilled in ways that other university entities are not. Like the undercommons, the third university is a fugitive space that entails refusal as a stance. For faculty from racialized backgrounds who have been manufactured into trains to transport knowledge back to our institutions, the third university asks us to use the tracks that were constructed but to move in a different direction. That is, we could break the tracks apart and reassemble them to move perpendicularly, diagonally, or even vertically. We could transport university knowledge and resources back to our communities in ways that bring material benefit to those who have been most dispossessed and locked out of these spaces that hoard knowledge. In trying to reconcile "what knowledge" the university deserves, a different question arises as follows: "*which* university?" I grapple with this question as an education faculty member who resides in the second university. By bringing in radical Black knowledge systems to my institution, am I trying to shock my students into the third-university space of marronage and fugitivity (and would they even survive it?), or am I excavating and delivering these systems like the colonial train? I often fear it is the latter.

I end this essay with ambivalence. Only theorizing fugitivity and refusal is not satisfying to me. I desire to have some closure that explores the maroon spaces where refusal resides. The colonial train is persistent and old. Bandits are able to stop the train temporarily and confiscate some of its contents, but another train is always on the way. Blown tracks are also able to undergo repair. Could second-university classrooms become maroon spaces? Could Uhuru exist outside of marronage? Should it? The aforementioned are questions that I, and hopefully other scholars who identify as BIPOC, continue to ponder, and will for quite some time. The interplay between the stage, the distance, and the train will continue to expose our contradictions . . . until we collectively and willingly organize toward a new reality.

6   A Shattered Window

Sandra L. Guzman Foster

The Beginning of It All

It was during my first year as an instructor at a large university in the Southwestern part of the United States that I experienced more overt racism and discrimination than I ever could have fathomed. As a former public-school teacher, I was initially excited about teaching future teachers in my role as a faculty member in a school of education. I believed my experiences in the K-12 classroom would be a valuable asset for the professional learning of pre-service teachers. However, it was during this time that I learned that my physical characteristics made me an easy target for mostly White pre-service teachers' resistance to everything about me including my identity as a Latina teacher educator.

In one specific course that I taught early in my career, the teacher candidates, the majority who were White, were required to critically examine and reflect upon their backgrounds, cultural assumptions, attitudes, and values, as well as how they viewed people who were culturally, linguistically, and socioeconomically different. Fundamentally, for most White teacher candidates, this course meant that they had to examine their Whiteness, something which was not easy for most of them to do because many had been socialized to ignore their racial identity. For many, this type of critical self-reflection about their White identity would also be unacceptable coming from a woman of color like me (Lugo-Lugo, 2012).

At the end of our second class meeting, three students, one older White male and two younger White females, approached me. I stopped packing my belongings to give them my full attention. Suddenly, they raised their voices at me. They told me they "did not like" the way the class was going. As they continued to complain, they moved closer to me, violating my personal space. I politely asked them to step back. They did not listen to me. They continued to complain about the required amount of reading and writing in the course. I stopped the conversation and asked them to leave the room.

On my way to the parking lot, the two White female students approached me, blocking my path on the sidewalk. They attempted to talk to me again, but I restated that the conversation was over. As I proceeded to walk to my car, the older White male student stopped me, and attempted to apologize for "blowing up." He stated that he needed to "vent" to me. He then emphasized that "things need to be changed" in this course or a formal complaint would be filed against me. I immediately ended our conversation. For the first time in my life, I felt physically threatened. I honestly thought I could handle this situation and in the moment decided not to tell anyone what had happened. However, my decision to not seek help would be a mistake I would later regret.

Before the third week of class, the older White male student sent me an e-mail. Through the thread, I learned that a meeting had taken place between my department chair, the teacher-education program coordinator, and several White students who were chosen to represent the group. The White male student stated that he felt uncomfortable attending this meeting without my presence because he did not like speaking about other people in an indirect manner. He pointed out that it is not a "good thing" to belong to a group that is typically seen as powerful (as he is an older White male), but "he had to do it" for the sake of the class. He claimed that he and his mostly White peers felt that the instructional methods used in my class were leading to a hardening of prejudice against other cultures. He referenced a video and readings assigned during the first two weeks of class. The video and readings addressed the presence of American Indian boarding schools, as well as the forced assimilation of American Indians and other groups in the United States through education. Teacher candidates in this course were asked to examine the consequences of these schools, especially in terms of how Indigenous children were forced to assimilate. They ultimately had to subtract their culture and replace it with European ideals and values. This White male student ultimately concluded that I was biased against White people, which he claimed would ultimately lead me to unfairly evaluate their assignments. He further claimed his White peers also felt that learning was not taking place because they had to make sense of everything themselves instead of being taught anything by me. They wanted me to tell them "how to" teach diverse children using assimilationist and quick-fix frameworks. However, they did not want to learn about the social implications of Eurocentric education on their work as teachers. He then claimed that he and his White peers felt that there was "something going on" in my personal life that was making it difficult for me to prepare and teach the class. They felt that it is entirely unfair for the class to suffer because of my "personal problems."

According to Perez (1993), "in the minority experience at the university level, it becomes commonplace that one is guilty of some kind of intellectual inadequacy or incompetence until one proves otherwise, or until one's politics conservative or progressive are approved" (p. 272), a presumption that is widespread for women of color scholars and teacher educators like me (Lazos, 2012). The White male student hoped that the outcome of this meeting and his e-mail would result in "improving the class" according to his and other White teacher candidates' demands. They wanted to hear more about "the methods" used to teach diverse children because they felt the current lectures and the readings had no relevance to their preparation for teaching. He said he would report the information from the meeting to his peers. He also suggested that during the next class, we could take time to work through these concerns. He assured me that he would ask his peers to participate in a manner that would be respectful to everyone. He further suggested that I not take any of this in a negative way but instead react in a "constructive and professional" manner.

Significantly, this White male student felt that it was his job to give me, his professor, a full report on the inadequacies of my teaching methods. He was using his age and his racial privilege as levers. I was also being "schooled" on how to be a "proper" professor. I then e-mailed my department chair. I wanted to know why I had not been notified of the meeting. Additionally, I informed him that I was offended by the comments from these students speculating about my personal life, all of which had no bearing on my performance. My authority and competence were openly challenged by these White teacher candidates and compromised without my knowledge. Although I was told by my chair that none of this was a "big deal" to any of us, I was still uneasy and disturbed by the outcome of this meeting. My experience was not an isolated case, as women of color in the academy have shared numerous accounts of their experiences where their competence has been questioned and challenged, and where White students often have exhibited hostile behaviors toward us in the classroom (Lazos, 2012; Turner, González, & Wong, 2011).

"This Would Not Be Happening . . . If You Were a White Male Professor"

The next day, I confided in a colleague who is also Latina. She was quick to point out: "This *would not* be happening . . . if you were a White male professor." Could it really be that the amount of work I required was "too much" and that White teacher candidates did not like the fact that a Brown woman was telling them what to do and how to do it? In most of my White teacher candidates' eyes, my gender and ethnicity/racialized identity obscured their recognition of my academic expertise, experiences, and credentials, as "I was a minority person first and an instructor second" (Aguirre, 1995, p. 17).

The next day, I received an e-mail from my department chair, encouraging me to meet with another professor who had studied the topic of student resistance. I met with Professor Johnson and shared my experiences. After listening, she responded as follows: "They know *exactly* what they are doing. Your students are resisting everything about you . . . including your teaching. I believe they are feeling threatened and challenged by you and they do not like it." We agreed that she would come to the class to confront the problem "head-on."

I introduced Professor Johnson at the beginning of our next class. She began by asking the teacher candidates to voice their feelings. Several White teacher candidates accused me of being racist toward White people, being incompetent in the subject, giving them too much work, practicing favoritism toward students who scheduled office hours with me, lecturing too much, telling them what to do, not knowing how to teach, and telling them lies about the American public-school system. They also said that I have created a hostile environment. They stated because of all of this, they "have not learned anything" in class. Professor Johnson asked them what they meant by "hostile." Many responded that they felt that topics related to racism, discrimination, Eurocentric education, and so forth, were all too much to take in. They felt these topics made White people "look bad," which they correlated to a hostile learning environment. As Weiler (1988) asserts, "Since White privilege is so much a defined part of the U.S. society, Whites are not even conscious of their relationship of power and privilege" (p. 76).

Then seemingly out of nowhere, some students came to my defense. They turned to their peers who just spoke and made comments such as the following: "She *does* care about us. She has an open-door policy for anyone who has any concerns. She is *not* racist. She has no control over your White guilt. She is very thoughtful. She is doing her job. We are learning from the readings. We are prepared for the midterm exam."

Professor Johnson then asked them if there was a problem with them accepting me for who I am. There was silence. She repeated the question. One of the two younger White females who had threatened me on the third night of class asked, "Are you asking if we are racist?" She replied, "I don't know; is that what you think I am asking?" According to Rains (1995), "Whites may fear being labeled a 'racist' if they somehow 'see' color. Some confuse color recognition with quality of treatment" (p. 92). No one responded.

Professor Johnson and I talked after class. She said their behaviors were typical of White student resistance and then proceeded to give me some material to read that addressed this issue. I thought the American education system had prepared me so that I could fit in for this position. That is, I was already part of two worlds: the White world and the Latinx world. This experience had caused much more anxiety and confusion than I ever imagined. I began to recall my schooling experiences. My education started with assimilation into the dominant culture as a result of my parents' own educational experience. The American public-school system had instilled in my parents that our language was something that had no value in their lives or in the public schools. As children, they were physically and mentally abused by their White teachers for speaking Spanish. My grandparents and parents were born in the United States. They were Americans who happened to speak Spanish. As they were punished when speaking Spanish to their friends, they eventually spoke English when they communicated with their mostly White teachers. My parents were simply communicating in the way they knew how. After they were married and had children, they were determined that we would not receive the same kind of punishment they received. Consequently, they taught us to speak English first with the intention of teaching us Spanish second. However, time passed by; we never learned how to speak Spanish fluently. As I now know, my parents wanted our English to be strong so we could hopefully "fit in" with the dominant White culture.

Today, it is not easy being a Latina who does not speak the Spanish language fluently, as people from my ethnic group often dismiss me. The American education system got it all wrong. Instead of embracing, acknowledging, and accepting the differences that children bring to school, our system dismisses them, and moreover, openly punishes and humiliates children who are culturally, ethnically, and linguistically different. For those of us who grew up in this generation, we are not only trying to survive among members of the dominant White culture, but we are trying to survive in our own culture because we are seen by some as "sellouts" because we do not speak our parents' native language.

After the meeting with Professor Johnson, my class was never the same. Every time I walked into the classroom, I was under constant scrutiny. My level of competence was always being questioned and challenged by several White teacher candidates. I was not recognized for my credentials or my teaching experience but only by my physical characteristics that marked me as an outsider. I became visible in both my body and in the texts I chose. I became subject to the authority/authenticity paradox that many of us face when teaching courses that cover topics that nobody wants to talk about (Ho, 2002, p. 67). I learned that White teacher candidates would treat me differently from their White professors; that everyone and everything that I culturally represented would be held against me (Turner & Myers, 2000). As I was rudely reminded:

> When individuals report discrimination, bias, etc. of ethnically distinct groups, too often university officials consider them as "isolated" incidents even though they result in stereotyping, condescension transmitted into compliment, and the second-guessing and undermining of the academic work of Latino/a professors, not to mention of their talents and humanity.
>
> (Padilla & Chavez Chavez, 1995, p. 7)

Such incidents are invisibly normal and endemic to the academic landscape. Characterizing them as "isolated" incidents result in perpetuating the status quo and stifling the dialogue that is needed to overcome them. According to the literature, "it is a disturbing portrait of academic life in American universities as experienced by Latino/a academics" (Padilla & Chavez Chavez, 1995, p. 7). As Njeri (1989) further asserts, the White interpretation of the world is objective, and the minority person's interpretation is political. Thus, no matter how I delivered information, White teacher candidates would always see me as a Latina whose intent was to misinform them with "lies" about the American school system.

After the midterm, I received an e-mail from the older White male student about his grades in the course. He believed that no matter what he did in class, I would assign him a letter grade of a B. He informed me that he was told by the committee that if he saw any changes in the way his assignments were being graded, that he was to inform them immediately. However, before he went to the committee, he wanted to give me "the opportunity" to address the issue with him first. I informed him that I had three other instructors grade his papers. Each was given a redacted copy of his paper, and that all three of the instructors assigned the same grade as the grade I assigned him. I then asked him if he wanted me to give a redacted copy to my supervisor for a fourth round of grading. He never responded to me after that exchange.

At the end of the semester, I received two types of responses in my course evaluations. One group found the class to be engaging, interesting, and one of the best they had ever taken. The other group was highly critical of my teaching because the course was dominated by literature focused on how concepts such as race, ethnicity, gender, and class are reflected in and reinforced by American public schools. According to the second group, I allegedly used the class to forward my "politically correct education agenda" of promoting works that addressed how education affects different social and cultural groups in different ways at the expense of other types of readings (Ho, 2002; Lazos, 2012). I was not surprised by these evaluations because women of color often receive lower course evaluations than White female and White male instructors (Lazos, 2012).

How Will They Treat Children Who Look Like Me?

In the end, I became extremely concerned about the kinds of teacher candidates who are leaving our teacher-preparation program. If they treat me with such disrespect, how would they interact with children and parents who look like me? Despite these concerns, I decided to teach the course again. Like the first time I taught the course, this round of White pre-service teachers also mostly resisted everything about me and the course. Clearly, they were not prepared to teach children who are culturally and racially different. Little did I know that I was in for my second rude awakening with this group of mostly White teacher candidates.

After the first night of class, I received an e-mail from an older White female teacher candidate, asking me a question about an assignment. At the bottom of her e-mail was a thread that had been sent to the entire class by another White student. The e-mail advised students to "save everything" I handed out in class in case "proper action" needed to be taken against me. Unlike the first time where I did not tell anyone about what I was experiencing, I did not hesitate this time around. I immediately forwarded the e-mail to my department chair. This time, I was encouraged by my chair to take care of this issue as soon as possible. I also met with a veteran Latina professor. She said the best way to deal with this is to bring it up in class and, and as she stated, "Nip it in the bud." She advised me as follows: "This is unacceptable behavior, and you are a person who deserves to be here, and they did not have the right to treat you with such disrespect."

At the next class meeting, I projected a redacted copy of the e-mail on the screen in front of the classroom so all of the teacher candidates could see it as they walked into the classroom. When it was time for class to start, I asked for a volunteer to read the e-mail and to interpret the message. A young White male volunteered. He read the e-mail to the class, and then said, "This message says we have too much work and something needs to be changed." Another White female student said, "This tells me that someone is planning to take action against you, but I'm not sure why." I asked, "Why would anyone attempt to report me before speaking with me first?" No one responded. I then stated that I was very disappointed that they had already made a judgment based on what others were saying about me when they had just met me. I pointed out that this was not a good characteristic to have if one aspires to become a teacher by asking the group, "Are you going to judge a student based on what you heard through the rumor mill before he/she sets foot in your class? Or are you going to have an open mind and give him/her a chance?" No one responded. I knew I had to do something to make this work. The last thing I wanted to do was silence my students who aspired to become classroom teachers. I knew what it felt like to be silenced. I knew that if I wanted this all to work, we had to learn to trust and respect each other, as well as create a safe place where all voices could be heard and where transformative dialogue could take place. I thought the best way to meet this goal was to model and practice empathy.

I asked the class to consider a time when they felt they were being treated unfairly because of who they are or as a result of their various identities. A Latino teacher candidate described how he has been racially profiled by the police. He has been stopped numerous times because he has long hair and drives a beat-up old car. A White female shared how she was kicked off her soccer team because the coach wanted a male to play in her position instead. A Latina teacher candidate described how her child looks more like her White husband; however, when she picks her son up from school, she is often mistaken by White adults to be the child's maid. As they were sharing their stories, I wrote how they felt on the board. Words like *anger, pain, frustration, betrayal, sadness, disbelief*, and so forth filled the board. I shared that these were some of the very same feelings I had experienced the previous semester, but that I was refusing to go through these feelings again with this new group.

I emphasized that this is not a multicultural class, nor is this a course where I will teach them "how to teach" diverse children. I informed them that in this class, they will be asked to critically examine their ideologies, their paradigms, their schooling experiences, their upbringing, and their cultural understandings, especially their role as moral agents in our schools. I reiterated that some of the content could be uncomfortable because our discussions may lead to the deconstruction of ourselves, something that is very difficult to do given that we live in a racialized society that also discourages critical reflection about race. I emphasized they would have to unlearn some things they may have long held as truths, but it was also important to examine their frames of reference before they entered the classroom as teachers to be effective teachers of all learners.

I knew that allowing my teacher candidates the opportunity to openly discuss and engage actively among each other was an integral part of the learning process. That is, good teaching requires risk-taking. In this case, I took a risk by asking my teacher candidates to venture beyond their normal level of comfort and areas of knowledge (TuSmith, 2002). Additionally, I took a big risk by throwing my vulnerability out there and asking for them to do the same.

Commanding Respect as a Latina Teacher Educator

> Even though Latino/a academics may have been disoriented by covert and overt prejudices, marginalized, and made to question their own humanity in the everyday experience of academic life, these individuals have instinctively reoriented themselves. They have reasserted and reclaimed their authenticity through words and actions.
>
> (Padilla & Chavez Chavez, 1995, p. 3)

It was important for me, as a Latina scholar and teacher educator, to let my mostly White teacher candidates know that I would not allow them to disrespect or silence me in any way. Martinez Aleman (1995) states the why powerfully:

> As individuals present in realities that dismiss us, ignore us, forget us, and are indifferent toward us, our choice is either to keep quiet and live professionally as affirmative action statistics or to speak, to make ourselves heard, or act affirmatively.
>
> (p. 71)

It may have been easier for me to embrace silence and not cope with such experiences, but I believe, as Martinez Aleman (1995) notes, "to choose silence is to embrace cultural complacency and to do this would only deny my personhood and my identity" (p. 74).

The most difficult part of this journey was the hard lessons I learned. First, I learned that whether we like it or not, "the politics of identity shape our interactions with our students and the very dynamic of learning within the classroom" (Leong, 2002, p. 124). The second lesson I learned is the reality that my identity would always be a factor no matter where I am in the academic world. That is, in the K-12 world and in the academy, I would always be under intense scrutiny simply because I am Latina (Perez, 1993). It was not just that my White teacher candidates made me feel different because I am a Latina, but it was that they equated my difference with assumptions of inferiority (Cruz, 1995).

These experiences have also helped to shape me into a stronger and wiser Latina scholar and teacher educator. As I continue my journey, I will not let such experiences keep me from growing and thriving. I am reminded of Perez's (1993) keen insights that "It is within our power as students, educators, and administrators to educate minorities and non-minorities alike to question the construction of national mythologies and predefined stereotypes or 'identities' that underlie our national romance" (p. 276).

Mine is but one experience among many Latinx scholars in higher education. To face adversity and survive everyday life in the academic world, valuing ourselves becomes a necessity. For many of us, valuing ourselves is the metaphorical glue that we adhere to protect our authenticity and preserve our integrity (Turner & Myers, 2000). I have learned from my experiences. Each moment feeds my spirit, my soul, my heart, and allows me to continue growing into a respected Latina scholar and teacher educator. Like Torres-Guzman (1995), I have learned to value the self by setting limits not on myself, but on those around me who attempt to devalue my every move, my expertise, and my essence as a human being. Like Martinez Aleman (1995):

> I am stuck by my lived contradictions: to be a professor is to be an Anglo; to be a Latina is not to be an Anglo. So how can I be both a Latina and a professor? To be a Latina professor, I conclude, means to be unlike and like me. Que locura? What madness!
>
> (p. 74)

As a Latina in the academic world, I am learning how to be a professor without compromising my identity. It is important for me to determine who I am rather than having my identity designated by others, especially Whites. If I allow these experiences to starve me of what I deserve, then I will be letting those who choose not to see beyond my beautiful brown skin, brown eyes, and my accent to take away my sense of self. No one deserves to take away something so dear and precious to my heart and soul.

I recognize that the American Dream comes with a price. My experiences have given me a deeper awareness of my identity as a Latina. I now have a greater appreciation for my origins and cultural values. It has become clear to me that in some people's minds, my identity overshadows my intellectual work, professional aspirations, and relations; consequently, they are trying to cloud my personal life and self-confidence (Torres-Guzman, 1995). I also realize that many other people actually support me and really care about how hard I have worked to build and maintain my credibility. Unfortunately, there are others still who believe that all I have accomplished in life is meaningless.

Implications

I share my experiences in hope that it will further dialogue that is desperately needed, as "We can let discomfort become a path to reflection and democratic action in our practice" (Padilla & Chavez Chavez, 1995, p. 14). A starting point would be for predominantly White colleges and schools of education to require more than one course on diversity and to actually infuse anti-racism into all required teacher-preparation courses. The goal would for teacher candidates to reflect consistently and critically on their identities to help them understand the sociopolitical contexts of schooling throughout their programs of study. For teachers to be able to teach all children, it is imperative for pre-service teachers, especially those who are White, to become aware of their racial identity and race-based privileges before they step into any classroom.

In addition, departments and programs need to deliberately sponsor conscious-raising sessions. These sessions would have to meet Style's (1996) primary criterion that learning environments should provide everyone, including faculty and students, with both mirrors and windows to learn. Windows provide new perspectives; they encourage participants to look beyond their existing views. However, mirrors are essential; they allow us to see ourselves and ourselves, giving us opportunities to culturally connect to the learning environment.

The problem with our current educational system is that racialized Americans have many windows but not enough mirrors while our White peers have too many mirrors on the dominant culture but not enough windows into different perspectives (Brewer, 1990, p. 4). As Turner and Myers (2000) assert, inclusiveness leads to unity. The vision of a truly inclusive academic climate must include space for all individuals to maintain their cultural identities while participating fully in the institution. The task of the university thus should be "to provide all with a range of safe environments and options where they can explore and develop terms which they find comfortable for interethnic/cultural contacts" (Duster, 1992, p. 15).

White teacher candidates who resist teacher educators from racialized backgrounds are only denying themselves the opportunity to learn from (let alone getting to know) people who are different from them. They need to be encouraged to open their eyes and their minds so that they see us (and respect us) as scholars and teacher educators. Most importantly, mostly White pre-service teachers need to open their minds before they step into K-12 classrooms because everything they do or say (or not) will impact their students' lives. We must teach White pre-service teachers that it is unacceptable to devalue communities, families, and students based on their cultural identities and languages. My grandparents' and parents' experiences with US public education are some of the many examples of the consequences of having White teachers who do not value where children come from or the rich cultures they bring to school.

7 Disproportionate Underrepresentation of Faculty of Color in Education

A Critical disAbility Studies in Education (dSE) Analysis

Hyun Uk Kim

Re/Living Trauma

I am overwhelmed with emotions as I reflect on my journey in academia. Until recently, I have intentionally avoided reliving my past and deliberately ignored what has happened to me as a faculty of color who was employed at a predominantly White institution in a racially segregated school of education. As petrified as I was to revisit my journey, I also found relief in sharing my story, as it was therapeutic in a way (Ellis, Adams, & Bochner, 2011). As a firm believer in the power of interpretive autobiography (Denzin, 1997), I narrate my story, my lived experience, and my autobiographic voice (Creswell, 1998) as a faculty of color who was employed at a predominantly White school of education. My purpose here is not to merely expose the visceral racial macroaggressions and academic bullying as defined as systematic long-term interpersonal aggressive behaviors by White education faculty members in positions of power in the academy (Sue, 2010) and how their behaviors have both pained and dehumanized me. The purpose is also to solidify my stance as a proud faculty of color and to also use my narrative as a means to exert my agency to ultimately inspire (and reassure) others who have also been long denied a voice (Denzin & Lincoln, 1998) in education. I also invite other education faculty and scholars from minoritized backgrounds to engage in the task of resisting academic bullying and macroaggressions in education and society as a means to promote true inclusion.

My narrative is embedded in the theoretical framework of disAbility Studies in Education (or dSE). As a dSE educator and scholar, I have always contextualized disAbility within political and social spheres in my pedagogical and scholarly endeavors. Here, I intentionally use the term disAbility over "disability" to dismantle and disrupt negative and misleading connotations of the original word while also maintaining the latter when referring to formal classification systems. As a dSE scholar,

I have been advocating for "social justice, equitable and inclusive educational opportunities, and full and meaningful access to all aspects of society for people labeled with disability" (Connor, Gabel, Gallagher, & Morton, 2008, p. 448), dismissing the common notion that anyone who does not fit the imaginary constructs of normality is deviant and dangerous (Davis, 1995). However, it did not dawn on me until I reflected on my identity as a person of color that I have also been the epitome of being dangerous and deviant to my White counterparts. That is, my "colored identity" did not fit their expectations of normality in their predominantly White institution, let alone in US society. This epiphany helped me juxtapose my identity as a scholar of color who embraces dSE disability in relation to a hostile White-dominant institution that claimed to promote equity and justice in its mission and values.

"Go Back to Your Country!"

On April 24, 2017, I was sworn into this nation as a naturalized US citizen. As I sat with a roomful of people, representing 27 different countries around the world, I could not help but ask myself one question as follows: "Now that I am no longer an alien, would I be treated as equally as other citizens in the United States?" For context, an "alien" admitted to the United States is a lawful permanent resident. Permanent residents are also commonly referred to as immigrants; however, the Immigration and Nationality Act (INA) broadly defines an immigrant as "any alien in the United States, except one legally admitted under specific nonimmigrant categories" (US Citizenship and Immigration Services Glossary, n.d., n.p.).

When I accepted a job from an institution of higher learning in the northeast in 2007 to teach practicing and pre-service teachers, I was thrilled at the prospect of teaching in the academy after having lived in Los Angeles for almost a decade. Soon after my partner and I arrived in the town where I would be teaching, we met a family who was willing to show us around their neighborhood for prospective housing options. As we familiarized ourselves with the area, we noticed an elderly White woman approaching us. She identified herself as a resident of the same townhouse complex we were visiting. She told us we were being too loud and disruptive. Noticing we were not speaking English, she also dared to say, "You! Go back to your country!" I said, in return, that I would "go back" to my country if she would also "go back" to hers. Also, this country she claimed to be hers actually belonged to Indigenous persons. Upon hearing my argument, she left us with a very sullen look on her face. In almost a decade of living in Los Angeles, I had not encountered any incidents of this kind and magnitude. It was only when I was relocated to the northeast part of the United States did I receive such an unwelcome reception from a fellow American. Unfortunately, this was neither the first nor the last incident from people who continued to consider me as an alien and intruder in their sacred spaces. I also soon saw connections in the nearly all-White academic workplace that racialized bodies are not fully welcome there, even though these spaces claim to be more egalitarian than segregated neighborhoods, for instance.

"She Should be the Second Author of Your Manuscript"

In May 2012, I was at work heating dinner in the kitchen, and also, getting ready for my evening class. Two senior White faculty members, with whom I will refer to as Amy and Pete, walked into the kitchen area. Amy suddenly claimed that I was guilty of plagiarism because I used a similar title for an existing article for an upcoming manuscript. Pete then further demanded that Amy should be listed as a co-author/second author of the article because she was the one who gave me the idea about the manuscript. He also told me that he should read the manuscript before I submit it to any journal. Caught completely off guard, I felt bullied and harassed by their accusations. Trying to maintain my composure, I told them I would think about what they said . . . and get back to them.

I shared the incident with my department chair, who, after listening to me, suggested that I file a formal grievance against both of them. I contemplated her suggestion for a few days because I was supposed to apply for promotion and tenure in the following autumn term. I feared that filing a complaint of this sort would significantly work against me. I decided to go with the formal grievance because I could not bear being bullied and harassed any longer. The only regret I had at that point was I should have taken action when it first happened rather than waiting.

To backtrack a bit, in 2008, when I was a new faculty member, Pete approached me and alluded that he would like to work with me. As a new faculty member, I was initially grateful that a senior faculty member wanted to collaborate with me. However, it soon became very clear that what he meant by "working together" was just editing my work but expecting me to list him as an equal contributor on a published manuscript. I consulted about the matter with Amy, a newer White faculty at the time, as to what I needed to do in this circumstance. She told me that as a junior faculty, "this sort of thing" happens a lot in academia. She seemed to understand the difficult situation that I was in. Nonetheless, feeling pressured and vulnerable as an untenured junior faculty, I reluctantly added his name to my manuscript and sent it to a publisher. The manuscript ended up being rejected. However, I was actually relieved about this rejection because I did not want to publish an article with someone who claimed any ownership when he deserved none. In 2012, I decided to work on the manuscript again, and included it in my annual-review dossier as one of my "in-progress" manuscripts. This action led

Pete and Amy, who happened to serve on my peer-review committee, to bully and harass me, and then try to claim ownership of my work.

"I Did It for Her" . . . and Other Acts of White Bullying and Patronization

Since 2008, I had also been developing an advanced training certificate program, a five-course sequence in the area of Autism Spectrum Conditions (ASC). The program had been discussed consistently at departmental meetings for about three years. Before submitting the proposal to the Curriculum Committee, we, as a department, were to review the suggestions made at the previous meetings and incorporate them into the full-program proposal. At a luncheon meeting in January 2012, Pete claimed that the proposal should be substantially revised to move forward. He also stated that I should consult with other faculty members who specialize in ASC at other institutions. Although he was one of the search committee members who hired me because of my expertise in ASC, he, in this moment, questioned my expertise publicly. Although there were nine other White faculty members at the meeting who knew about the proposal, none of them spoke up, as if they agreed with what Pete had to say. Immensely humiliated, ridiculed, and feeling defeated, I felt I had no choice but to withhold the proposal at the last minute.

The following week, I received an e-mail from one of the students who was enrolled in an ASC course. Her note read as follows: "Due to the lack of development in the certificate program in autism, I will have to withdraw from the course." Later, I found out that she was one of Pete's advisees, and he had directly discouraged her and other students from taking the course. Pete continued to share with his advisees that there was "a lack of development" in the ASC program. I was scheduled to offer two ASC courses during the summer before launching the entire program in the subsequent autumn term; however, both were cancelled due to low enrollment. That summer, I sat down with the department chair. She had met with Pete before meeting with me. She told me that he said to her the following: "I did this for her [me]." While he belittled, ridiculed, and humiliated me publicly in front of my peers, he claimed that he did what he had done . . . only because he was supposedly "looking out for me."

Until I finally fought back against Pete, I blamed myself for everything. White senior faculty members' offensive and malicious bullying immensely affected my physical and emotional well-being and performance, rendering my work environment to be extremely toxic. The workplace became unbearable to the point that I became physically ill whenever I came to work. I thought I had to redeem myself with more work and better teaching. It never occurred to me that I could fight back or be assertive, let alone to stand up for myself.

As a Korean woman, I was raised to value humanity, respect my elders, and offer deference to authority figures (Yim, 2002). All of these are influenced by the many aspects of Confucius's ideology. That is, my compliance and deference to power and authority reflect my cultural heritage and values. However, to White people like Pete, it was likely misconstrued as incompetence and misinterpreted as obedience to their White power and authority. This moment is when I realized that I needed to "leave my culture behind" to be taken seriously by Whites. That is, I had to be as assertive as I possibly could be to send a clear message that I would not be bullied racially by them any longer.

After years of silence and self-blaming, I was determined to articulate my pain and the impact of ongoing harassment and academic bullying in a formal manner. I finally filed a formal grievance against these two senior White tenured faculty members in August 2012, which was also the year that I was supposed to apply for tenure and promotion. With this formal grievance against these people, who also served on my peer-review committee, I knew that being assertive and articulating my pain publicly would cost me my tenure, but I had already decided I would leave the institution either way to restore my rights as a scholar and my dignity as a human being.

Ironically, this university claims that it:

> is committed to maintaining a multicultural academic community in which the dignity and worth of each of its members are respected, and that it is the policy of the University that abuse or harassment, of or by students, faculty, staff, and guest or visitors, will not be tolerated.
>
> (n.d., n.p.)

However, this formal grievance brought me absolutely nothing. The following spring, I received a letter stating that my tenure and promotion application had been denied by the institution. I did not appeal the decision, not because I agreed with the outcome but because I knew my voice meant nothing at this institution. It was not worth it to further invest my energy here.

In May 2014, I taught my last class at this majority White school of education that granted me my first teaching job in higher education. On May 30, 2014, I vacated my office with the mindset that I did not want to ever teach in higher education again. I had no intention of returning to the academy, as I did not want to relive a painful and demoralizing past. Days became months (and months became a year) when I realized that I missed one thing dearly: the joy of teaching. Although Pete tried to take away my humanity with his so-called collegial actions, there was one thing he could not take away from me was my passion for teaching and learning.

I needed a year to recuperate from the damage done to me. I ultimately decided that I needed to relocate to feel human again. Most importantly, I learned about the impact my cultural background has in US higher education and decided I had to be more assertive to be legitimated by Whites. In the spring of 2015, I was offered a job at a private institution in the Southeast region of the United States. At this institution, I was not just one of the few faculty of color but one of many. My colleagues were also collegial. Major adjustments from my end were required to adapt to this environment because I was not used to be treated as a colleague or as an equal. However, my honeymoon here did not last long, though. One day, a White male colleague asked me how to pronounce my first name. When he could not pronounce *Hyun Uk* correctly, he asked me, "Can I call you *kimchi?*"

Diversity and Inclusion

According to Myers (n.d.), "Diversity is being invited to the party. Inclusion is being asked to dance (n.p.)." In addition, Pat Romney contends that "Equity is having a voice in the play list" (personal communication, October 13, 2017). My voice in the song selection called "inclusive academia" and "liberal education" has been completely dismissed. Nobody has been interested in hearing from me or asking me if there was any song that I wanted to hear with them. An open invitation to the party is thus a must for true inclusion. However, are we being asked to dance with others? Is everyone able to articulate the list of songs that everyone could dance to and with others? Our dance matters. Our song matters. Therefore, our voices should matter too.

In reflection, I was invited to my first institution's party to fulfill its various diversity initiatives so it could make it appear that they cared about equity by having more faculty of color. Despite these concerted efforts, we remain significantly underrepresented in higher education. For instance, as of 2015, I was among fewer than the just 4 percent of Asian/Pacific Islander females of all full-time faculty at degree-granting postsecondary institutions in the United States, whereas 42 percent are White males and 35 percent are White females; the figures are more homogeneous in the field of teacher education (NCES, 2017). Indeed, most predominantly White institutions of higher education focus only on recruiting minoritized faculty rather than doing the more critical work of retaining and supporting them (Thompson, 2008).

As an Asian immigrant, I am also immediately positioned as an "alien" in this country. As a faculty of color, I am readily situated as the Other in predominantly White institutions. I am still in search of finding my legitimate place in this country and institutions of higher education. Similarly, it has not been long before students with disAbility labels were finally invited to the party. Public Law 94–142, also known as the Education for All Handicapped Children Act, was enacted to "invite" students with various exceptionalities to US public schools in 1975, which was designed to guarantee a "free and appropriate public education" to all children with disAbility labels. Although this legal mandate has changed the landscape of education considerably for students with disAbility labels, the overrepresentation of children from racialized backgrounds in special education classrooms has been a recurring and persistent concern since Dunn (1968) identified the problem for the first time in the late 1960s:

> About 60 to 80 percent of the pupils . . . are children from low status backgrounds – including Afro-Americans, American Indians, Mexicans, and Puerto Rican Americans; those form nonstandard English-speaking, broken, disorganized, and inadequate homes.
>
> (p. 6)

One explanation for the persistent overrepresentation of students from racialized backgrounds in special education is that their teachers who are predominantly White, middle-class, and female may not understand (or care to even try to understand) the experiences and needs of students who are not like them (Fuller & Shaw, 2011; Ladson-Billings, 1995), and thus, refer them to special education. These acts at the initial teacher-referral stage, which involve many forms of cultural bias, mislabeling, and racism, contribute to racial and ethnic disparities in special education that ultimately perpetuate a multitude of equity gaps (Skiba et al., 2008).

The disproportionate alienation and hostility, as well as mis/labeling of faculty from minoritized backgrounds by White faculty, have similar parallels. Personally, for me, the ways by which several White senior faculty members bullied, demeaned, and mislabeled me, as well as the lack of institutional support and retention efforts, were the main factors that led me to temporarily leave academia. Let me backtrack. I did not leave; I was pushed out. Hollis (2017) contends that faculty members without power who happen to be women from minoritized backgrounds are more vulnerable to academic bullying. We are eventually prone to leaving higher education entirely. Ironically, my experiences contrast with how I approach my courses with aspiring teachers, where I have been conceptualizing differences as natural, acceptable, and ordinary, and that inclusion is a *must* in truly promoting social justice (Baglieri & Knopf, 2004). However, I did not see the obvious connection between my identity and exclusion in higher education, and the fact that racism is a societal response to assumed or real differences from a White norm (Mirza, 1998).

Throughout US history, societal perspectives and treatment toward people with disAbility and racialized labels have, to some extent, changed. Historically, people with exceptionalities have been tortured, displayed as freaks, and institutionalized. They eventually have been "included" in society, but they are still on the fringes of mainstream institutions (Adams, Bell, & Griffin, 2007). The pejorative term of "handicapism," which is defined as "a set of assumptions and practices that promote the differential and unequal treatment of people because of . . . physical, mental, or behavioral differences" (Bogdan & Biklen, 1977, p. 14) has many parallels to racism (Bogdan & Biklen, 2013). For instance, for me, being among mostly White faculty members induced both unequal and differential treatment because of my assumed or real differences. Rather than being included as an equal participant in this community, I was viewed in highly deficit terms, and subsequently was treated as inferior to White faculty.

Davis (2006) contends that it is not that people with disAbility labels who have inherent problems; rather, it is the way that normality is constructed in this society that creates problems for people with disAbilities. Davis further posits that the conceptualization of "a norm" or average could be attributed to the French statistician Adolphe Quetelet, who had formulated the concept of both physical and moral constructs and means as imperative to make sense of the world around us. When the concept of a "norm" is operative in a given society like in the United States, it implies that the majority of the population should be part of a set of assumed normative constructs. Hence, there is a false notion of, for instance, "abled" versus "disabled" bodies. This perspective is reflected in the medical model of "disability," which defines "a disability" as a problematic condition that resides in the individual, and moreover, associates having a disAbility as a personal tragedy (Oliver, 1996). In this view, it is permissible and almost natural in a given society to have a negative social perspective for people with disAbility labels. In education, those with disAbility labels are marginalized and stigmatized by many educators who label students not fitting into dominant paradigms as deviant (Stainback & Stainback, 1984). Educators thus will hold negative attitudes toward students with various exceptions and other social differences in school settings as long as these narrow notions of what is "normal" persist (Lipsky & Gartner, 1996). Similarly, in the culture of academia that is distinctly White, as well as ableist, classist (i.e., affluent and middle-class), and heterosexist, White administrators, faculty members, and students will largely presume those who do not fit within normative constructs to be incompetent (Gutiérrez y Muhs et al., 2012).

dSE, on the other hand, asserts that disAbility is a social construct. That is, it is our societal beliefs and practices that "disable" certain individuals (Baglieri, Bejoian, Broderick, Connor, & Valle, 2011). dSE further presumes the competence of all persons, and focuses predominantly on inclusive education and practices (Connor et al., 2008). Indeed, presuming competence is a necessary condition for the full and meaningful inclusion of people with disAbility and other minoritized labels (Biklen & Kleiwer, 2006). Further, Biklen and Burke (2007) posit that to fully include students with disAbility labels in a given classroom, their participation should be not conditional but a must whereby "the student must be seen as someone more than a body to fill the chair" (p. 172). Similarly, faculty from racialized backgrounds are often used to be hired to "fill the chair" so we are able to help diversify the campus and fulfill shallow diversity goals. However, there must be a strong institutional commitment where our participation means more than using our physical presence to claim that diversity goals have been attained. That is, we must be able to articulate our "song list," and also, make clear that we want to listen to and/or dance with others. Additionally, there must be a stronger commitment for institutional transformation that requires all faculty, particularly White women and White men (and gender nonconforming individuals who are White), to learn from and with their colleagues from minoritized backgrounds "rather than replicate divisive survival strategies of the past" (Gutierrez y Muhs et al., 2012, p. 13).

Final Thoughts

I began this chapter with extremely personal and extraordinarily painful narratives that had happened to me as a faculty member in a predominantly White school of education that was part of a university claiming to value diversity and inclusion. I hope these narratives do not discourage anyone who is considering a career in academia as a teacher educator. Rather, I narrated my experiences to do the opposite. Although I have had several "bumpy rides" throughout my initial journey into higher education, I am now able to reflect back, and say that I am at a place where I am fully enjoying my journey. To be clear, while my experiences are better at my new institutional home, academic bullying and microaggressions have not gone away, and moreover, the playing field has not been leveled completely where I am at. I would say, however, that I am more prepared to handle all of the various "curve balls" thrown at me daily. Now, I know how to better advocate for myself, and, also, to speak up. Rather than ignoring my culture and trying to hide my heritage, I educate other faculty members explicitly and diligently, particularly those who are White, about my cultural background for their awareness, as well as for our mutual understanding.

Whereas many White Americans used to regard my silence as incompetence and compliance, my White colleagues now mostly acknowledge that this is who I am, and in general, presume that I am competent rather than incompetent. It may be not only because I am more assertive with articulating my opinion, but also because I am now surrounded by people who are willing to listen to (and learn) from me. They seem genuinely interested in what I have to offer to this school of education. There is also a strong institutional commitment to supporting and mentoring all members of the faculty to make its institution as inclusive as possible.

For instance, a recent e-mail from the President at my institution reads as follows:

> We recognize the humanity of each individual and understand why equity is required to have a just world. . . . We are confident that if we remain steadfast, we can learn and grow together-developing equity mindsets. . . . Let's keep the strong momentum going around building a thriving and just community committed to equity and inclusive excellence.
>
> (H. Drinan, personal communication, December 01, 2017)

It was originally not the institution's initiative. Rather, it was brought forward by students in 2015 with specific demands to make the institution as inclusive as possible. As part of an ongoing commitment to inclusive excellence, I attended a mandatory all-day seminar to explore diversity, equity, and inclusion as it relates to my work as a teacher educator. I will attend the next iteration of the seminar to expand the focus to equity and excellence in teaching and learning. In these dialogue-based seminars, all participants learn from each other because we are all in this work together.

Second, as a "disability" is a social construct, so is the idea of what educators consider to be "normal." The overrepresentation of racialized bodies with "disability" labels in K-12 and the underrepresentation of faculty from similar backgrounds in higher education seem to be completely different constructs. However, these are the same issues, as they are about how we respond to "differences" in those who look, talk, and behave in ways that we see as "different." Unless we make a concerted effort to question and challenge the very idea of normality in our schools and society, we will continue to be haunted by the same issues repeatedly for many years to come. It is my sincere hope that sharing my experiences will encourage fellow scholars in education, especially those of us from marginalized backgrounds, to constantly question the concept of what is "normal." I also hope we will learn to celebrate our similarities rather than differences as we move closer to shared efforts to create and sustain a more just society and working environment for everyone, especially for those of us who have been labeled as different.

8 From the Mekong River to the Merrimack River

One Lao American Refugee's Journey Through the Academy

Phitsamay Sychitkokhong Uy

When the Personal Becomes Professional

It was over two decades ago when I started my journey as an "accidental academic." An elementary teacher at the time, I had attended a Lao education conference in Minneapolis, Minnesota. There, I found out that Lao American and other Southeast Asian American youth in the area were dropping out of school at alarming rates with conservative estimates at 60 percent. I began to ask myself questions like "Why is this trend happening? What are people doing to address this issue?" The response from the community was astounding with remarks such as "We don't know. None of us work for or with the school district." When I returned home and told my roommate who was a UCLA graduate student about the significant dropout rate of Southeast Asian American youth, she told me, "That's what a dissertation is for. When you have a compelling question that you care about and have the time and energy to study, then you go study it." My reply to her was "What do I, as a Lao American refugee, know about conducting a research study, let alone writing a dissertation?" At that time, I also did not know of any Lao American researcher or professor in my personal or professional network.

I am the first person in my family to attend college. I received a bachelor's degree in human resource management. I received a master's degree in curriculum and instruction, a second master's degree in administration, planning, and social policy, and a doctorate in education. The previously mentioned achievements were far more than what my refugee family hoped for and could have ever expected from me. As Southeast Asian American immigrant and refugee scholars in US institutions of higher education are significantly underrepresented among all ranks, my journey is one of many firsts. For example, I did not have the guidance afforded to many of my White classmates who had family members and friends to guide and support them. While there are many stories that I could share about my educational and professional journey, this chapter will highlight how I navigated various microaggressions (Sue, 2010) first as a doctoral student at an Ivy League education program and then as a tenure-track faculty member in a predominantly White college of education. I will describe my use of autoethnography and vignettes to capture my narrative experiences. Then I will discuss the theory of social capital (Bankston, 2004; Noguera, 2004) as a theoretical lens to contextualize my experiences. I follow with a description of the salience of my Lao refugee identity and how it centers both my personal and professional journey. I will highlight the strategies I have used to address microaggressions and structural barriers, as well as how I have created productive and safe spaces for myself within the academy.

Autoethnography

Dyson (2007) adeptly describes autoethnography as a "way of knowing" and "a narrative form of writing and inquiry" (p. 40). Similarly, Hickey and Fitzclarenge (1999) describe autoethnography as follows:

> Narratives provide the sources of meanings that people attribute to their experience. Stories not only express meaning given to experience but also determine which aspects of experience are selected for expression. In this sense, narrative or story provides the primary frame for interpretation of experience.
>
> (p. 8)

When I started to construct my educational journey, I realized that my story was explicitly interwoven with other Southeast Asian American refugee narratives within the United States and with other racialized experiences. In reflecting on my narrative experiences, I am acting as someone who has seminal characteristics of an auto-ethnographer as a "boundary-crosser" who also has a "dual identity" (Reed-Danahay, 1997, p. 3). In writing this chapter, I connect my personal journey to similar ones experienced by other immigrant and refugee scholars of color in the field of education. I blur the distinction between the two as I move back and forth between looking across my journey and highlighting certain stories (Dyson, 2007, p. 38). To comply with the core principles of autoethnographic methodology, I am revealing my voice as the author and academic up front. In sharing my story, I am exposing myself to a degree of risk, in particular, the perception that I lack objectivity and am relying on self-reported incidents. However, I concur with Dyson's (2007) argument that "writing in [the] first person brings with it a personal accountability" (p. 40).

Social Capital

Social capital has become a widely used framework in education to understand the variation in achievement levels between various ethnic and racial groups (Bankston, 2004; Noguera, 2004). It is also a useful framework for examining achievement within groups, as members within or between specific populations may have access to different resources that inform different educational outcomes for them. According to Coleman (1988), social capital is developed when people form relationships or networks and exchange resources with one another, whether as members of a dyad or a network. Social capital may manifest in many forms, including information channels and social norms (Louie, 2004). In a network of people, social norms govern behaviors by sanctioning members whose perceived or real behavior strays from what is deemed to be acceptable. However, social norms could be seen as a resource when a group's standard set of behaviors happen to benefit the individuals with/in the group.

It has been well documented that parents, teachers, and friends all serve as sources of social capital for an individual. In this chapter, I will focus on the social capital that friendships and peer groups have provided me (Koyama, 2007) to support my academic achievement as a doctoral student at Harvard University and then as a tenure-track (and now a tenured) faculty member at University of Massachusetts Lowell. Researchers have documented how through peer relationships, children and youth develop social skills, obtain information about the world, and learn how to navigate the world (Berndt, 1999; Hartup, 1993; Ryan, 2000). In my case, my friendships have been influenced by a host of school-related behaviors (Bukowski, Newcomb, & Hartup, 1998; Heaven & Ciarrochi, 2008), including having influenced my decisions to engage in certain academic or social activities (Berndt, Laychak, & Park, 1990).

What "Refugee Camp" Are You From?

Laos is the most heavily bombed country per capita in the history of our world. From 1964 to 1973, the United States dropped more than two million tons of ordnance on Laos during 580,000 bombing missions, equal to a planeload of bombs dropping every eight minutes all day over nine years (Khamvongsa & Russell, 2009). During the Secret War in Laos, the bombings were meant to support the Royal Lao Government against the Pathet Lao and to disrupt the traffic along the Ho Chi Minh Trail. The bombings destroyed many villages and caused hundreds of thousands of Lao civilians to seek refuge in neighboring countries and abroad.

During the 1970s and early 1980s, neoconservative advocates were pushing for America's involvement in nations that had "potential" for democracy. Countries in Southeast Asia were ripe for intervention and influence since civil wars were splitting the countries into two factions: pro-democracy versus pro-socialist/communist. The Pathet Lao, Khmer Rouge, and Viet Cong were being supported by China and were on one side, while the Lao Royal Government (Laos), King Sihanouk (Cambodia), and the South Vietnamese government (Vietnam) were supported by the United States and their allies on the other side. US citizens were also divided in their support for America's international policing policies. President Richard Nixon and his advisors did not think that the small factions of democratic Southeast Asian leaders could win a war against communist forces without the help of the United States. Their arrogance cost thousands of lives and contributed to the forced migration of hundreds of thousands of people. My family was one of those families seeking refuge in a Thai refugee camp, called Ban Thong, near Chiangrai, Thailand.

Since my father was hired by the US Central Intelligence Agency to run reconnaissance intel along the Ho Chi Minh Trail, he was considered an American sympathizer. When the United States pulled out of Vietnam and Southeast Asia, many of the communist forces like the Pathet Lao targeted dissenters and democratic supporters for their "re-education camp list." This list was notorious for putting the members in so-called "seminars," with some members not returning to their families afterward. My father, hearing the rumors, planned to escape this fate. In July 1977, my father snuck out of Laos with my two older brothers across the Mekong River. A month later, my mother bribed a cargo captain to hide us (including my sister and me) in pickle barrels to cross into Thailand where we would be reunited with my father and two brothers. One day, we were questioned by Thai authorities for legal papers. As a result, we were placed in the Ban Thong refugee camp. We stayed in that camp for two years before receiving refugee status from the United Nations High Commission on Refugees (UNHCR) that allowed us to be sponsored in the United States.

Incidentally, growing up as a young child, I thought *everyone* went to a refugee camp. I would ask my elementary classmates in Connecticut, "What camp did you go to?" The Lao kids would compare stories of the refugee camps they were at like how we would wait in line for the Red Cross to hand out food rations, or how some soldiers would provide us with candy when they saw us. Meanwhile, the White kids looked at us as if we were weird. Many said that they went to YMCA camps; was that our type of camp too?

Growing up in a Lao refugee family, I was not cognizant of how much discrimination my parents faced. We struggled economically like other poor families in the United States. We lived in subsidized housing projects and were on welfare until my parents found jobs to support our family. Our struggles were also marked with post-traumatic stress disorder (PTSD). Southeast Asian refugee families are at least twice as more likely to suffer from PTSD than the average US citizen. More specifically, scholars have found that at least 14 percent of Southeast Asian American refugees suffer from PTSD (Kroll, Habenicht, Mackenzie, Yang, & Chan, 1989; Field, Muong, & Sochanvimean, 2013), compared to just under 7 percent of all US citizens (Kessler, Chiu, Demler, Merikangas, & Walters, 2005). Moreover, PTSD in Asian American communities not only affects the individual but also their families and communities in what is known as the phenomenon of intergenerational trauma (Endo, 2018b).

A key difference between Southeast Asian Americans from refugee backgrounds and other Asian American immigrants is that their socio-cultural experiences have direct impacts on their psychosocial well-being. The higher rate of PTSD among Southeast Asian Americans is because large numbers of Southeast Asian refugees were fleeing political perse-cution, "re-education camps," famine, torture, and displacement that stemmed from the Vietnam War, the Cambodian "Killing Fields," and the Secret War in Laos. In their attempts to escape, many families were split up, and some family members died along the way. The "boat peo-ple" often fell victim to Thai pirates, who often attacked and abused the men and raped the women. Moreover, many children died of malnutri-tion (Chan, 1991).

With this all as the backdrop to my family's escape from Southeast Asia, it was no wonder that my family also held a culture of silence about the civil war in Laos. This silence contributed to my lack of understand-ing about why we were refugees and how we came to the United States. In fact, my family never talked about politics because of their continual fear of persecution. There was a lot that I did not know, and unfortu-nately, the K-12 curriculum that my peers and I were subjected to did not teach me much about America's involvement in Southeast Asia. However, what I do know for sure is that the Southeast Asian American refugee experience directly shapes how I view the world, how I teach, and how I relate to other immigrant and refugee children and their families. While my experiences and identities make me appreciative of the opportunities that I have here in the United States, it also gives me the responsibility of paying it forward.

My father and mother emphasized to my siblings and me the value of formal education. They ensured that all of their children received at least a high-school education. I had assumed that all Lao parents felt the same way as my parents did, so I was bewildered by the large dropout rate among Lao American and other Southeast Asian American youth that I found out about in Minneapolis at the conference referenced ear-lier in this chapter. Therefore, when my roommate was accepted into a newly created graduate program with a concentration focused on com-munities and schools at Harvard University, led by nationally recognized education scholar Pedro Noguera, she insisted that I apply so that I could examine the factors that contributed to many Southeast Asian Americans being pushed out of school.

I will be the first to admit that the Harvard University brand and name was intimidating to me. I assumed that it was for "smart" people . . . and not a Lao refugee like me. I was told as such during my sophomore year of college by my Filipina roommates when I responded to an Asian casting call for a Joe Pesci movie based at Harvard titled *With Honors*.

While my two Filipina friends got cast as extras to play Harvard students, I was told that I did not "look like" a Harvard student; therefore, I was not cast. So, if it was not for my roommate, Carolyn, I would not have even dared to consider this opportunity. The name and price tag alone for attending Harvard University were two major deterrents to me. However, Carolyn made an appointment for me to meet Noguera to discuss the possibility of applying. I did. Noguera's interest in my research topic and my background gave me the confidence to apply to the program. I was completely forthcoming in my application and wrote that I was taking care of my father who was undergoing chemotherapy, and thus, could not afford to attend the program without financial assistance. Noguera advocated for me to receive one of the coveted Harvard Presidential Fellowships that former President Larry Summers had recently established under his tenure before he moved on to an advisory capacity at the federal level.

Being Seen as "Statistically Insignificant"

Once I entered the doctoral program at Harvard University, my confidence waned again. I had been accepted into the Administration, Planning, and Social Policy Program in the Harvard Graduate School of Education. My colleagues were some of the best and brightest minds in the field of education. However, I felt like an imposter. Perhaps it was "the other Phitsamay" that they really accepted? You know, the real Thai Phitsamay (my mother named me after her favorite Thai actress) . . . and not the Lao American refugee imposter? However, my plan was that I was going to "fake it" until I was discovered. What I discovered instead was a lot of White-savior complexes (Cole, 2012) toward immigrant and refugee communities among several White students in the program. Several White faculty members also exhibited a stunning lack of awareness about the diversity among the Asian American community. I experienced many microaggressions from White faculty and students throughout my doctoral studies. Sue et al. (2007) define "racial microaggressions [as] brief and commonplace daily verbal, behavioral, or environmental indignities, whether intentional or unintentional, that communicate hostile, derogatory, or negative racial slights and insults toward people of color" (p. 271).

One of the most significant microaggressions that occurred to me happened in my second-year statistics course. A White male instructor was using a National Center for Education Statistics (NCES) dataset to show the change in the percentage of students who dropped out in different cohorts. He had a graph with these demographics of students: "Black, Hispanic, and American Indian." *No Asian students were in the graph.* I asked him the following: "Where are data on the Asian students?" He told me Asian students were "statistically insignificant" and therefore not used in his analysis. I sat there perplexed. How could he think that our Asian American students were "statistically insignificant?" He obviously did not know about Lowell High School in northern Massachusetts, which had 4,000 students, with over a quarter of them being of Asians ancestry. He also did not know that among the 4.4 million English language learners (ELLs) in the K-12 schools nationwide, that Chinese (mostly Mandarin) was the number-two language spoken by ELLs, followed by Vietnamese at number three, and Hmong at number five.

To counter this microaggression, I set out to prove that Asian American students were statistically significant, and also, several needed many types of academic and structural support. My pilot study examined how Southeast Asian American youth from refugee backgrounds were dropping out of school at alarming rates (Uy, 2009). That same White male instructor told me that dropout rates were an issue only for "Black and Hispanic" students. I found a district that had over 5,000 Asian American students. However, since most school districts do not provide disaggregated data, I had to cull through each line to determine if a student was Southeast Asian American and enrolled in the same year of my cohort model. I created an ethnicity proxy by using country of birth and languages spoken at home, but this model left out many Southeast Asian American students who were born in the United States and primarily spoke English at home.

Data disaggregation has been an advocacy priority for Asian American and Pacific Islander advocates in their quest to get better services for our community. Many students from this group have been systemically rendered invisible because they are lumped under a singular "Asian" category. That is, their needs are concealed by the larger pan-ethnic Asian umbrella, which consists of more than 48 ethnic groups. Many school districts do not see a need to disaggregate data for the Asian American and Pacific Islander community because of the persistent model-minority image and the myth of racial sameness (Louis, 2005). These images of Asian American and Pacific Islander students often lead many White educators and leaders to embody color-neutral views of this diverse population.

Another example of feeling invisible on campus was whenever there was a discussion on race, the discourse was framed as Black and Brown on the one side and White on the other side. For instance, in class, we would often discuss issues around poverty. White students would compare Black and Latinx children to Whites. We had a whole class on the history of education where the White female instructor highlighted all the marginalized communities such as American Indian, Black, and Latinx. Again, there was no discussion of Asian American students. So, where did Asian American students go to school during segregation? The instructor made no mention that the city of San Francisco had segregated its Chinese American schoolchildren from 1859 until 1871 (Takaki, 1998), or that it was the *Lau vs. Nichols* Supreme Court decision that helped develop programs for all ELLs, not just Chinese American bilinguals, in 1974. Our Asian American students thus were invisible in the curriculum and throughout classroom discussions.

When mostly White education faculty members embody such color-neutral and narrow lenses in discussing issues of identity and race, it makes it difficult for students from racialized backgrounds to feel validated in the classroom. I know that I felt marginalized. If it were not for the other students who were BIPOC in the Harvard Graduate School of Education, I would not have survived in my doctoral program. Some of the older doctoral students from BIPOC backgrounds formed study groups to support each other. They extended the invitation to younger students to join as space became available. Everyone started meeting together to talk about our experiences. We then started organizing. One result was the formation of an Alumni of Color Conference that is now nearing 20 years of existence. The dean at the time, a White female, did not think we needed an Alumni of Color Conference. She stated that there already was an Alumni Association and an Alumni Conference; that we should "just be part of the community." She did not see a need for solidarity among the alumni who were from racialized backgrounds. However, we continued to push back and got the support of some senior faculty members to advocate for us. I really think the dean at the time was clueless to the fact that students from racialized backgrounds indeed have a much different experience in higher education than White students. It was in these spaces that discussions of the revolving door of faculty of color happened, and how the university put the burden on these faculty to support all students from racialized backgrounds. The earlier arrangement absolves the White faculty and the White-run institution from its responsibility to create systems and support structures that would be culturally responsive to all of us.

Continuing to Address Invisibility

Unfortunately, I had similar challenges with racialization as a tenure-track faculty member at the University of Massachusetts Lowell. With a rich history filled with immigrants and refugees, Lowell claims the second-largest Khmer/Cambodian community in the nation. Despite the varied racial and ethnic diversity in Lowell, the university has approximately 10 percent Asians students and 34 percent of students from other racialized backgrounds in their undergraduate programs. In my College of Education, those numbers are even lower. In the seven years I have taught there, I have only taught the following students as teacher candidates: five Asian Americans, one Latinx, one American Indian, and one Black. Of the 14 faculty members at the time, three were Asian American, one was Black, and one was Latino.

Moreover, like the other women of color faculty, I was overloaded with service expectations. In contrast, I noticed that three senior White faculty members seemed to have no service expectations, at least at the departmental level. Thus, I was working in a college where many junior faculty members were carrying the bulk of the work for the entire college. For me, I was serving on two university-wide committees: 2020 Strategic Planning Commission and the Faculty Senate, as well as three college-level committees: Dissertation Award, Leadership Faculty Team Committee, and the M.Ed. Recertification Committee. Despite this heavy load, two major benefits from being on the university-wide committees are as follows: (1) getting to know faculty across the university, which in turn, (2) helped me better understand university systems and networks. However, the college-level committees were laborious. When I spent a lot of time in meetings, it meant that I had less time to focus on my research projects and writing, two tasks that were vital to my tenure.

I was fortunate enough to have been surrounded by a strong social network. I am confident that the support of my colleagues at the Center for Asian American Studies (CAAS) ensured the tenure status that I now enjoy. One support that my senior colleagues provided me was to co-author journal articles and grants. Another support was their monthly meetings, where senior Asian American faculty would ask important questions such as the following: "How are you doing? *What* are you doing? Do you need any help?" They provided advice on what my workload should be and how to better navigate the politics of our predominantly White institution. Questions I asked them were those such as the following: "Can I say no to more committee assignments or invitations? What should I do about those privileged White students?"

There were many questions that I did not know to ask about the tenure process itself. The "hidden curriculum" that surrounds the tenure process was so elusive because the Provost's Office only offered guidance in general terms like regularly publish "high-quality" research, teach well, and serve the community. They also advised us to defer to the standards of our college and discipline. Young faculty need their dean, department chair, and senior colleagues to more clearly state what the tenure expectations are. Unfortunately, I was getting conflicting messages within my college. I had two senior White faculty members who were on the Personnel Committee giving me tenure advice. One told me to "Be productive [which meant six publications] and focus on getting good teaching evaluations because we are a College of Education and care about our pedagogy." In contrast, another White senior faculty member said, "Produce a dozen publications, but don't focus on teaching since no one gets tenure because of teaching." Having these two different opinions expressed to me made it difficult for me to understand the expectations that I was going to be evaluated on.

Implications

Given my experiences, I would like to offer the following advice for predominantly White colleges and schools of education to implement to better retain, support, and advance their faculty from diverse backgrounds:

1. **Establish a formal mentor program:** it would behoove these institutions to provide a formalized mentor program that could do what my Center for Asian American Studies (CAAS) colleagues did for me. New faculty members should have at least one clear mentor who would check on them periodically instead of waiting for annual conversations to occur with the dean or department chair. They should also help the faculty member identify a mentor in the scholar's field to cultivate a professional network outside of their home institutions. As a first-generation faculty of color, I did not know how to protect my time and to prioritize my research agenda. I was overloaded with service at the departmental and university levels. However, it was my choice to continue serving my national Southeast Asian community, though. Yet, why was I being questioned about the need to go to DC every year to facilitate the Leadership and Advocacy training of Southeast Asian American community members to their Congressional representative? Why did I have to review the Gates Millennium Scholarship or the APIASF Scholarship Fund? Academic programs and university need to value community-engaged service (as they usually claim to publicly value it) instead of questioning it.

2. **Kerry Rowland's Faculty Development for Success Program:** one national online writing support group that has worked for a few of my colleagues and me is Kerry Rowland's Faculty Development for Success Program. She provides a how-to guide about making writing a regular part of a scholar's daily work, especially in the beginning years. Ideally, the institution could pay for institutional membership to enable interested faculty members to work in community with other scholars who are in similar stages of their careers and who will support each other's writing goals. This program is also efficient because it has asynchronous online support with benchmarks.

3. **Professional development:** many of us consider ourselves fortunate if we are at an institution that pays for one conference per year. Early career scholars, especially those who are BIPOC, need to get their names and work out as much as possible. It would be very beneficial for the university to pay for one conference and the college/school to pay for another. That way, scholars are able to attend both national and regional conference proceedings to talk about their work and network within and across professional organizations.

4. **Have a transparent tenure process:** it seems that the tenure process is cloaked in mystery when it does not have to be, especially for

colleges and schools of education. If the college or school wants journal publications, then say it explicitly. Advice like "be productive" is not useful for any scholar. "Publish six journal articles in Tier 1 and Tier 2 journals as first or second author" is a much more concrete goal for us to work toward.

As the only tenured first-generation Lao American faculty member in an education department in the United States in this current moment, I am also committed to ensuring that more Southeast Asian American scholars fill the halls of the academy. To do so, I have started an online support group for doctoral students with whom I am meeting at campus events and various national conferences. I am supporting them by articulating the doctoral journey, the academic job search, and the tenure process. I am also connecting them to each other. I know how helpful it was for me to have a network of people supporting me on my educational journey. Having an online community has also reduced feelings of isolation that they often experience at their home institutions.

My commitment also extends to Southeast Asian American community members and youth who are not in academia. My service to the Southeast Asian American community includes providing cultural competency trainings to local school districts, speaking in congressional briefings on data disaggregation at the state and national levels, and advocating for more funding of Asian American and Native American Pacific Islander-Serving Institutions (AANAPISI) programs at the federal level. As a teacher educator, it is also important for me to educate White teachers, administrators, and other educational leaders about the experiences of Southeast Asian American immigrant and refugee communities. It is especially essential at this time when so many struggling Southeast Asian American students do not get the chance to continue to pursue higher education because their families are being demonized and torn apart. My mission is to ensure that educators and policymakers see my Southeast Asian American community and youth as high potential and high talent, and not as being "at risk."

9   Still Searching
My Present Reality

Keitha-Gail Martin-Kerr

I Am Who I Am

I am Jamaican
Came to America
In search of . . .
Still searching . . .
It is not only the rainbow wheel on my computer screen that is spinning.
Working in a predominantly White institution as a Black immigrant woman
Keeps me spinning
Like the wheel on my computer screen
A top
A windmill
I am a compass trying to find my direction
Looking for familiar faces, language, ways of being
Looking for alignment
Oriented
Humanized
Liberated
Not disorientation
Not objectification
Not oppressed
Still searching
Re-routing
Make a U-turn in 450 feet
Use the second lane from the left and keep left
As a Black teacher educator, is my destination to be here?
Still searching . . .

Situating the Context

I endured varying layers of complexities and challenges when my employer in a college of education in a predominantly White university in the Midwest region of the United States decided to partner with a highly controversial alternative-licensure program. It is important for me to forefront that most of the faculty in the department, even the White ones, were against partnering with this program for several reasons. Everyone strongly expressed their reservations during many public meetings. Some openly stated that they and their graduate assistants would refuse to teach in the program if the partnership with this program was launched. It was a heated debate with the faculty and the White university administrators. A few faculty members even threatened to resign from the university if the partnership continued; others threatened to stage a boycott. In the end, the university's White administrators ignored the concerns of the faculty and established a partnership with this alternative-licensure program. When all of this was unfolding, I was a part-time Ph.D. student working full time in a teaching position at this institution. I was one of seven people of color in the whole department. I was also the only person of color who was an immigrant, a single mother, a person without the terminal degree (at the time), and of a different social class from the other faculty members in my program area. To make sense of all that was happening to me at the time, I draw on the work of Fanon (1986) and Freire (1993) to better understand the racism and the oppressed-oppressor relationship that I faced at one particular moment in my life as a Black, social-classed teacher-educator working at a White-dominated college of education in the Midwest in the United States.

Oppressed-Oppressor

Freire (1993) theorized the relationship between the oppressed and the oppressor as it relates to being human. For Freire, people's true vocation is humanization, which is the process of everyone becoming more fully human. Humanization is at stake because of dehumanization; that is, humanization remains a struggle for many. Some people still are being dehumanized through systems of injustice and exploitation; these people are the oppressed. Dehumanization is a distortion of allowing certain individuals from being fully human. Through a system of injustice, the oppressed are dehumanized by their oppressors. The oppressed then struggle to become fully humanized. Dehumanization not only affects the oppressed but also the oppressors who have exploited the former. The oppressors live in a false reality that has them believing that they must dominate others in order to get ahead themselves. The oppressed are constantly trying to be more human. In an effort to emancipate themselves from the traumatizing effects of being dehumanized, the oppressed frequently imitate the behaviors and tactics of their oppressors. Freire (1993) cautioned for the oppressed not to become oppressors in order for us to regain our own humanity.

For Freire, those who are oppressed should not internalize the behaviors of our oppressors, as doing so would continue the destructive cycle of dehumanization. He argued that the oppressed need to liberate ourselves and also our oppressors. Indeed, the oppressed have the responsibility to restore humanity to both groups. Freire believed the oppressors, who exploit the oppressed through their power, do not have the strength to liberate themselves or the oppressed. He argued that liberation comes only from the strength of the oppressed. The oppressed have to fight for liberation through acts of love. We have to fight to love the loveless; that is, we must show love to our oppressors.

Objectification

To theorize how my body reacted in a moment of blatant racial injustice, I draw on the work of Fanon. In *Black Skin, White Masks*, Fanon (1986) wrote about his Black body being distanced from itself under the White gaze. Objectification is the process of distancing the body from itself. Through the process of objectification, the Black body is not seen by White people as whole; rather, it is seen as an object with separate parts. The Black body's interaction with and reaction to racism lead to objectification, which treats the body as a thing less than human, a thing that can be manipulated.

Fanon (1986) notes:

> And then we were given the occasion to confront the white gaze. An unusual weight descended on us. The real world robs us of our share. In the white world, the man of color encounters difficulties in the development of his body schema. The consciousness of the body is solely a negating activity. It is a third-person consciousness. An atmosphere of certain uncertainty surrounds the body.
>
> (p. 90)

In reference to certain uncertainty, Bhabha (1994) also writes the following: "The atmosphere of certain uncertainty that surrounds the body certifies its existence and threatens its dismemberment" (p. 45). While the body is being objectified, it is simultaneously being historicized. The Black body carries with it many legends, stories, and myths of its ancestors (Fanon, 1986). The Black body also stores knowledge. It operates at the subconscious level but is also felt in the flesh. The Black body actively learns, processes, and stores corporeal and intellectual knowledge. The Black body is racialized and historicized as it interacts and reacts upon meeting the White gaze.

In what follows, I briefly recapture *the moment* from my memory. Thereafter, I will deconstruct my personal narrative through the lenses of the oppressed-oppressor. I will further elaborate on what it means to lead and liberate others and myself. I then will theorize my experiences based on the concept of objectification. Last, I make suggestions for retaining and supporting racialized faculty in predominantly White colleges and schools of educations. I finish with advice that I would give my younger self and other young Black scholars/racialized scholars like me.

A Memory

I sat in a program-area meeting taking notes on agenda items such as the course schedule, funding, and graduate assistantships. I rarely pay attention during these program-area meetings. The folks who usually need to talk are senior professors who must, as they claim, only teach during specific days of the week. They refuse to teach on Mondays or Fridays, as these are their "writing days." At the end of the meeting, Tom, a White male and the leader of the program area, walked over to me and said, "Because of programmatic changes, you will only have a 75 percent workload for next semester. If you want to work 100 percent, you will have to work 25 percent in the alternative-licensure program." I stuffed my computer in my bag and fussed around with a few papers in my bag to remain calm and composed. I could not look up at Tom. I was afraid the tears would just roll down my face if I made any eye-contact with him.

My head spun. Where will I get the money to pay the mortgage? Send Zion to school? Send money to my parents in Jamaica? Buy food? Pay for the lights, gas, and phone bills? I also wondered to myself, "I guess I have to call and disconnect the cable. But, what about Zion? She likes to watch TV." I think I am going to lose my mind. I cannot work only 75 percent, as I will not be able to make ends meet.

I also cannot work in a program that places mostly White teachers in classrooms after only 10 weeks of teacher-preparation coursework. Teaching in this program would go against my beliefs. Teachers need to be properly educated before they are allowed to teach children. I cannot be part of this program. I do not want my name associated with a program that places mostly White teachers in urban schools to teach primarily students from racialized backgrounds after only a few weeks of what they call "accelerated" teacher preparation. However, I needed an additional 25 percent workload to make ends meet. Yet, I also could not find myself to oblige to Tom's request from an ethical standpoint.

Several other faculty members were present at the program-area meeting. Did they know about these plans? Did they discuss this all over e-mail before Tom gave me the news? Were they all in agreement with Tom? Am I the only one who sees this arrangement as unfair? I am a full-time employee at the university. How does a senior White faculty member have the power to change my appointment? How long was this arrangement being planned? I always get excellent scores on my course/

teaching evaluation. I also have served on multiple departmental, college, and university committees. Why would Tom decide to change my work-load? Did he change Liz's? She has a 100 percent teaching position that is similar to mine. What about Matt; did his appointment also change? Did Tom tell Liz and Matt, both White folks, that they also had to work in this program to meet their contractual obligations?

I picked up my computer bag and told myself, "I have to get out of here. I need to breathe. I need to talk to someone to maintain my sanity." I stepped in the hallway. Loneliness slapped me in the face. I saw no one around who looked like me. I heard no one who sounded like me. I know I am walking but it feels like I am drowning. Treading water. The current is pulling me in. I am under. Up. Down. Up. Down. I need to survive. I fight to get out alive.

Deconstructing My Story: Oppressed-Oppressor

I had worked full time at this specific university as a teacher educator since the year 2011. Based on my contract, I should be given at least three months of notice if the university decided to change my contract or relieve me of my duties, which was not the case in this situation. In a brief encounter, Tom told me that I could either work 75 percent or I could take the position as lead instructor for the alternative-licensure program in order to fulfill my 100-percent appointment. This is a classic case of institutionalized racism where the rules that govern an organization do not apply to Black bodies. It was difficult to believe that Tom forgot that an employee has a contractual agreement with the university. He acted on the invisible and collapsed relationship that a racist institution, the university itself, has with Black bodies. Bonilla-Silva (2010) cogently notes the type of racism I was experiencing as follows: "Contemporary racial inequality is reproduced through 'New Racism' practices that are subtle, institutional, and apparently nonracial" (p. 3).

Tom evidentially thought he was being benevolent by offering me any type of 100-percent employment, even though his approach was in viola-tion of the university's contractual arrangements with its thousands of employees. However, would he have asked one of his White colleagues who were also vehemently against the alternative-licensure program to actually teach in it? I highly doubt it. It was easy for him to ask me because he knew that I was not in a position to tell him "No" because of my status as a Ph.D. student, a non-tenure-track instructor, an immi-grant, a single mother, and a Black person.

Separate from manipulating me because of my race and other dis-enfranchised statuses, he also played on the capitalist logic on which the university operates, which is to pay the Black body the least while expecting the most labor from her. There are classist, sexist, and racial inequalities embedded in this type of capitalism: "racism and sexism are very much linked to capitalist production. . . . I don't see the possibility of overcoming racism and sexism in a capitalist mode of production" (Shor & Freire, 1987, p. 167, as cited in Darder, 2002, p. 13). Based on this argument, it could be inferred that Tom used my status as a Black woman, as well as a single mother, immigrant, and graduate student without a Ph.D., to serve the capitalist mission of the university.

I distinctly remembered the moment when Tom told me my appointment "options." I knew Tom did not come up with these two options arbitrarily or instantly. I knew it was a well-thought-out plan that was also supposed to be well-executed. He knew he had me where he wanted me: between "the devil and the deep blue sea," which is a Jamaican expression for one having no viable options. When Tom positioned me between "the devil and the deep blue sea," he tried to view me as an object for his manipulation. His actions could be read as an attempt to strip me of my humanity. In his attempt to dehumanize me, he actually reaffirmed my humanity. According to Jean-Paul Sartre, "no one can treat a man like a dog without first regarding him as a man" (In Memmi, 1965, p. xxvii).

Several thoughts raced through my mind as I heard the two options echoing over and over in my mind. In that very moment, I recognized the injustice. I knew that this entire process was inherently unfair. Through acts of injustice and unfairness, the oppressor seeks to dehumanize the oppressed. Freire expressed that in the process of dehumanization, the oppressed become conscious of the state of oppression, and realize they have been robbed of their own humanity. Freire further explained that the oppressor, through taking the humanity of the oppressed, has also dehumanized himself/herself. Freire's theory helped to make sense of my experience because I was aware of the injustice that was imposed on me. I recognized it as an unfair act that was thoughtfully planned and executed by a White man who was in a position of power and authority.

Deconstructing My Story: Objectification

I sat in the program-area meeting taking notes. My body was at ease in this space. I operated with a sense of normality. My body performed what it was expected to do in a program-area meeting. It sat in a chair and took notes like everyone else. I mentioned in my earlier narrative that I rarely spoke in these spaces, as I desired to be silent in these meetings. There would be lots of thoughts that I would want to utter aloud, but I would not articulate them because of my position as a part-time Ph.D. student, faculty member who was not on the tenure-track, Black woman, single mother, and immigrant. I know my White colleagues have "woven me out of a thousand details, anecdotes and stories" (Fanon, 1986, p. 91). I was objectified in this space. Fanon further states that below the corporeal schema, there is the historic-racial schema. As the only Black body in this meeting, I desired silence because of the history that my body brings to this space. My body singles me out when I am in the presence of my mostly White colleagues. I just did not want to share my thoughts with them. I did not want them to use it in another way to distance me or make me the outlier; the one that does not belong in this space because of the color of my skin and the history that it brings to this place.

When Tom told me about the new terms of my appointment, I remembered stuffing my computer in my bag. I then shuffled papers in my computer bag to remain calm. My body responded to Tom's words through void busyness. His comment disoriented my body. I acted in denial in order to orient myself. I bought myself time to compose my body by packing up my computer bag. I placed all my energy into packing the bag instead of owning how I felt in the moment. My body acted "busy" under racist comments; my emotions remained composed. Being Black affects the way I operate when I am upset. If I spoke to Tom in the moment, I would likely be perceived by him as the angry Black woman.

My body performed the way I was programmed to act when I am upset in and within the academy. I refused to make eye-contact with Tom and tried to control my outward emotions. I did not allow Tom to see how I was feeling. I de-compartmentalized my bodily actions from my raging emotions to protect my whole being from crumbling in front of a White male. My body felt as if it could not function freely in this moment. I had to slow down my thoughts. I had to also slow down my actions, deliberately thinking about each action and thought because I knew Tom was waiting for me to react. I did not want him to see how I felt because the Black body is not free to take up any space in a predominantly White institution. My body was dismembered by Tom's comments. I felt my head spinning. I walked and I felt like I was drowning. I found it hard to breathe. I felt the need to talk to someone to maintain my sanity. Loneliness punched me in my face at this moment. My body was separated from being whole because of Tom's words, which severed me like a knife. I was in a moment of existential crisis, as I worried that I was losing my mind, and yet, had to remain calm in the space.

Implications and Discussion

Before any predominantly White college or school of education attempts to recruit faculty and scholars from racialized backgrounds, they need to think about how they will respect and support racialized bodies. Put simply, racialized bodies actually want to be a part of the college/school and institution. We want to feel a sense of belonging and have a voice in making major decisions. When the institution is ready to open up its doors to us, there should be a mentoring system in place for junior scholars with a senior White faculty, who is an ally for racialized Americans. Recruiting us is not enough if there is not a support system for us.

From my experiences, existing policies and practices around diversity have not worked. People have to be the ones to mobilize the policies they want to work. Many times, when Indigenous persons and people of color are mentioned in human-resource policies, it is usually only with respect to equal opportunities for hire. The reality is we are typically not hired. If we are, the institution is usually not ready to engage with us because of our different backgrounds and perspectives. Policies alone are also ineffective. The types of programs I have seen operationalized to successfully recruit, retain, support and advance scholars like me are based on dialogues and institutional initiatives. The dialogues and initiatives that have worked are the ones started by White colleagues who are true allies. These White folks begin the conversation by first identifying and acknowledging the Whiteness around them. They worked to deconstruct and disrupt Whiteness in the institution, curriculum, and policies. They have continuous dialogue about internalized White supremacy and how to be allies to racialized bodies. These dialogues are learning spaces where White people learn to understand their role in maintaining the status quo, which supports both imperialistic ideologies and White supremacy.

Through these deep challenging conscious-raising dialogues and reflection, action items such as recruiting, retaining, and advancing faculty from underrepresented are usually birthed. For these conversations to be truly transformational, they need to take place at all levels: administrative, departmental, and through individual employees. They have to happen in structured and unstructured meetings: faculty meetings, program-area meetings, and departmental social gatherings. Most times, it is important to bring in an outside consultant who has researched this topic to conduct focused interviews and then provide professional development on the institution's racial climate issue to get the conversation going or to maintain the need for continuous examination of race and racism in and through the institution.

Advice to My Younger Self

As I think about the advice I would give to my younger self, I think about a younger scholar of color whom I now mentor with great pride. The conversations we have with one another each time we meet would sound like this.

I would hear my cell phone ping. I look it; it is a text message from Kia

KIA: K-G, I know you are busy, but I really need to talk something through with you. Can we meet?
K-G: I am available to chat now or face-to-face on Tuesday at 2:00 p.m.

The first advice I would give to my younger self is to find a senior scholar who identifies as BIPOC who is willing to listen and help you think through difficult situations. More than likely, that person has gone through similar issues that you have.

I imagine we met at our regular spot, which is a coffee shop down the street from the university. We sat in the same seats we were in the last time we were here. It is like our special place that holds our secret conversations. We are not sure if we should mutter to ourselves much less to each other . . . but we do anyway.

KIA: I am not sure about something. I do not even understand what is happening. I am not even sure if I am making a thing out of nothing. I am just struggling with this issue. I cannot even explain it. I cannot capture in words what it is.

K-G: Spill it out! If you are struggling so much with it, let us talk about it.

The second piece of advice that I would give to my younger self is if struggling with an issue, talk about it with someone who is trustworthy. Do not underestimate the psychological burden that the issue might have on one's professional life. It is best to talk it through with someone and get some advice to make better sense of the situation. Most times when racialized scholars in education experience racism or acts of microaggression, they do not have the words to capture the nuances of the situation and how it made them feel. However, the more we talk about these incidents, the more language we will have to describe what we experienced and how these acts make us feel.

I dig in my bag trying to find my purse. I need to order two cups of coffee for us. I cannot feel my purse. I begin to empty contents from my handbag, old receipts, notepad, my car key, and a book I am re-reading.

KIA: Let me see that book. What's it about?

K-G: It's called *Racism without Racist* by Bonilla-Silva. I read it already. I just wanted to re-read the chapter on Obama. You can borrow it if you want.

The third piece of advice I would give to my younger self is to read widely and deeply on the topics of race and racism. Get familiar with the work of Gloria Ladson-Billings, William H. Watkins, Rev. Dr. Thandeka, Richard Milner IV, Pedro Noguera, Anne Anlin Cheng, and many more.

KIA: So, as I was trying to explain, during class yesterday, this White student made me feel . . . I do not even know how to say it. But what she said came across as if . . . you know what I mean?

K-G: I think I understand what you are trying to say. Did she make you feel as if you are not qualified to teach her, or you do not know what you are talking about, or you have not read all that she has read or traveled where she has gone?

The fourth advice I would offer to my younger self is that before each class or each meeting is engaging in self-pep talking. *Remind yourself: you have the right to be in this space, you have the right to speak, and the right to be heard. It is important that you do not tell students to stop referring to you as Professor Martin-Kerr or tell them to not call you Dr. Martin-Kerr. You earned it. You deserve it. Own it. Do not engage in self-deprecating humor. Do not put yourself down. Operate in confidence by speaking about all of the research, theory, and practice that you know.*

KIA: I tried to explain the situation to my boss, a White male. He said I need to stop playing "the race game."

K-G: There is no "race game!"

The last advice I would give to my younger self is to remind her that there is no "race game" for Black people. Being Black is a reality that is (and will always be) a part of us. It is not a game. It is who we are. And racism is a structural and systemic reality that Black people face on a day-to-day basis.

10 "You Need to Be More Social"

Controlling Images of Black Women in Tenure Dossiers

Stephanie L. Burrell Storms

Gender, Race . . . and the Tenure Dossier

The tenure dossier is a detailed portfolio that includes evidence of a faculty member's cumulative record in teaching, research/scholarship, and service (Burnham, Hooper, & Wright, 2010). Most US colleges and universities use the dossier to make decisions about promotion and tenure for pre-tenured faculty. According to Burnham et al. (2010), many untenured faculty members find this process to be overwhelming and ambiguous due to "the lack of precise directions about the preparation and documentation process" (n.p.). Evidence of teaching effectiveness may include items such as a philosophy statement, course syllabi, and student evaluations.

Studies show that a professor's race and ethnicity influence how students evaluate the person's course quality and instructional effectiveness (e.g., Littlefield, Ong, Tseng, Milliken, & Humy, 2010). In one study, African American women faculty were rated the lowest on perceived characteristics such as competence, legitimacy, and interpersonal skills, as the authors found that White students' deeply harbored racial stereotypes against Black people influenced these overwhelmingly negative ratings (Bavishi, Hebl, & Madera, 2010). Furthermore, White students tend to expect African American instructors who teach race-focused courses to be biased in their instructional delivery (Littlefield et al., 2010). Similarly, Fiske and Neuberg (1990) report that "when a student does not know a professor, students are likely to use surface cues, such as race/ethnicity and gender, to make judgments about them" (as cited in Bavishi et al., 2010, p. 246). Findings such as the aforementioned show the importance of addressing poor ratings from students in tenure dossiers. Such a task is especially critical for African American women faculty who make up just 3 percent of all full-time faculty in US institutions of higher education (NCES, 2017).

My Journey

Becoming a tenured associate professor was not an easy or a traditional path for me. I am a Black cisgender woman who grew up both working-class and poor. In addition, I am a first-generation college student who attended public institutions from kindergarten through graduate school. My father did not graduate from high school and my mother went to college after I completed my baccalaureate degree. She is now a retired elementary school teacher and assistant principal. It was my mother and former K-12 teachers who influenced my love for education. I pursued degrees in psychology and community counseling to help students like myself, mostly first-generation students of color, succeed in college. My first "real" job, as my mother would say, was a tenure-track counseling faculty position at a community college. I was awarded tenure and promotion to associate professor a year early based on positive evaluations of my advising, teaching, and service. The process was less onerous at the community college than at the four-year level because there were no research or scholarship requirements for faculty. Also, the guidelines for tenure and promotion there were much clearer than at many four-year universities. I left that position after ten years to pursue my doctoral degree in the area of social-justice education. It was during that time when a professor suggested that I consider teacher training as my next career choice. Instead, I accepted a position at my current institution as Assistant Director for the Center for Academic Excellence (CAE).

After one year in the CAE, I was offered a visiting assistant professor position in the Graduate School of Education and Allied Professions (GSEAP) in the Educational Studies and Teacher Preparation (ESTP) Department. One year later, I was offered (and accepted) a tenure-track faculty position as an assistant professor in multicultural education. My current institution is Catholic (Jesuit), private, and predominantly White. This was my first experience at a religious and private institution. It was the first time I faced the "publish or perish" expectation. I thought I understood what was expected of me to attain tenure until I received a negative evaluation of my teaching effectiveness during my third-year review. Suddenly, the "hidden curriculum" of the tenure and promotion process was real for me. In this chapter, I will explore what Collins (2000) famously coined as controlling images of Black women in analyzing how several White colleagues and White students formally evaluated my instructional effectiveness and professional competence.

Conceptual Framework

Black feminist thought (Collins, 2000) is a lens for me to theorize, understand, and name my experiences through the tenure and promotion process. Collins argues that Black women, due to our double-bind (Walkington, 2017) status in the United States, experience "gendered racism – a combination of both racism and sexism" (p. 266). Gendered racism could be best described through socially constructed "controlling images" of Black women. Collins (2000) identified four distinct stereotypes as follows that are commonly used by Whites to justify our continued marginalization in the United States: the mammy, the matriarch, the welfare mother, and the Jezebel or the whore. She theorizes that privileged groups who hold the power to define and describe social norms in US society willingly characterize "nondominant" groups as the architects of their own oppression. For Black women specifically, these powerful images rooted in slavery still function today, and influence our ability to gain recognition, inclusion, and equity in our professional lives. For this study, I focus on the first three sets of controlling images.

Collins (2000) describes the mammy characterization as a "faithful, obedient domestic servant" (pp. 72–75) who accepts her marginalized role in a stratified power system. In higher education, Black women are expected to "give deference to their white and male counterparts, allow for students along with colleagues to question their professorial competence, and then expect black women faculty and graduate students to comfort those who question their abilities" (Walkington, 2017, p. 53). Black women professors who challenge this image through asserting themselves are often deemed as uncaring toward their students and may consequently receive lower ratings in student evaluations of their courses and instruction.

The matriarch is described as aggressive, domineering, and unfeminine – or the failed mammy. In higher education, White students may describe Black women professors in evaluations as according to the "angry Black woman" trope, or as authoritarian, cold, and unapproachable. White students often choose to approach their White professors with their "concerns" about the classes we teach because they are confused and upset that their construction of Black women professors as matriarchs are false; that we are unwilling to be mammy-like in our interactions toward them. The dynamics could also result in our White colleagues formally and informally rating us poorly on our assumed interpersonal skills.

Unlike the matriarch, the welfare mother lacks aggression; she is instead described as lazy. Black women faculty who are seen as less available to their students than White faculty or unwilling to answer e-mail messages immediately may see comments in their course/teaching evaluations labeling them as idle and lazy. In addition, those Black women faculty who are not awarded tenure may be blamed by their White colleagues for not "doing enough" because we are expected to be "de mule of de world" (Collins, 2000, p. 270) or doing the work that some White and male colleagues are unable or unwilling to do (i.e., mentoring students who identify as BIPOC, extra service work, and so forth).

Inquiry

I use an autoethnographic approach to describe and analyze my personal experiences with gendered racism through the formal evaluation of my tenure dossier (Ellis et al., 2011). Autoethnography as a mode of inquiry could be described as a "self-narrative that critiques the situatedness of self with others in social contexts" (Spry, 2001, p. 710). That is, autoethnography allowed me to "retroactively and selectively write about past experiences" (Ellis et al., 2011, p. 13). Autoethnography also helped me uncover and make meaning of the painful lived experiences that I had with being subjected to gendered racism throughout my tenure-review process. According to Diggs, Garrison-Wade, Estrada, and Galindo (2009), "an important challenge to racial [and gender] oppression is sometimes well expressed in the form of storytelling, giving voice to the knowledge and experiences that are often unrepresented in society" (p. 317). Autoethnography intersecting with Black feminist thought made sense for me in the articulation of my experiences in that both are rooted in discourse from those on the margins and also challenge the dominant group's perceptions of reality (Spry, 2001).

I also analyzed my course evaluations (2009–2011), peer-review evaluations (2009–2011), and artifacts in my tenure dossier (2009–2014) as data sources. The student evaluations were collected from the course I taught titled "Teaching and Learning within Multicultural Contexts." I focused on this course because the literature suggests that faculty of color who teach race-based courses are more likely to receive lower ratings on student evaluations (Littlefield et al., 2010). This also is a required course for teacher candidates pursuing the Master of Secondary Education degree and specializations in Teaching English as a Second or Other Language/Bilingual Education and Educational Technology. It was an elective for candidates in our Childhood Education and Teaching and Foundations programs. I taught the course six times between 2009 and 2011.

I taught this course from a social-justice education perspective, which I define as a critical approach to education that examines how power and privilege are used in institutions to reproduce social inequality in society (both unintentionally and intentionally) based on social group membership (Picower, 2012). I have used several textbooks such as *Rethinking our Classrooms: Teaching for Equity & Justice* (Au, Bigelow, & Karp, 2007) and *Multicultural Education: Issues and Perspectives* (Banks & Banks, 2010). In addition, teacher candidates read articles that focused on identity and privilege, power and oppression, curriculum development, and teaching for social justice. Assignments included a critical autobiographical paper, a critique of instructional materials for various types of bias, a social-action lesson plan or class activity, and a field experience to help candidates connect theory with real-world practices and experiences in schools and communities.

The dossier for pre-tenured faculty is written and updated every year for our schoolwide peer-review committee to evaluate. I have used my dossier to examine how I described my teaching philosophy and responded to student and peer evaluations. The student and peer evaluations were used to understand how their discourse reflected the theoretical framework used for this inquiry. The constant comparative method of analysis was used to assess the fit of the "controlling images" framework (Collins, 2000) to my lived experiences (Fram, 2013). Therefore, my goal was not to develop theory here but to systematically compare the data sources to develop categories and themes that illustrate my experience with gendered racism during the tenure and promotion process.

The Peer-Review Committee and Process

In GSEAP, each pre-tenured faculty member completes and then adds to a dossier on an annual basis so that tenured faculty on the schoolwide peer review committee (PRC) are able to conduct a formative assessment to evaluate the quality of the candidate's teaching, scholarship, and service. The dossier is also used as a summative assessment. Besides providing feedback on our progress toward tenure and promotion, it is also used to determine whether we are eligible for merit-pay increases, and moreover, whether or not we will receive a contract for the following academic year. The PRC designed a rubric based on the information in the faculty handbook to evaluate our dossiers. The rubric was given to all pre-tenured faculty to help us determine what kind of "evidence" we might consider including in our dossiers when writing about our teaching, research/scholarship, and service. The committee schedules a group meeting with all pre-tenured faculty once per year to discuss the process and to address questions we may have. The committee is made up of five tenured faculty, each elected from one of our four departments, and one at-large member. From 2009 through 2011, the membership of the committee was predominantly White and female, reflecting the faculty population in the school in general.

Faculty members submit their dossiers in the spring semester in binders and also electronically to the Associate Dean. A file box accompanies the dossier that includes evidence such as syllabi, teaching evaluations, and one's publications. These documents are kept and secured in the Dean's Office. After all dossiers are submitted, the members of the PRC read each one. The committee meets and discusses each dossier. The person who is assigned to write the letter given to the pre-tenured faculty member takes notes during the discussion to help them prepare the written document. The letter includes feedback, as well as ratings on teaching, research/scholarship, and service, which is shared with the Dean. The letter also includes a section that provides recommendations on the format/content of the dossier that is only shared with the pre-tenured faculty member. Once the faculty member under review receives the letter, it is recommended that we meet with the person on the PRC who wrote the letter to ask any questions about its content. All tenured faculty members are able to submit letters to the PRC in support (or not) of pre-tenured faculty, but it is the PRC role to provide formative and summative feedback.

My Pre-Tenure Review Process: An Unwelcome Surprise

The PRC process described earlier took place for the first time during my third year. The evaluation process prior to this one was less formal, as most faculty felt the feedback was not helpful to our development and growth. The new process initially seemed rigorous but fair. I was anxious to read my letter because the third year is considered a significant one in which one would have a clearer sense of progress toward tenure and promotion. One would also learn about reappointment in terms of if renewal would (or would not) be recommended for subsequent years.

I clearly remember going to my office in the morning when the letter arrived. I opened it, read the first paragraph, and thought, to myself, "This is going to be okay." The next paragraph focused on my teaching. As I read the letter, two comments stood out to me. The first was "many students' criticisms are not addressed." The second stated, "Dr. Burrell's obvious passion for the topic she teaches may be compromising her ability to effectively communicate her ideas to students." At the end of the teaching section, the PRC members voted that I did not meet teaching expectations. The actual vote was as follows: two voted that I "did meet expectations," four voted that I "did not meet," and there was one "abstention." In the moment, I was angry and confused. How did I meet teaching expectations during my first and second years, but not in my third year? I felt sick and scared. I thought I was going to be fired. I sat in my office and cried. I called a colleague in my department who tried to comfort me by stating the PRC was probably trying to give me critical feedback.

In the course evaluations the PRC reviewed, students generally described me as intimidating, opinionated, emotional, and unapproachable; the previous items are all examples reflecting the matriarch controlling image of Black women (Collins, 2000). In addition, I found seven (total) of these comments in evaluations from one course. For example, one student wrote, "She often shuts down contrary viewpoints and inadvertently can intimidate students." Another further reported, "[She is] very opinionated at times; [gives] aggressive feedback." Another wrote, "Teacher was uptight, sensitive to teaching this subject. Needs to distant herself from this field." Yet another wrote, "Sometimes too emotional about comments made. Could find her remarks insulting. Felt material was bias & a lot times I was made to feel guilty about who I am." Finally, several students reported that I was, for instance, a "Poor communicator, inaccessible, unavailable," and showed "Poor social & e-mail skills."

When I met with the White female faculty member who was assigned to write my letter, she suggested that I become "more social" with students to help raise my evaluation scores. Once again, I was dumbfounded. I left her office feeling misunderstood and alone. At my university, teaching and scholarship are heavily weighted in tenure and promotion decisions. Faculty members must reflect on their course/teaching evaluations, acknowledge any patterns of concerns raised by students, and discuss how they have or will respond to them. I thought I acknowledged and responded to the students' feedback effectively. I began to wonder, as scholars of color have suggested, whether "my interests, values and knowledge in social justice education [are] working against me" (Diggs et al., 2009, p. 314).

None of my colleagues on the PRC asked me how I felt about the vicious comments that my mostly White students wrote about me. None of them gave me concrete or helpful suggestions about how to write about my teaching experiences in my dossier. Moreover, there was no advice given during group meetings about how to respond to negative student comments in course evaluations, especially those that were appearing to be sexist, racist, classist, homophobic, and so forth. After my third-year review, I did not feel safe sharing the challenges I faced in my social-justice education courses with my White colleagues.

Discussion and Implications

The goal of this inquiry was to explore how several controlling images of Black women (Collins, 2000) appeared in my student and peer evaluations in my pre-tenure dossier. Data revealed the matriarch image of Black women directly impacted how I was perceived as a Black faculty member at this predominantly White institution by White faculty and White teacher candidates. These findings also reflect previous research in that mostly White students/teacher candidates and colleagues gave me lower ratings on my "interpersonal skills" based on stereotypical and oppressive images of African American women faculty (Bavishi et al., 2010). Furthermore, White students generally, reported that I, a Black woman, was biased in how I taught social-justice education without critical reflection about their own positionality in their interpretive frameworks that would lead them to believe this in the first place (Littlefield et al., 2010).

Learning how to respond to gendered racism in tenure dossiers is a must if Black women faculty and other racialized scholars in education wish to survive the brutality of the tenure-and-promotion process. I recommend several strategies to combat the "hidden curriculum" in terms of responding to gendered racism in tenure dossiers. First, use your teaching philosophy as a theoretical framework to describe the "why and the how" behind your teaching. For example, I wrote the following: "I believe teacher candidates need to critically analyze their prior experiences with diversity and social justice issues and reflect on their biases prior to learning how to teach students because teachers' attitudes influence their practice in the classroom." There is credible research that supports the previous statement, which leads to my second recommendation. Use the literature to support your argument and while writing your dossier. Approach your dossier like any other manuscript that you write. Do not apologize for your approach to teaching. However, if possible, include research that highlights the impact of what you do in the classroom.

Next, use quantitative data from your student evaluations creatively. I asked a full professor outside my department to read my dossier before submitting it. One idea this professor gave was highlighting a particular finding in my evaluations that I did not think of using beforehand. We use the IDEA student ratings of instruction as our quantitative form of assessment. There is one statement in the evaluation that asks students to rate the following statement on a 5-point scale as follows: "I really wanted to take this course." This statement measures student motivation to enroll in the course. My colleague pointed out the range of ratings I received and suggested I highlight it in my dossier. The range I received for one course was between 2.9–3.6 (out of 5-point scale). I wrote the following in my dossier:

> I love teaching ED/SL 441, but at times it presents a dual challenge for me, of presenting material in a way that is accessible and relevant to a fairly homogenous student population, while, simultaneously, retaining the academic rigor of the course. In addition, on the "I really wanted to take this course" question my scores range between 2.9–3.6. To engage students in ED/SL 441 (and all my courses), I model the tenets of social justice education pedagogy.
>
> (See figure 1)

The goal was not to blame students for my lower evaluations but rather to indicate the context for the resistance I might face when teaching about social-justice concepts in the course. Once again, there is research to support my statement (e.g., Justice & Barker, 2007), as responding to oppressive statements in the tenure dossier also represents the various types of pedagogical challenges that faculty like me experience.

After my third-year review, I attended a faculty-development institute on writing the teaching dossier. I spent a week at Windsor University learning about the process of collegial evaluations of teaching in higher education, and how to write about my own teaching effectively. The institute gave me hope that I could demonstrate my effectiveness in the classroom. I shared what I learned with my colleagues in and out of my school of education. The dean of GSEAP and the center for teaching at my university paid for my travel expenses. I recommend this type of professional development for anyone, especially if you believe you do not have the support you need on your own campus to be successful.

My final recommendations are viewing other dossiers and forming a "dossier prep group." Ask to see dossiers from others who were awarded tenure on your campus, especially those who teach courses about social justice. For example, I approached a Black woman who taught a course on critical-race theory because I assumed we may have faced similar experiences with student feedback. One sample dossier from someone in my field and one outside of it were helpful when I sat down to write my own case.

I also formed a dossier group with colleagues who wanted to build their dossiers using a community-practice model (Smith, Calderwood, Storms, Gill Lopez, & Colwell, 2016). We met monthly to discuss topics such as how to write a teaching philosophy, how to design the box that included evidence, and discussed the rank-and-tenure guidelines. Faculty from across the university were invited to participate. The final group included the following demographics of pre-tenured faculty: two White females, one Black woman, and one Asian male from professional schools, as well as and the director from the center for teaching who was a tenured full professor and a White female. The group provided each member with the support needed before submitting our dossiers to the rank-and-tenure college-wide committee. We all were awarded tenure.

The previous recommendations target individual faculty. However, massive changes need to occur at the institutional level. Rank-and-tenure committees, as well as administrators, need to be aware of these issues and enact policies and practices that combat gendered racism and other forms of institutional biases. Placing this responsibility solely on the shoulders of faculty who are BIPOC is not the answer. Blaming the victim will only lead to more marginalization. However, understanding our experiences at historically White institutions will help reduce racial-battle fatigue (Smith, Yosso, & Solórzano, 2006) and promote the retention and well-being of diverse faculty (Pittman, 2010). We need to continue to conduct similar research until all forms of oppression are properly addressed in higher education, especially in predominantly White schools of education that explicitly promote missions of equity and inclusion.

11 Iconic Modernism and Gendered-Racialized Realities

Sheila W. Stamm

"Go Back to Where You Came From" . . . Is Met With Silence

I vividly recall an incident that occurred to me early in my career in the academy. A White colleague held up his hand while I spoke during a faculty meeting on diversity and the preparation of new teachers. He said, "Go back to where you came from." Silence followed. As the only racialized American in the meeting, I had to tell the participants who later apologized, including the department chair, that they should have *said* something at the meeting and ultimately held their colleague in check for his troubling remark. Little has changed for me since then. In many respects, my interactions in the academy have only worsened as I have advanced in my career.

So we are clear about the identity politics shaping my social existence as an American, I am a descendant of: (1) *the first* generation of Africans abducted from their homelands (and strong enough to survive a long and treacherous journey across the Atlantic) who arrived on the nation's eastern shores and were held captive against their will, (2) *the first* generation people native to the eastern shore whose lands were seized and homes relocated (American Indians), and (3) *the first* generation Europeans who crafted the idea of abduction and displacement of people for economic gain, then created arbitrary social categories to perpetuate beliefs of Otherness to justify this decision. Since birth, I have variously been called everything from "Negro," "Colored," "Black," "Afro American," "African American," and (more recently) simply one among many "people of color" or "racialized" Americans disenfranchised in the United States. I was also frequently called the "N" and "B" words that occurred along with the many critical encounters related to these socially contrived notions of race, as well as class and gender.

The lens used to analyze critical encounters is based on my direct experiences dealing mostly with the many *concrete ceilings* created by the duality of my race and gender. Born and raised in the South at a time of heightened social change focused on equity and social justice, I attended segregated K-12 schools. I clearly remember seeing race-separate water fountains as a child. Among the first African Americans to enroll "by choice" in what was then called a "White school," I experienced first-hand the removal of physical and legal barriers that had limited access and opportunities for those labeled as Black.

I also have witnessed the residual effects of unexamined assumptions in its aftermath. I recall how a group of clever locals outraged by federal mandates desegregating schools found a loophole and gerrymandered school lines so that Blacks who attended previously all-White schools "by choice" could return to segregated situations. However, given time limits specific to compliance, my siblings were able to graduate from the federally compliant desegregated school. I take solace in knowing that my brother and his classmates were successful in having White school officials remove the large confederate flag painted on a wall of the high school's gym and rename the sports team formerly known as "The Rebels." My sister was also among the few Black students selected statewide to attend a mathematics and science institute at one of the top research universities and graduated two years later from the White high school as *their* first Black valedictorian. Simultaneously, to show the extent to which *public* officials were willing to defy federal mandates, I graduated *after* desegregation from a high school where 99 percent of its students were categorized as Black. The sole student classified as White was from a family too disadvantaged economically to pay for private education.

Given White flight to a local private school following the federal mandate, we were systematically left with limited resources at the school we attended. However, having gained access previously, we were more aware of the inequitable funding distributions within the county's public schools and knew of the type of resources provided to Whites. Working with a few peers, this knowledge was brought to all. We were subsequently labeled as "ring leaders" for orchestrating a student walk-out in peaceful protest of funding inequities. As one of the leaders of this effort, we successfully negotiated items not previously provided including, among others, school lockers to store our books, uniforms for sports teams, and an athletic bus for "away games." Still, neither the federally compliant school that my siblings attended nor the segregated one gerrymandered by local policymakers where I attended were offered the tennis courts and swimming pools like the public school in the north of the district, where 100 percent of its students were White.

As a dean of education decades later, I easily recognized the subtexts involved (and the frequency with which faculty colleagues who were White, including department and program chairs) questioned my advocacy for racialized Americans in K-12 including the education of American Indians, as well as my desire to take immediate action among policymakers in eradicating statewide opportunity gaps. These same White colleagues were quick to say the opportunity gap "is your [my] problem" and refused to take responsibility for educator preparation specific to cultural competency. On more than one occasion, I heard someone say something along the lines of, "You must feel like Obama." These moments reflected their contentious nature in which when I said "absolutely yes" to affirming diversity, but they argued "no" – even if most of them agreed that our community needed and wanted our help.

Systematically, my lived experience that informed professional practice such as teacher preparation was often silenced, therefore limiting our school of education's collective ability to be truly innovative in offering educator-preparation programs truly supportive of inclusive practices. Consider that having come of age during the Civil Rights Movement in the 1960s, I understand the desire for unity and inclusivity. How a few people asked not what their country could do for them but what *they* could do for the nation. I vividly recall the murder of President John Fitzgerald Kennedy (JFK), Rev. Martin Luther King, Jr. (MLK), and the former president's little brother "Bobby" whose lives were taken while trying to give back. I had often wondered about the irony of how their last initials, when combined, referenced the "KKK." I recall the outrage by several Whites over civil-rights changes specific to racial discrimination: the water hoses and dogs trained (and told) to attack people who looked like me or their reactions to Blacks who dared sit at the counter in a segregated restaurant in North Carolina. I recall how the governor Alabama stood defiantly in the doorway, refusing to let Black children in a school building, as well as the church bombing that killed three little Black girls. I remember the three young men brutally murdered in Mississippi (one Black and two Whites; one was Jewish). I remember the story of another young man also brutally murdered in Mississippi and whose mother in Chicago allowed *Ebony* to photograph her grieving over his bloated body on the magazine's cover so that all could see what White supremacists had done to her son.

Through televised evenings with Walter Cronkite (a man with journalistic ethics so rare in modern times), I witnessed firsthand the events of this era, including countless body bags arriving home from Vietnam. I witnessed how a few brave citizens like my father and mother could fight against injustices and discrimination with dignity as peaceful warriors. In the midst of it all, I enjoyed the Beatles perform on the Ed Sullivan show, saw NASA's space flights around the Earth and a man walking on the moon, danced to Ike and Tina Turner, listened to *Santana* and the *Last Poets* while proclaiming "I am Black and I am Proud" with James Brown. I grew up with Motown and televised revolutions. I witnessed Watergate, followed by the impeachment of Nixon, who gave the current man in office a photograph, which he now claims spurred the idea that he, too, could one day be president.

Since that time, I have devoted my life and career to education and the arts, and along the way, have been (among others) a teacher in K-12, director of agencies in three states (two of them Southern), twice tenured, a full professor, and faculty in public and private institutions of higher education in three regions. I have led a faculty senate, served as an academic dean in three institutions of higher education, been a board member for another, and a commissioner of higher education in a Midwestern state. Correspondingly, I worked across sectors and in partnership with artists, designers, architects, scientists, engineers, lawyers, local boards, philanthropists, corporate, and political leaders of both parties, as well as policymakers and community leaders. Nonetheless, the road to these accomplishments provides a cautionary tale for other racialized Americans seeking careers in higher education, especially in predominantly White colleges and schools of education.

Conceptual Framework

The absence of racialized Americans – especially those who are women – in higher education, is clearly visible in many hallways and well-documented in the literature (e.g., Carter et al., 1996; Turner, González, & Wood, 2008; Wilson, 1989). Yet, despite years of US institutions of higher education attempting to address diverse hiring practices, little progress has occurred. While the literature highlights some diversification among the faculty ranks, few instances provide a deeper analysis of campus dynamics among those at the executive level. While it is abundantly clear that racialized Americans (particularly women who identify as BIPOC) are absent among senior-level positions (e.g., June, 2008; Valverde, 2003; Wilson, 1989), the unique experiences of these leaders and their benefit to supporting campus diversity are not fully explored. After all, it is at the senior level where change most effectively occurs in addressing equity issues from an institutional and systems-level perspective. Leaders who are from racialized backgrounds with specific lived experience therefore occupy critical spaces helpful in responding to political nuances, addressing external forces affecting institutional progress specific to diversity, and shaping campus policies and practices supportive of inclusivity. They also manage performance assessments and grievances affecting the careers and advancement of faculty, staff, and students – many of whom are also racialized Americans. It is therefore at this executive level where manifesting constructive change supportive of generations to come could really occur for institutional, academic, and student affairs.

In my case, Collins's (2000) Black feminist thought is used to frame the views herein. I concur that conversations about inclusivity and the lives of racialized Americans are inseparable from the historical contexts of the people who directly experienced these encounters. Further, the tripartite existence of race, gender, and class among Black women (whose public persona resides on the edges of society) provide a unique socio-political lens to analyze, discuss, and explore the intersections of socialized constructs. Thus, by exploring the unique personal experience of perceptive Black women who know and have lived the historical underpinnings, we are able to have a deeper understanding of how racialized identities occur in the United States, and moreover, the ways by which ideologies of difference manifest themselves within the social milieu. Moreover, by indwelling within the matrix of privilege and domination, Black women provide a distinctive ethnographic gaze for analyzing (and could provide insightful inquiry on) the uniquely "American" experience. In essence, we experience the experience of historical reaction to race, gender, and class.

Historical Contexts of Difference

Race, as opposed to genetic diversity, is a social construct that has no biological meaning or reality (Montagu, 1942). The scientific evidence is unequivocal among anthropologists, biologists, and geneticists. Racism – still a reality – is nonetheless so deeply embedded in our culture that it directly or indirectly affects every aspect of life. Most certainly, racism still abounds in US institutions of higher learning. Injustices against racialized Americans and others are manifest in the demographics and experiences of students, faculty, and leaders. That this type of racism is often systemic or institutional rather than personal is irrelevant. What matters most is that systemic/institutional (e.g., policies/practices) and personal racism evolved and continues to exist not only to preserve and protect power and control, but to disenfranchise those who are deemed as "less than" Whites. It is, to quote the title of Ashley Montagu's seminal 1942 book, *Man's Most Dangerous Myth*.

The roots of racism as it manifests in the United States today are deeply embedded in American history. These ideas have their genesis in the one-drop rule adopted in Virginia to arbitrarily categorize children born of mixed heritage to mothers of African descendants – many of whom clearly *looked just like them* – from all others born to mothers of European ancestry. The one-drop rule subsequently denied those of mixed African ancestry any legal claim to their birthrights and access to the cultural capital of their White fathers including money, land, education, and social status. The rule essentially stated that "one drop" of African blood was enough for a person to be considered Black and allowed wealthy White plantation owners a legal basis to continue holding those of mixed heritage from first-generation Africans captive. The modern marginalization of Blacks in the United States who descended from the first-generation Africans has its origins in this one-drop rule, which continues to influence the social consciousness of American citizens. This consciousness contributes to the unexamined assumptions and belief structures based on the hue of one's skin, along with the continued practice of racial categorization.

Despite the Civil War, Civil Rights Movement, and the election of President Barack H. Obama, the icons of the past – confederate symbols and other contemporary expressions of sympathy for scientifically discredited ideologies – permeate our modern political discourse. As White supremacy finds sanction within President Donald J. Trump, his troubled legacy persists and grows in the US Congress, schools, and society at-large. Efforts continue to disenfranchise racialized American voters and discontinue or defund various health, education, and other social-support programs. Iconic modernism thus describes the current effort to resurrect a period of unquestioned White supremacy, albeit in a mutated form.

Iconic and Modern Barriers to "Success" in Higher Education

Overt and residual manifestations of racialized thought forms, whether conscious or unconscious, in *all* phases of the US higher education career process, from the interviewing stage to those who are now part of the academy in leadership positions. Although leadership issues are the focus of this chapter, my experiences regarding typical barriers in the selection process provide several useful contexts. For example, when interviewing for leadership positions, I consistently encountered women and men in higher education who do not look like me, who vigorously scrutinized or challenged my qualifications (e.g., for example, questioning how my accomplishments were achieved "in such a short amount of time"), who verbally articulated deeply held assumptions about my competence, and who made critical mistakes documented in the literature when assessing the potential of new leaders. These phenomena further disadvantage leaders from racialized backgrounds who must also overcome their added perspectives on gender and race (if not also age and other factors). Many individuals serving on search committees wished actively and clearly to support the status quo either by working intentionally or inadvertently to "clone" themselves by finding leaders who replicated Whiteness. In such cases, identity politics was most assuredly in the room. After years of being both the interviewee and interviewer on search committees, it is clear that unexamined or unchallenged assumptions of "Otherness" interfere with hiring decisions and ultimately prohibit our collective success in securing and retaining talented personnel.

Without a significant understanding of these undercurrents, search firms and the institutions seeking to diversify leadership pools risk overlooking and supporting viable candidates from varied backgrounds. Allies are therefore needed at multiple levels to ensure the continued advancement of leaders from racialized backgrounds. One thing is for certain: if racialized Americans are never appointed as department chairs or academic deans, it is highly unlikely that we will see much change among executive positions in higher education. The dual politicized space shaped by skin tone and gender in the United States creates what Wilson (1989, p. 85) referred to as the "double jeopardy of oppression" that women of color encounter in environments that are dominated by White males. Yet, these very women are often in the best position to lead both student and faculty affairs because of their lived experiences.

Once hired, many Indigenous women leaders and women leaders of color are often locked in their positional roles without access to critical information that is helpful to their continued growth as leaders, as well as in negotiating salaries, managing difficult personnel situations, and seeking advancement. Many are culturally isolated and lack adequate support from faculty and other campus leaders. They tend to endure incredible stress from working long hours and campus fatigue from having to ward off false attacks on their character. Their overcapacity risks their advancement. Their health and well-being compromised, many opt to leave for positions elsewhere or exit higher education altogether based on the hostile levels of campus receptivity. These leaders must also work to manage public perceptions in ways that their White peers do not, and moreover, must carefully weigh the long-term implications of decisions they make from a sociocultural perspective. If they make unpopular decisions, these leaders risk further scrutiny without the benefit of being able to freely articulate the nuances either to direct reports, their peers, or other campus leaders.

The iconic modernist approach that complicates the work of equity-focused leaders is an increasingly common practice in higher education of faculty using "a vote of no confidence" to block advancement politically and displace leaders, especially those who are from racialized backgrounds. Another approach is mobbing or upwards bullying among direct reports designed to discount leaders who are seen as most progressive in changing the status quo or advancing an unpopular agenda (e.g., those leaders who are in turn-around situations). If left unchecked, the bullying process sets equity-focused leaders up for failure by allowing their peers and subordinates to call their abilities into question. Saying publicly that individuals hired do not "measure up" to expectations is a common way to set leaders from racialized backgrounds up for failure. Often, one's success is blocked by direct reports who carefully construct distorted narratives about their leaders and encourage others to join in this negative messaging. These narratives are then shared with those to whom the leader reports to discredit the person's work and to redirect conversations for personal and self-serving reasons rather than in support of the institution. Colleagues who are more experienced in the institutional setting (who disagree with the leader's hire and/or agenda for change) also tend to use valuable insider knowledge and withhold information to derail decisions, conversations, and the long-term success of leaders new to these institutions.

By way of example, consider the schemes described in an anonymous letter sent by a remorseful White faculty member to a university provost describing the tactics s/he and "a small but persistent and influential number of faculty (and a few staff)" used against a dean (Black female) to "actively and aggressively . . . destroy her credibility and set her up for failure." According to the letter, tactics included (personal communication, undated):

1. "Intensely scrutinize her every word and deed; complain to colleagues and higher or other authority about the dean whenever possible; question or challenge virtually every decision."
2. "Isolate the dean as much as possible and accuse her of micromanagement or adversarial-ness when she asks to be kept informed or provides direction."
3. "Pester her with e-mail and other requests intended to consume her time."
4. "Deprive her of information needed to make informed and/or timely decisions by withholding information in whole or in part and/or disclosing it only grudgingly or at the last minute (e.g., conceal issues requiring attention until they reach a serious stage)."
5. "Do only what is literally requested rather than what our experience informs us to do or deviate from instructions (to do instead what we would like) and later claim her communication isn't clear."
6. "As suitable opportunities arise, urge students to complain."

Other tactics disclosed included:

1. "Attempt to befriend and thereby woo new individuals to their "worldview" (e.g., lavish praise, attribution, and other kindnesses on them)."
2. "Subtly (and sometimes not so subtly) portray [the dean] in an unfavorable light (e.g., as an adversary, micromanager, or intervenor; as someone to blame)."
3. "Minimize, discount or ignore the contributions of [the dean]."
4. "Selectively pit . . . new leaders against her and each other."

According to the letter, racial animus and preservation of the status quo were primary motives.

The extent to which this type of behavior manifests in institutions of higher education generally is unknown. Yet, these events often reflect the leadership experience of women who are racialized Americans – me included – notwithstanding laws specific to the discrimination of those in a protected class.

In a post-Obama era, racialized Americans who are also Black women in top leadership positions are especially vulnerable to toxic work environments characterized by bullying, mobbing, micro and macro aggressions, insubordination, and smear campaigns predicated on innuendo, misperception, half-truths, and outright lies. The professional literature amply documents these as techniques classically applied in higher education settings (e.g., DeAngelis, 2009; Solórzano, Ceja, & Yosso, 2009; Sue, 2010). Given the aforementioned realities, those holding leadership positions need adequate support and understanding from institutional boards, executive leaders, general counsel, human resource management, and the local community to succeed.

Reflections Gained While Leading From the Edge

Unquestionably, to be a woman and a racialized American in the academy is to be challenged both for *who* you are and *what* you are capable of accomplishing. To be an artist *and* intellectual makes the situation even more difficult. To be this while leading agendas of unity and inclusivity within a predominantly White school of education *inside* an institution of higher education led mostly by White women and White men is even more complex. To be *all* of the mentioned pieces is to have a strong sense of self – the audacity to *be* who you are while challenging conventional practices. To lead well in this environment is to be creative and visionary, while embracing difference and also understanding (and expecting) that most peers will think and do otherwise.

Complicating matters is how tenuous the American dream is for those in the middle class; the residual effects of living with limited resources in many institutions of higher education; and the professionalization of education in predominantly White colleges and schools of education in the United States. Clearly, we collectively face new challenges of our past while responding to the current internationalization of students and working with faculty who either do not know (or cannot understand) the complexities of American history, or who buy into the erroneous mythologies created from the intergenerational mixing of cultures. It has been my experience that colleagues in predominantly White schools of education especially use moments of national political change as an excuse to ignore diversity. For example, following President Obama's election, a colleague who had only recently received American citizenship said that our campus conversations about diversity were no longer needed given that I (also meaning all Blacks) had "gotten what you wanted." Another of Jewish faith from Russia, who ironically taught literature for teachers in a large public district where many students enrolled are Black, asked me, "Why are Blacks so prejudiced against Whites?" I also experienced Whites in the academy describe their encounters with students and faculty who were Black as triggering feelings of "reverse discrimination."

Given that these individuals reside in predominantly White schools of education focused on solutions to the opportunity gap in K-12, the most pressing advice I am able to offer is for all to *know* the history behind events, policies, and practices in the United States supportive of unity and inclusion. *Understand* the genesis of the American experience and familial relationships between and among American Indians, Whites, and Black descendants from first-generation Africans brought here by force. *Recognize* the origins of "Otherness," xenophobia, and how racialized categorizations were used to perpetuate White supremacy, and to further justify criminal and immoral actions against humanity. Knowing this history is essential to interrogating the iconic modernist conservative ideologies defining the national landscape currently, which are highly *reactionary to* inclusivity. Know that these views are in the public sector and hallways of institutions of higher education and schools of education that espouse policies of inclusivity when they really mean that the Americans they racialize "need not apply."

I recall a conversation with a search firm representative who was angered by the practice of colleges and universities going through a national search while knowing that the search committee would select an inside candidate. I encountered another representative who, upon questioning, admitted that the university wanted to improve its diversity numbers by asking me to interview for a leadership position as a finalist. The practice of seeking qualified racialized Americans to interview while knowing that they will not receive the position is a common strategy used by some institutions of higher education to provide a public illusion of inclusion while maintaining the status quo. Knowing this possibility, it is my advice for all to question hiring policies and practices while *inside* these institutions. Work to ensure equitable access and opportunity is maintained either by you and/or a leader who is fully informed of US history, brave enough to counter the prevailing norms, and who is able to use a position of authority to question myths about racialized Americans (particularly those who are Black). Work immediately to address those who interfere with searches.

Additional advice I will offer is as follows:

1. Fight injustices in the workplace while being careful not to become those people you end up fighting against. Advocate for a deeper reverence for humanity and maintain a strong spiritual core that is more ethical, wise, and strategic than those who work against your success. Remember to take the high road. Recognize that programs, units, and institutions of higher education are in *your* care. What you do (and do not do) matters for those yet to come.
2. Protect access and opportunity to high-quality education for the generations to come. Without students, there is no point in talking about

higher education. An already frail society becomes a fragile civilization where important gains previously made are ignored or lost.

3. See allies among leaders who understand the critical encounters faced and who are willing to use their positions of authority and cultural capital to advocate on your behalf.

4. Preempt negative encounters swiftly by reporting these immediately to offices of human resources and direct supervisors (e.g., deans and provosts if you are faculty, provost and presidents if you are a dean or in another leadership role). In essence, quickly tell your story, preferably in writing, before someone else does. It has been my experience that those with malicious intent will tell a distorted version equivalent to character assassination. Legally, offices of human resources and academic leaders must act on matters affecting those in a protected class. However, *tell the truth*. Present facts as objectively as possible. Leave the emotion out of everything.

5. Preempt poor assessments that reflect biased statements from students and colleagues by carefully analyzing these as the ethnographer you were trained to be. Situate findings within the literature and use citations in your responses to them.

6. Keep a contemporaneous audit trail of all critical encounters, events, and documents to ensure these could be sufficiently analyzed and used to combat naysayers who fabricate stories that challenge your right to teach and/or lead effectively in the workplace. Contemporaneous accounts have greater credibility than those created after the event.

7. Know that the frequency and intensity of critical encounters matter to you, your health, and your loved ones. Recognize signs of burnout and fatigue. Use sabbaticals, vacations, and (if needed) seek positions elsewhere so that you are able to renew, rejuvenate, and advance to a healthier work environment.

8. There is nothing wrong with nomadic intelligence gained from working in multiple institutions of higher education. Such intelligence allows you to become fluent in reading environments and recognizing encounters before they occur so that these critical moments could be placed within context among leaders who are able to assist in strategically addressing these situations. However, keep in mind that some hiring committees will see someone moving around too frequently in a negative light. Know when to move. Five to seven years in the same role is preferred – although given the number of toxic environments encountered, I often have to leave a setting more quickly.

9. The point is, know when enough is enough. Be strong enough to leave *on your own terms*.

10. Rely on loved ones and a professional network of colleagues in similar positions across the nation to help you analyze and respond to

problematic situations. Shared knowledge is essential in maintaining a balanced perspective and lifestyle.

11. Get your own legal counsel. Keep them on retainer, particularly if you are in a leadership position. Remember that legal counsels and offices of human resources at institutions of higher education are there to protect the institution and not you. Think of your own personal legal counsel as a similar type of life insurance that you hope will never be used but is there (just in case).

12. Give back to others often and in their early careers – especially if you advance through the ranks and have leadership positions. Even junior faculty are able to give back to postdoctoral fellows and students. However, remember to be mindful of the type of capital espoused in higher education for these positions so you are able to reap the benefits at all times.

13. Work within the academic unit/department but reside at the campus and community levels. Make sure those outside the department and within the local community know who you are. Become familiar with them. Work collaboratively and form alliances by serving on committees supportive of the larger community. Doing so will help combat the mythologies created by colleagues at the departmental and unit levels, and moreover, will provide a sense of contribution and accomplishment during difficult times.

14. For those in leadership positions: it is essential to understand that you occupy a seat of authority that affects the lives and careers of faculty and students. Work to address biased assessments while upholding high standards of excellence regardless of anyone's background. Do not be afraid to speak and work with intention, focus, and resolve.

15. Remember that *you* define yourself and not your career. Neither do we own institutions; we are merely stewards. If we do our jobs well, the campus will be there long after we are dust and be more inclusive than when we arrived.

Finally, in *The Seven Pillars of Wisdom*, T. E. Lawrence (1935) wrote the following words of wisdom:

All men dream: but not equally. Those who dream by night in the dusty recesses of their minds wake in the day to find that it was vanity: but the dreamers of the day are dangerous men, for they may act their dreams with open eyes, to make it possible.

(n.p.)

If you want change, then you must effect change. Act your dream by day . . . but with eyes open.

Figure 12.1 Iconic Pillars: Remain strong and stay true to your core values.
Credit: Sheila W. Stamm

Conclusion – From Relics of Racial Oppression to Sites of Authentic Inclusion

Challenges and Possibilities

Rachel Endo

Contexts, Optics, *and* Outcomes Matter

Several predominantly White colleges and schools of education in the United States, and the universities where they are situated, symbolize relics of racial oppression. These sites cannot credibly or effectively serve as advocates on behalf of or for racialized populations until there are significant shifts in how they are governed and structured. The 12 authors of this collection have narrated how they, as racialized scholars in education, have experienced distinct types of racialization echoing prior historical moments of racial exclusion and symbolic violence. They speak to what it means to show up in professional spaces embedded in Whiteness as racialized bodies of difference. In addition, being the only one or just among a few scholars of color in predominantly White academic units further intensifies their experiences with racialization. Without regular encounters with ethnically and racially diverse individuals in the classroom or workplace, White faculty and students/teacher candidates in education programs may act on or concoct distorted views of racial difference when a racialized body becomes their colleague, leader, or instructor (Lugo-Lugo, 2012). Having more regular contact with diverse individuals in professional settings will, at least in theory, help reduce racialized and other types of biases that are apparent in relatively homogeneous settings such as predominantly White colleges and schools of education (Banks & Banks, 2010; Sue, 2010). There are added benefits of bringing together diverse people and their perspectives into an academic environment such as in professional programs in education, as "It is . . . virtually impossible to demonstrate respect for diversity when working in a homogeneous culture. Only when presented with different views can one demonstrate respect for different perspectives" (Higgerson & Joyce, 2007, p. 158). However, predominantly White education programs must aspire to do more than simply include or seek out racialized bodies only to fulfill self-serving needs. The stakes are high to approach diversity, equity, and inclusion initiatives in education with humility and integrity.

This final chapter does not offer absolute and clear-cut solutions, although several authors individually elected to offer their own implications for practice by bringing together and connecting their specific institutional contexts, ranks, and sociocultural identities. Some authors also ended on a more ambivalent note, unsettling dominant forms of narration by refusing to offer prescriptive solutions to complex problems. This final chapter will offer three critical frameworks for interpreting and re/reading the multiple contexts of racialized experiences as follows: (1) recognizing the sociocultural and sociopolitical contexts of narrative experiences, (2) identifying common deficit views toward bodies of difference that permeate the ideologies of many predominantly White US colleges and schools of education, and (3) situating the causes and consequences of disparate outcomes in these spaces with attention to closing equity and perception gaps to support equitable and inclusive spaces. In this chapter, I also draw from alternative paradigms for explicating experiences to encourage individuals in White-dominated education programs to reflect critically on and tackle their own unique equity-focused problems of practice.

More Than "Just a Story" to Tell: Why Narrative Context(s) Matter

There may be an urge to reduce these 12 diverse narratives and others like them to isolated examples of cross-cultural conflicts, cultural misunderstandings, or the lack of fit between an individual and the academic unit/institution. However, individualistic views of racialized experiences are problematic because they ignore experiential patterns occurring across certain demographic groups. For example, the eight authors of this collection who identify as women of color education scholars narrated experiencing similar types of gendered racism (Collins, 2000) in predominantly White US colleges and schools of education, despite coming from different backgrounds and institutional contexts. They drew from various scholarly frameworks to illustrate patterns of how their pedagogies and professional competence have been critiqued and scrutinized similarly by their White colleagues and White students/teacher candidates. Across their narrative profiles, gendered racism could be read as impacting women of color education scholars in similar ways including being blatantly and/or subtly berated, infantilized, and objectified or sexualized by Whites in professional settings. Their experiences are connected to a long history of gendered and racialized oppression in the United States where women of color have been constructed in White America's imaginary as immoral, sexually licentious, and subhuman. That is, in the eyes of many Whites, including educated professionals such as their colleagues, women of color are unruly bodies in need of containment and discipline (Carter et al., 1996; Collins, 2000). Thus, narrative experiences, particularly those from multicultural and racialized perspectives, should be framed and situated in their proper sociocultural and sociopolitical contexts (Connelly et al., 2003) to understand that modern-day forms of racialization cannot be estranged from historical accumulations and racialized iconography.

Context also matters when interpreting or reading racialized experiences because most colleges and schools of education in the United States have a faculty, leadership, and student core that is mostly White but promote publicly missions supportive of diversity, equity, and inclusion (Gasman et al., 2011). Therefore, scholars like the authors of this study who enter spaces of Whiteness bring valuable insights about growing up and living in a racialized society. For one, the authors' experiences have multiple and relevant parallels to the realities that diverse children, families, and individuals encounter under current and former systems of racial oppression in ways that are not widely understood by White leaders, scholars, and students/teacher candidates. Many of the authors have descended from communities where their ancestors were forced to attend state-sanctioned segregated schools. Others whose families are newer Americans have experienced the residual impact of exclusionary and segregationist racial projects in the United States (Omi & Winant, 1994), even if they attended racially integrated schools. Furthermore, many education scholars from racialized backgrounds, like the 12 authors of this collection, bring socioculturally specific expertise and insights into professional credential and licensure programs about home-school relations, identity development, parental engagement, and student success in ways that enhance and expand how predominantly practicing and pre-service K-12 professionals view issues around diversity, equity, and inclusion. Thus, the knowledge that racialized scholars in education bring to these settings is sorely needed, especially as many predominantly White US colleges and schools of education continue to grapple with questions about their credibility and legitimacy in a multicultural and racialized society.

Interrogating Deficit Views of Racialized Bodies

Despite the rich experiences and knowledge that they bring to their institutional settings, racialized scholars frequently report being treated and viewed by their White colleagues and students/teacher candidates as inferior to Whites (Gasman, 2016; Matias, 2013), a theme that cut across all chapters in this collection. A deficit view is a general assumption that racialized Americans are intellectually inferior and undeveloped compared to Whites. A common example of a deficit view in K-12 education is the widespread belief by many White teachers that most Black children are difficult to teach or unteachable because of stereotypes that people who are Black tend to come from broken and dysfunctional families with few adult role models at home (Howard, 2013). Indeed, anyone could hold a deficit view of another person. However, within the context of education and racial equity, it must be recognized that Whites, as the primary group dominating the K-12 teacher workforce and teacher-preparation programs, exert a great deal of influence in the lives of many in terms of applying deficit frameworks to label certain people using clinically accepted terms such as "disruptive" and "emotionally disturbed" that also have explicit and implicit racialized underpinnings. More specifically, White educators at all levels often make high-stakes decisions that damage, delay, and interrupt a person's academic trajectory significantly (Blanchett, 2006; Harry & Klingner, 2006).

Within the academy, deficit views similarly depict faculty from racialized backgrounds, especially specific subgroups like women of color, as less competent and more emotionally unstable compared to their White counterparts (Gasman, 2016; Gutiérrez y Muhs et al., 2012; Holling, 2019). Similarly, within the specific context of most US education program that are largely populated by current and former classroom teachers or school leaders who are White, deficit perspectives are ones where racialized scholars are viewed as defiant, disruptive, intimidating, lazy, loud, not collegial, oppositional, uncaring, uncivil, unmotivated, and unprofessional (Aguirre, 1995; Bavishi et al., 2010; Lugo-Lugo, 2012). When challenging interactions, situations, and tensions arise in these spaces that often connect to racialized bodies bringing attention to or critiquing inequitable practices, there is a tendency to blame or shame racialized scholars without analyzing the larger contexts of how spaces of Whiteness often silence and stifle racialized bodies.

To begin dismantling the array of deficit views that abound in US colleges and schools of education, the following must be understood by all individuals in these spaces: "No learning situation is culturally neutral" (Ginsberg & Wlodkowski, 2009, p. 10). More specifically, when racialized bodies enter exclusively or predominantly White spaces as faculty/instructors, learners, and occasionally as leaders such as chairs, associate deans, and deans, their mere presence may be unsettling to Whites in ways that may evoke curiosity, fear, and in some cases, outright resentment. When consumed with fear or uncertainty about the racially different, White Americans may react in irrational ways (Coffee, Stutelberg, Clements, & Lensmire, 2016) toward their colleagues, leaders, and students who are Indigenous and of color. When viewed as threats to Whites, racialized bodies are often disciplined including through non-verbal expressions of censure, physical removal from a space, and verbal reprimands or slights (Sue, 2010). Other psychologically punitive means such as excluding, ignoring, and isolating them may also occur in ways that are similar to how many White teachers attempt to control and regulate K-12 students who represent racialized bodies of difference (Endo, 2019).

Differential Expectations and Disparate Outcomes

Most predominantly White education programs, including the academic spaces where the authors have entered and, in some cases, left because they have been pushed out, condemn publicly the rampant inequities and opportunity gaps that persist in the K-12 schools. They often boast of offering academic programs for aspiring and current K-12 practitioners that center diversity, equity, and social justice as their core values. For example, consider the conceptual framework of one predominantly White school of education in the Midwest:

> We believe . . . there is interdependence between schools and society. Society and schools should exist to promote social equity. Therefore, program participants develop an understanding of the role education has played and plays in shaping society. They learn to recognize that gender, ethnicity, and socioeconomic status often determine both the quality and quantity of education individuals receive. As a result, the programs' current and future educators and leaders actively seek to counter forms of racism, sexism, classism, and other types of discrimination.

Colleges and schools of education like the one mentioned and similar to the ones where the authors have been affiliated with are operating within multiple contradictions. For example, in the year 2010, the previously quoted school of education had 15 faculty and staff of color, but as of the year 2017, all of these individuals had departed from the university. While their individual reasons for leaving varied, all 15 were subjected to similar types of racially derogatory treatment by their White colleagues, leaders, and/or students/teacher candidates. Out of eight total faculty of color among this cohort, six were denied promotion or tenure, even though the majority of them had clearly met all written expectations. In contrast, no White faculty member had ever been denied promotion or tenure in this school, even though some of these individuals did not meet minimum written expectations. Yet, despite these contexts, this White-dominated school of education has claimed publicly that diversity, equity, and inclusion are central to its mission and values.

Predominantly White US colleges and schools of education like the one mentioned are likely to have track records replicating multiple forms of cultural and racial biases toward their own colleagues and students/teacher candidates who identify as BIPOC. The severe underrepresentation of racialized scholars is further intensified when analyzing who is and is not represented among the ranks of leadership and tenured faculty. As several of the authors have noted, in these spaces, there is also a litany of differential expectations and non-performance-related judgments of their competence and professionalism. For example, in addition to navigating the "hidden curriculum" of various aspects of academic life, several of the authors have been pressured to defend or justify their pedagogical approaches and service activities in diverse communities. That is, racialized scholars in education often find themselves being questioned by their White colleagues and leaders for doing exactly what they were hired by their institutions to do: to bring diverse perspectives to the academic enterprise and to serve as cross-cultural liaisons with underrepresented and underserved communities. Unfortunately, these realities align with race-based disproportionality concerns in K-12 education, where mostly White classroom teachers tend to hold their Indigenous students and students of color to different expectations and standards compared to White students (Blanchett, 2006; Harry & Klingner, 2006).

Racialized scholars who persist in these environments often battle challenging and dead-end conversations with mostly White institutional leaders and senior colleagues, many who appear to be unable and unwilling to listen to their concerns or take any meaningful action to support them. Consequently, some are eventually pushed out of the academy or are moved around within an institution, both of which have cumulative and negative effects in terms of one's career stability and professional reputation. As Jones (2019) notes, faculty from racialized backgrounds often leave the academy for these reasons:

> Dissatisfaction with tokenism and isolation, denial of tenure, inability to effect institutional change, lack of personal and professional fulfillment, and failure of their institutions to create campus climates that tangibly embrace diversity, equity and inclusion among faculty and administrators.
>
> (p. 47)

Critical Frameworks for Tackling Equity-Focused Problems of Practice

In authentically inclusive and equitable environments, racialized scholars in education would feel empowered to share candidly their experiences on their own terms rather than to fulfill a White person's curiosity or the self-serving needs of their home institutions such as to momentarily celebrate an education scholar of color's accomplishments to pass an accreditation visit. They would be able to speak directly to issues that may be delaying or interrupting racial progress within their academic units and institutions without fear of individual or institutional reprisal. Like many of their White colleagues, they could see themselves at their current institutions for the long term. As most colleges and schools of education in the United States identify themselves as being dynamic learning communities, creating these types of spaces would enable rich conversations to ensue that would ideally inspire a collective will for an academic unit or campus to tackle their own unique equity-focused problems of practice. For such an environment to be successful, everyone, particularly persons who in positions of power by rank, social identity, and status, must fully engage in this work with cultural humility, which "involves the ability to maintain an interpersonal stance that is other-oriented (or open to the other) in relation to aspects of cultural identity that are most important to the [individual]" that ultimately requires collaboration and "respectful openness" (Hook, Davis, Owen, Worthington, & Utsey, 2013, p. 253). Cultural humility stands in stark contrast to the notion of cultural arrogance, misappropriation, and thievery, which is the tendency for White Americans, especially in education programs, to appropriate uncritically, co-opt, and profit professionally from the intellectual property and sociocultural symbols produced by racialized communities, educators, and scholars (Seto, 1995). When learning from and listening to racialized scholars in education, attention must be paid to issues of positionality and power, or the simple recognition that not everyone has always had equal and equitable opportunities to define themselves and share their experiences freely.

To begin the process of reimagining and restructuring these racially stratified spaces, faculty and leaders in White-dominated education programs and universities must foremost be willing to admit that they, whether intentionally or not, are directly and indirectly responsible for creating and replicating multiple race-based disparate outcomes through past and present decisions made at both the individual and institutional levels. They must further acknowledge how the behaviors, competence, and worth of racialized scholars are often assessed or judged formally and informally in ways that perpetuate racially derogatory understandings of culture, difference, and identity. Disparate outcomes appear in various forms, beyond obvious disparities such as compensation gaps or workload inequities. As several of the authors have described, they have frequently been held to biased and differential standards compared to their White colleagues. Often, the expectations are not made clear from the start, or they receive mixed messages about performance criteria, causing uncertainty about how they will be judged for certain high-stakes milestones such as reappointment and tenure. New or unwritten rules are often applied to their situations in ways that inequitably hold them to different or higher standards compared to their White colleagues.

Those in leadership positions are uniquely positioned to identify these and other types of challenges and equity gaps in consultation with the individuals who are most impacted by them. Leaders who allocate financial or human resources in these spaces also influence how initiatives related to diversity, equity, and inclusion are incentivized and prioritized in their academic units. Working in consultation with various stakeholders who are most impacted by these efforts could determine how future initiatives and priorities are resourced. Finally, discussing candidly what restitution might look like by those who have been impacted by racially oppressive policies, practices, rituals, and routines may be necessary for any attempt to re/build trust and restore positive working relationships that would foster a climate of belonging and inclusion.

Looking Back *and* Moving Forward

Those who are committed to creating environments that center equity and inclusion must be willing to allow those with direct lived racialized experiences to take the lead on cocreating and recreating dynamic learning environments that are supportive of many ways of being and knowing. A clear sign of meaningful progress will be when White-dominated education programs do more than simply seek out racialized bodies who appear to fit within White standards of acceptability and respectability or to exploit their knowledge for self-serving individual or institutional purposes. Equity-minded and inclusive leaders actively and proactively find ways to incorporate and validate diverse perspectives into all aspects of an academic division's structure to advance collective goals and institutional mission. They consistently use their institutional positions and social positionalities to advance racialized scholars into various formal and informal leadership roles that will influence the direction of their institutions and various micro-units for years to come. In this process, respect must be shown for the various ways by which racialized scholars from varying backgrounds, experiences, ideologies, and politics show up in spaces of Whiteness, as well as to cocreate environments where they are able to contribute and participate fully in these environments. Indeed, optics *and* outcomes matter.

References

Adams, M., Bell, L. A., & Griffin, P. (Eds.). (2007). *Teaching for diversity and social justice*. New York, NY: Routledge.

Aguirre, A., Jr. (1995). A Chicano farm worker in academe. In R. V. Padilla & R. Chavez Chavez (Eds.), *The leaning ivory tower: Latino professors in American universities* (pp. 17–27). Albany, NY: State University of New York Press.

Ahad, B. S. (2015). Imagining communities in Dave Chappelle's Block Party. *Journal of Popular Culture, 48*(6), 1108–1129. https://doi.org/10.1111/jpcu.12351

Anyon, J. (1980). Social class and the hidden curriculum of work. *The Journal of Education, 162*(1), 67–92. https://doi.org/10.1177/002205748016200106

Apple, M. W. (2014). *Official knowledge: Democratic education in a conservative age*. New York, NY: Routledge.

Au, W., Bigelow, B., & Karp, S. (2007). *Rethinking our classrooms: Teaching for equity and justice* (Vol. 1., 2nd ed.). Milwaukee, WI: Rethinking Schools.

Awad, G. H. (2007). The role of racial identity, academic self-concept, and self-esteem in the prediction of academic outcomes for African American students. *Journal of Black Psychology, 33*(2), 188–207. https://doi.org/10.1177/0095798407299513

Baglieri, S., Bejoian, L. M., Broderick, A. A., Connor, D. J., & Valle, J. (2011). [Re]claiming "inclusive education" toward cohesion in educational reform: Disability studies unravels the myth of the normal child. *Teachers College Record, 113*(10), 2122–2154.

Baglieri, S., & Knopf, J. H. (2004). Normalizing difference in inclusive teaching. *Journal of Learning Disabilities, 37*(6), 525–529. https://doi.org/10.1177/00222194040370060701

Baker, M. (2011, October). *Center of controversy: Africana studies and research center leadership tumult creating conflict*. Retrieved from www.ithaca.com/news/center-of-controversy-africana-studies-and-research-center-leadership-tumult/article_682fb3ac-f9cc-11e0-a5cb-001cc4c002e0.html

Banks, J. A., & Banks, C. A. M. (Eds.). (2010). *Multicultural education: Issues and perspectives* (7th ed.). Hoboken, NJ: John Wiley & Sons.

Bankston, C. L., III (2004). Social capital, cultural values, immigration, and academic achievement: The host country context and contradictory consequences. *Sociology of Education, 77*(2), 176–179. https://doi.org/ 10.1177/003804070407700205

Bavishi, A., Hebl, M. R., & Madera, J. M. (2010). The effect of faculty professor ethnicity and gender on student evaluations: Judged before met. *Journal of Diversity in Higher Education, 3*(4), 245–256. https://doi.org/10.1037/a0020763

Benitez, M., Jr. (2010). Resituating culture centers within a social justice framework: Is there room for examining Whiteness? In L. D. Patton (Ed.), *Culture centers in higher education: Perspectives on identity, theory, and practice* (pp. 119–134). Sterling, VA: Stylus.

Berndt, T. J. (1999). Friends' influence on students' adjustment to school. *Educational Psychologist, 34*(1), 15–28. https://doi.org/10.1207/s15326985ep3401_2

Berndt, T. J., Laychak, A. E., & Park, K. (1990). Friends' influence on adolescents' academic achievement motivation: An experimental study. *Journal of Educational Psychology, 82*(4), 664–670. https://doi.org/ 10.1037/0022-0663.82.4.664

Berry, J. W., Poortinga, Y. H., Breugelmans, S. M., Chasiotis, A., & Sam, D. L. (2011). *Cross-cultural psychology: Research and applications* (3rd ed.). Cambridge, UK: Cambridge University Press.

Berry, T. R., & Stovall, D. O. (2013). Trayvon Martin and the curriculum of tragedy: Critical race lessons for education. *Race Ethnicity and Education, 16*(4), 587–602. https://doi.org/10.1080/13613324.2013.817775

Bhabha, H. (1994). *The location of culture*. London, UK: Routledge.

Biklen, D., & Burke, J. (2007). Presuming competence. *Equity & Excellence in Education, 39*(2), 166–175. https://doi.org/10.1080/10665680500540376

Biklen, D., & Kleiwer, C. (2006). Constructing competence: Autism, voice and the 'disordered' body. *International Journal of Inclusive Education, 10*(2–3), 169–188. https://doi.org/10.1080/13603110600578208

BIPOC project (n.d.). Retrieved December 13, 2018 from www.thebipocproject.org/about-us

Blanchett, W. (2006). Disproportionate representation of African American students in special education: Acknowledging the role of White privilege and racism. *Educational Researcher, 35*(6), 24–28. https://doi.org/10.3102/0013189X035006024

Bogdan, R., & Biklen, D. (1977). Handicapism. *Social Policy, 7*(5), 14–19.

Bogdan, R., & Biklen, D. (2013). Handicapism. In M. Wappett & K. Arndt (Eds.), *Foundations of disability studies* (pp. 1–16). New York, NY: Palgrave Macmillan.

Bonilla-Silva, E. (2010). *Racism without racists: Color-blind racism and the persistence of racial inequality in America*. Lanham, MD: Rowman & Littlefield.

Branscombe, N. R. (2011). Thinking about one's gender group's privileges or disadvantages: Consequences for well-being in women and men. *British Journal of Social Psychology, 37*(2), 167–184. https://doi.org/10.1111/j.2044-8309.1998.tb01163.x

Branscombe, N. R., Doosje, B., & McGarty, C. (2002). Antecedents and consequences of collective guilt. In D. M. Mackie & E. R. Smith (Eds.), *From prejudice to intergroup emotions: Differentiated reactions to social groups* (pp. 49–66). Philadelphia, PA: Psychology Press.

Brewer, C. (1990). *Minority student success in college: What works?* Olympia, WA: Evergreen State College.

Brown, K. D. (2013). Trouble on my mind: Toward a framework of humanizing critical sociocultural knowledge for teaching and teacher education. *Race Ethnicity and Education, 16*(3), 316–338. https://doi.org/10.1080/13613324.2012.725039

Brown, K. D., & Brown, A. L. (2010). Silenced memories: An examination of the sociocultural knowledge on race and racial violence in official school curriculum. *Equity & Excellence in Education, 43*(2), 139–154. https://doi.org/10.1080/10665681003719590

Brown, K. D., & Brown, A. L. (2012). Useful and dangerous discourse: Deconstructing racialized knowledge about African-American students. *The Journal of Educational Foundations, 26*(1/2), 11–28.

Brown, M. K. (2003). *Whitewashing race: The myth of a color-blind society.* Berkeley, CA: University of California Press.

Brown, S. (Ed.). (2014). *Discourse on Africana studies: James Turner and paradigms of knowledge.* New York, NY: African Diaspora Press.

Browne, S. (2015). *Dark matters: On the surveillance of Blackness.* Durham, NC: Duke University Press.

Bukowski, W. M., Newcomb, A. F., & Hartup, W. W. (Eds.). (1998). *The company they keep: Friendships in childhood and adolescence.* Oxford, UK: Cambridge University Press.

Burnham, J. J., Hooper, L. M., & Wright, V. H. (2010). *Tools for dossier success: A guide for promotion and tenure.* New York, NY: Routledge.

CAEP handbook. (2018). Retrieved October 13, 2018 from http://caepnet.org/~/media/Files/caep/accreditationresources/final-2018-initial-handbook-5-22.pdf?la=en

Camangian, P. R. (2015). Teach like lives depend on it: Agitate, arouse, and inspire. *Urban Education, 50*(4), 424–453. https://doi.org/10.1177/0042085913514591

Caraballo, L., Lozenski, B., Lyiscott, J., & Morrell, E. (2017). YPAR and critical epistemologies: Rethinking educational research. *Review of Research in Education, 41*(1), 311–336. https://doi.org/10.3102/0091732X16686948

Carmichael, S., & Thelwell, M. (2003). *Ready for revolution: The life and struggles of Stokely Carmichael (Kwame Ture).* New York, NY: Simon & Schuster.

Carter, D., Pearson, C., & Shavlik, D. (1996). Double jeopardy: Women of color in higher education. In C. Turner, M. Garcia, A. Nora, & L. I. Rendon (Eds.), *ASHE reader: Racial and ethnic diversity in higher education* (pp. 460–464). Needham Heights, MA: Simon & Schuster (Original work published 1987).

Casey, Z. A., Lozenski, B. D., & McManimon, S. K. (2013). From neoliberal policy to neoliberal pedagogy: Racializing and historicizing classroom management. *Journal of Pedagogy/Pedagogický Casopis, 4*(1), 36–58. https://doi.org/10.2478/jped-2013-0003

Cervantes-Soon, C. G. (2012). Testimonios of life and learning in the borderlands: Subaltern Juárez girls speak. *Equity & Excellence in Education, 45*(3), 373–391. https://doi.org/10.1080/10665684.2012.698182

Chan, S. (1991). *Asian Americans: An interpretive history.* Philadelphia, PA: Temple University Press.

Cobb-Roberts, D., & Agosto, V. (2011). Underrepresented women in higher education: An overview. *Negro Educational Review, 62/63*(1–4), 7–11.

Coffee, A., Stutelberg, E., Clements, C., & Lensmire, T. (2016). Precarious and undeniable bodies: Control, waste, and danger in the lives of a white teacher and her students of color. In S. Hancock & C. Warren (Eds.), *White women's work: Examining the intersectionality of teaching, identity, and race* (pp. 45–67). Charlotte, NC: Information Age Publishing.

Cokley, K. O. (2003). What do we really know about the academic motivation of African American college students? Challenging the "anti-intellectual" myth. *Harvard Educational Review*, 73(4), 524–558. https://doi.org/10.17763/haer.73.4.3618644850123376

Cole, T. (2012, March). *The white-savior industrial complex.* Retrieved from www.theatlantic.com/international/archive/2012/03/the-white-savior-industrial-complex/254843/

Coleman, J. S. (1988). Social capital in the creation of human capital. *American Journal of Sociology, 94*, S95–S120.

Collins, P. H. (2000). *Black feminist thought: Knowledge, consciousness, and the politics of empowerment.* New York, NY: Routledge.

Collins, P. H. (2005). *Black sexual politics: African Americans, gender, and the new racism.* New York, NY: Routledge.

Connelly, F. M., Phillion, J., & He, M. F. (2003). An exploration of narrative inquiry into multiculturalism in education: Reflecting on two decades of research in an inner-city Canadian community school. *Curriculum Inquiry, 33*(4), 363–384. https://doi.org/10.1046/j.1467-873X.2003.00270.x

Connor, D. J., Gabel, S. L., Gallagher, D. J., & Morton, M. (2008). Disability studies and inclusive education – Implications for theory, research, and practice. *International Journal of Inclusive Education, 12*(5–6), 441–457. https://doi.org/10.1080/13603110802377482

Cooke, N. A. (2019). Impolite hostilities and vague sympathies: Academia as a site of cyclical abuse. *Journal of Education for Library & Information Science, 60*(3), 223–230. https://doi.org/10.3138/jelis.2019-0005

Crenshaw, K. (1989). Demarginalizing the intersection of race and sex: A Black feminist critique of antidiscrimination doctrine, feminist theory, and antiracist politics. *The University of Chicago Legal Forum, 140*, 139–167. https://doi.org/10.4324/9780429500480

Creswell, J. W. (1998). *Qualitative inquiry and research design: Choosing among five traditions.* London, UK: Sage.

Cridland-Hughes, S. A., & King, L. J. (2015). Killing me softly: How violence comes from the curriculum we teach. In K. Fasching-Varner & N. D. Hartlep (Eds.), *The assault on communities of color: Exploring the realities of race-based violence* (pp. 99–103). Lanham, MD: Rowman & Littlefield.

Cross, W. E., Jr. (1995). The psychology of nigrescence: Revising the Cross model. In J. G. Ponterotto, J. M. Casas, L. A. Suzuki, & C. M. Alexander (Eds.), *Handbook of multicultural counseling* (pp. 93–122). Thousand Oaks, CA: Sage.

Cruz, D. M. (1995). Struggling with the labels that mark my ethnic identity. In R. V. Padilla & R. Chavez Chavez (Eds.), *The leaning ivory tower: Latino professors in American universities* (pp. 91–100). Albany, NY: State University of New York Press.

Cushing-Leubner, J., & Lozenski, B. D. (in press). "I'm in the ocean! I'm in the ocean!!" Standing with youth at the waters of heritage literacy. In K. Schmitz & N. Grant (Eds.), *Radical youth pedagogy: Flipping the culture of the classroom.* New York, NY: Peter Lang.

Darder, A. (2002). *Reinventing Paulo Freire: A pedagogy of love.* Boulder, CO: Westview.

Davis, L. J. (1995). *Enforcing normalcy: Disability, deafness, and the body.* London, UK: Verso.

Davis, L. J. (2006). Constructing normalcy: The bell curve, the novel, and the invention of the disabled body in the nineteenth century. In L. Davis (Ed.), *The disability studies reader* (2nd ed., pp. 3–19). New York, NY: Routledge.

DeAngelis, T. (2009). Unmasking 'racial micro aggressions.' *Monitor on Psychology*, 40(2), 42–46. Retrieved from www.apa.org/monitor/2009/02/microaggression

Delgado Bernal, D. (2002). Critical race theory, LatCrit theory, and critical race-gendered epistemologies: Recognizing students of color as holders and creators of knowledge. *Qualitative Inquiry*, 8(1), 105–126. https://doi.org/10.1177/107780040200800107

Delgado Bernal, D. (2008). La trenza de identidades: Weaving together my personal, professional, and communal identities. In K. P. Gonzalez & R. V. Padilla (Eds.), *Doing the public good: Latina/o Scholars engage civic participation* (pp. 135–148). Sterling, VA: Stylus.

Denzin, N. (1997). *Interpretive ethnography: Ethnographic practices for the 21st century.* Thousand Oaks, CA: Sage.

Denzin, N., & Lincoln, Y. S. (Eds.). (1998). *Strategies of qualitative inquiry.* Thousand Oaks, CA: Sage.

DiAngelo, R., & Sensoy, Ö. (2014). Getting slammed: White depictions of race discussions as arenas of violence. *Race Ethnicity and Education*, 17(1), 103–128. https://doi.org/10.1080/13613324.2012.674023

Diggs, G. A., Garrison-Wade, D. F., Estrada, D., & Galindo, R. (2009). Smiling faces and colored spaces: The experiences of faculty of color pursing tenure in the academy. *The Urban Review*, 41(4), 312. https://doi.org/10.1007/s11256-008-0113-y

Dillard, C. B. (2006). *On spiritual strivings: Transforming an African American woman's academic life.* Albany, NY: State University of New York Press.

Du Bois, W. E. B. (1916). The immortal child. *The Crisis*, 12(6), 267–271.

Du Bois, W. E. B., & Marable, M. (2014). *Souls of black folk.* New York, NY: Routledge (Original work published 1903).

Dumas, M. J. (2014). 'Losing an arm': Schooling as a site of black suffering. *Race Ethnicity and Education*, 17(1), 1–29. https://doi.org/10.1080/13613324.2013.850412

Dumas, M. J. (2016). My brother as "problem": Neoliberal governmentality and interventions for black young men and boys. *Educational Policy*, 30(1), 94–113. https://doi.org/10.1177/0895904815616487

Duncan-Andrade, J. (2009). Note to educators: Hope required when growing roses in concrete. *Harvard Educational Review*, 79(2), 181–194. https://doi.org/10.17763/haer.79.2.nu3436017730384w

Dunn, L. (1968). Special education for the mildly mentally retarded: Is much of it justifiable? *Exceptional Children*, 35(1), 5–22. https://doi.org/10.1177/001440296803500101

Duster, T. (1992). *The diversity project: Final report.* Berkeley, CA: The Institute for the Study of Social Change, University of California.

Dyson, M. (2007). My story in a profession of stories: Auto ethnography- an empowering methodology for educators. *Australian Journal of Teacher Education*, 32(1), 36–48. doi: 10.14221/ajte.2007v32n1.3

Dyson, M. (2015, April 17). Racial terror, fast and slow. *The New York Times*. Retrieved from www.nytimes.com/2015/04/17/opinion/racial-terror-fast-and-slow.html

Eisner, E. W. (1994). *Cognition and curriculum reconsidered* (2nd ed.). New York, NY: Teachers College Press.

Ellis, C., Adams, T. E., & Bochner, A. P. (2011). Autoethnography: An overview. *Forum Qualitative Social Research*, *12*(1), Art 10. Retrieved from http://nbn-resolving.de/urn:nbn:de:0114-fqs1101108

Ellison, R. (1953). *Twentieth-century fiction and the Black mask of humanity: Shadow and act.* New York, NY: Vintage Books.

Endo, R. (2018a). *The incarceration of Japanese Americans in the 1940s: Literature for the high school classroom.* Urbana, IL: National Council of Teachers of English.

Endo, R. (2018b). Reading civil disobedience, disaffection, and racialized trauma in John Okada's No-No Boy: Lessons learned 75 years after executive order 9066. *Children's Literature in Education*, *49*(4), 413–429. https://doi.org/10.1007/s10583-017-9328-4

Endo, R. (2019). Male of color refugee teachers on being un/desirable bodies of difference in education. *Equity & Excellence in Education, 52*(4), 448–464. https://doi.org/10.1080/10665684.2019.1684220

Espiritu, Y. L. (1992). *Asian American pan-ethnicity: Bridging institutions and identities.* Philadelphia, PA: Temple University Press.

Fanon, F. (1986). *Black skin, white masks.* London, UK: Pluto (original work published 1952).

Feagin, J. (2013). *The White racial frame: Centuries of racial framing and counter-framing* (2nd ed.). New York, NY: Routledge.

Field, N. P., Muong, S., & Sochanvimean, V. (2013). Parental styles in the inter-generational transmission of trauma stemming from the Khmer Rouge regime in Cambodia. *American Journal of Orthopsychiatry*, *83*(4), 483–494. https://doi.org/ 10.1111/ajop.12057

Fiol-Matta, L. (1996). Teaching in (Puerto Rican) tongues: A report from the space in-between. *Women's Studies Quarterly*, *24*(3/4), 69–76.

Fiske, S. T., & Neuberg S. L. (1990). A continuum of impression formation, from category-based to individuating processes. In M. P. Zanna (Ed.), *Advances in experimental social psychology* (pp. 1–74). New York, NY: Academic Press.

Fram, S. M. (2013). The constant comparative analysis method outside of grounded theory. *Qualitative Report*, *18*(1), 1–25. Retrieved from https://nsuworks.nova.edu/tqr/vol18/iss1/1/

Freire, P. (1993). *Pedagogy of the oppressed.* New York, NY: Continuum (Original work published 1968).

Fuller, K., & Shaw, M. (2011). Overrepresentation of students of color in special education classes. *Journal of Elementary and Secondary Education*, *2*(7), 1–11.

Gasman, M. (2016, September 26). An Ivy League professor on why colleges don't hire more faculty of color: 'We don't want them.' *The Washington Post*. Retrieved from www.washingtonpost.com/news/grade-point/wp/2016/09/26/an-ivy-league-professor-on-why-colleges-dont-hire-more-faculty-of-color-we-dont-want-them/

Gasman, M., Kim, J., & Nguyen, T.-H. (2011). Effectively recruiting faculty of color at highly selective institutions: A school of education case study. *Journal of Diversity in Higher Education*, *4*(4), 212–222. https://doi.org/10.1037/a0025130

Ginsberg, M. B., & Wlodkowski, R. J. (2009). *Diversity and motivation: Culturally responsive teaching in college* (2nd ed.). San Francisco, CA: Jossey-Bass.

Giroux, H. (2009). *Youth in a suspect society: Democracy or disposability?* New York, NY: Springer.

Green, A. L., & Linders, A. (2016). The impact of comedy on racial and ethnic discourse. *Sociological Inquiry*, *86*(2), 241–269. https://doi.org/10.1111/soin.12112

Gregory, T. (2019, January 11). 'A lot of these kids need role models': Following 1st-year black teacher Jonathan White through his first months at CPS. *The Chicago Tribune*. Retrieved from www.chicagotribune.com/news/ct-met-male-black-teacher-first-year-chicago-20190103-story.html

Gutiérrez y Muhs, G. G., Niemann, Y. F., González, C. G., & Harris, A. P. (Eds.). (2012). *Presumed incompetent: The intersections of race and class for women in academia*. Louisville, CO: University Press of Colorado & Utah State University Press.

Hall, E. T. (1976). *Beyond culture*. New York, NY: Anchor Press.

Harney, S. M., & Moten, F. (2013). *The undercommons: Fugitive planning and black study*. New York, NY: Minor Compositions.

Harris, C. I. (1993). Whiteness as property. *Harvard Law Review*, *106*(8), 1707–1791.

Harry, B., & Klingner, J. (2006). *Why are so many minority students in special education?* New York, NY: Teacher College Press.

Hartman, S. (2008). Venus in two acts. *Small Axe: A Caribbean Journal of Criticism*, *12*(2), 1–14. http://dx.doi.org/10.1215/-12-2-1

Hartup, W. W. (1993). Adolescents and their friends. *New Directions for Child and Adolescent Development*, *1993*(60), 3–22. https://doi.org/10.1002/cd.23219936003

Heaven, P. C., & Ciarrochi, J. (2008). Parental styles, conscientiousness, and academic performance in high school: A three-wave longitudinal study. *Personality and Social Psychology Bulletin*, *34*(4), 451–461. https://doi.org/10.1177/0146167207311909

Hermes, M., Bang, M., & Marin, A. (2012). Designing Indigenous language revitalization. *Harvard Educational Review*, *82*(3), 381–402. https://doi.org/10.17763/haer.82.3.q8117w861241871j

Hernandez, F., & Endo, R. (Eds.). (2017). *Developing and supporting critically reflective teachers: Diverse perspectives in the twenty-first century*. Rotterdam, Netherlands: Sense.

Hickey, C., & Fitzclarenge, L. (1999). Educating boys in sport and physical education: Using narrative methods to develop pedagogies of responsibility. *Sport, Education and Society*, *4*(1), 51–62. https://doi.org/10.1080/1357332990040104

Higgerson, M. L., & Joyce, T. A. (2007). *Effective leadership communication: A guide for department chairs and deans for managing difficult situations and people*. Bolton, MA: Anker Pub.

Ho, J. (2002). When the political becomes personal: Life on the multiethnic margins. In B. TuSmith & M. T. Reddy (Eds.), *Race in the college classroom: Pedagogy and politics* (pp. 62–70). New Brunswick, NJ: Rutgers University Press.

Holling, M. A. (2019). "You intimidate me" as a microaggressive controlling image to discipline womyn of color faculty. *Southern Communication Journal*, *84*(2), 99–112. https://doi.org/10.1080/1041794X.2018.1511748

Hollis, L. P. (2017). This is why they leave you: Workplace bullying and insight to junior faculty departure. *British Journal of Education*, *5*(10), 1–7. Retrieved from www.eajournals.org/wp-content/uploads/This-Is-Why-They-Leave-You-Workplace-Bullying-and-Insight-to-Junior-Faculty-Departure.pdf

Hong, G. K. (2018, January). *Virtual violence: Refusing redress in Gina Kim's "Bloodless/Dongducheon"*. In Critical Race and Ethnic Studies Graduate Group & Center for Writing Literacy and Rhetorical Studies Graduate Minor. Presentation conducted at the University of Minnesota.

Hook, J. N., Davis, D. E., Owen, J., Worthington, E. L., Jr., & Utsey, S. O. (2013). Cultural humility: Measuring openness to culturally diverse clients. *Journal of Counseling Psychology*, *60*(3), 353–366. https://doi.org/10.1037/a0032595

Howard, T. (2013). How does it feel to be a problem? Black male students, schools, and learning in enhancing the knowledge base to disrupt deficit frameworks. *Review of Research in Education*, *37*(1), 54–86. https://doi.org/10.3102/0091732X12462985

Hua, L. (2018). Slow feeling and quiet being: Women of color teaching in urgent times. *New Directions for Teaching and Learning*, *2018*(153), 77–86. https://doi.org/10.1002/tl.20283

Hune, S. (2011). Asian American women faculty and the contested space of the classroom: Navigating student resistance and (re)claiming authority and their rightful place. In G. Jean-Marie & B. Lloyd-Jones (Eds.), *Women of color in higher education: Turbulent past, promising future* (pp. 307–335). Bingley, UK: Emerald.

Iyer, A., Leach, C. W., & Crosby, F. J. (2003). White guilt and racial compensation: The benefits and limits of self-focus. *Personality and Social Psychology Bulletin*, *29*(1), 117–129. https://doi.org/10.1177/0146167202238377

JanMohamed, A. (2015). *Toward a political economy of death OR the threat/fear of death as the fundamental mode of coercion*. Rhodes University. Retrieved from www.ru.ac.za/media/rhodesuniversity/content/uhuru/documents/Abdul_JanMohamed_paper.pdf

Johnson, L., & Bryan, N. (2017). Using our voices, losing our bodies: Michael Brown, Trayvon Martin, and the spirit murders of Black male professors in the academy. *Race Ethnicity and Education*, *20*(2), 163–177. https://doi.org/10.1080/13613324.2016.1248831

Jones, L., Jr. (2019). Endless exodus: Faculty of color leave the academy in search of fulfillment. *Diverse: Issues in Higher Education*, *36*(11), 46–48. Retrieved from https://diverseeducation.com/article/150672/

June, A. W. (2008). Pipeline to presidencies carries lots of women, few members of minority groups. *Chronicle of Higher Education*, *54*(23), 18. Retrieved from www.chronicle.com/article/Pipeline-to-Presidencies/18988

June, A. W. (2015, November 13). The invisible labor of minority professors. *Chronicle of Higher Education*. Retrieved from www.chronicle.com/article/The-Invisible-Labor-of/234098

Justice, D. H., & Barker, D. K. (2007). Deep surveillance: Tenure and promotion strategies for scholars of color. *Profession*, *2007*(1), 174–180. http://doi.org/10.1632/prof.2007.2007.1.174

Kaplan, K. (2009). Unmasking the impostor. *Nature*. Retrieved from www. nature.com/naturejobs/science/articles/10.1038/nj7245-468a

Kessler, R. C., Chiu, W. T., Demler, O., Merikangas, K. R., & Walters, E. E. (2005). Prevalence, severity, and comorbidity of 12-month DSM-IV disorders in the national comorbidity survey replication. *Archives of General Psychiatry*, 62(6), 617–627. https://doi.org/10.1001/archpsyc.62.6.617

Khamvongsa, C., & Russell, E. (2009). Legacies of war: Cluster bombs in Laos. *Critical Asian Studies*, 41(2), 281–306. https://doi.org/10.1080/1467271 0902809401

Konadu, K. (2017, July). We are an African people. *Kwasi Konadu*. Retrieved from www.kwasikonadu.info/blog/2017/7/31/we-are-an-african-people

Koyama, J. P. (2007). Approaching and attending college: Anthropological and ethnographic accounts. *Teachers College Record*, 109(10), 2301–2323.

Kroll, J., Habenicht, M., Mackenzie, T., Yang, M., & Chan, S. (1989). Depression and posttraumatic stress disorder in Southeast Asian refugees. *The American Journal of Psychiatry*, 146(12), 1592–1597. https://doi.org/10.1176/ajp.146. 12.1592

Kumashiro, K. K. (2000). Toward a theory of anti-oppressive education. *Review of Educational Research*, 70(1), 25–53. https://doi.org/10.3102/00346543 070001025

Ladson-Billings, G. (1995). But that's just good teaching! The case for culturally relevant pedagogy. *Theory into Practice*, 34(3), 159–165. https://doi. org/10.1080/00405849509543675

Ladson-Billings, G. (2006). From the achievement gap to the education debt: Understanding achievement in US schools. *Educational Researcher*, 35(7), 3–12. https://doi.org/10.3102/0013189X035007003

Ladson-Billings, G. (2008). "Yes, but how do we do it?" Practicing culturally relevant pedagogy. In W. Ayers, G. Ladson-Billings, G. Michie, & P. A. Noguera (Eds.), *City kids, city schools: More reports* (pp. 162–177). New York, NY: The New Press.

Landry, B. (2006). The theory of intersectional analysis. In B. Landry (Ed.), *Race, gender, and class: Theory and methods of analysis* (pp. 1–15). Upper Saddle River, NJ: Pearson/Prentice Hall.

la paperson. (2017). *A third university is possible*. Minneapolis, MN: University of Minnesota Press.

Lawrence, T. E. (1935). *Seven pillars of wisdom*. London, UK: Double Day Doran & Company.

Lazos, S. R. (2012). Are student teaching evaluations holding back women and minorities? The perils of "doing" gender and race in the classroom. In G. Gutiérrez y Muhs, Y. Flores, Y. Niemann, C. González, & A. Harris (Eds.), *Presumed incompetent: The intersections of race and class for women in academia* (pp. 164–185). Louisville, CO: University Press of Colorado & Utah State University Press.

Leong, K. J. (2002). Strategies for surviving race in the classroom. In B. TuSmith & M. T. Reddy (Eds.), *Race in the college classroom: Pedagogy and politics* (pp. 189–199). New Brunswick, NJ: Rutgers University Press.

Lipsitz, G. (2006). *The possessive investment in whiteness: How white people profit from identity politics*. Philadelphia, PA: Temple University Press.

Lipsky, D., & Gartner, A. (1996). Inclusion, restructuring, and the remaking of American society. *Harvard Educational Review, 66*(4), 762–796. https://doi.org/10.17763/haer.66.4.3686k7x734246430

Littlefield, L. N., Ong, K. S., Tseng, A., Milliken, J. C., & Humy, S. L. (2010). Perceptions of European Americans and African Americans instructors teaching race-focused courses. *Journal of Diversity in Higher Education, 3*(4), 230–244. https://doi.org/10.1037/a0020950

Louie, V. S. (2004). *Compelled to excel: Immigration, education, and opportunity among Chinese Americans.* Stanford, CA: Stanford University Press.

Louis, B. (2005). The difference sameness makes: Racial recognition and the 'narcissism of minor differences.' *Ethnicities, 5*(3), 343–364. https://doi.org/10.1177/1468796805054960

Lozenski, B. D. (2017). Pedagogies of Black eldership: Exploring the impact of intergenerational contact on youth research. *Multicultural Perspectives, 19*(2), 65–75. https://doi.org/10.1080/15210960.2017.1302337

Lozenski, B. D., & Ford, G. E. (2014). From individualism to interconnectedness: Exploring the transformational potential of a community generated methodology. In B. Ngo & K. K. Kumashiro (Eds.), *Six lenses for anti-oppressive education: Partial stories, improbable conversations* (pp. 291–310). New York, NY: Peter Lang.

Lugo-Lugo, C. R. (2012). A prostitute, a servant, and a customer-service representative: A Latina in academia. In G. Gutiérrez y Muhs, Y. Flores, Y. Niemann, C. González, & A. Harris (Eds.), *Presumed incompetent: The intersections of race and class for women in academia* (pp. 40–49). Louisville, CO: University Press of Colorado & Utah State University Press.

Maggie Kuhn (n.d). *National women's hall of fame.* Retrieved August 30, 2017 from www.womenofthehall.org/inductee/maggie-kuhn/

Marable, M. (2004). *Globalization and racialization.* ZNET. Retrieved from https://zcomm.org/znetarticle/globalization-and-racialization-by-manning-marable/

Martinez Aleman, A. M. (1995). Actuando. In R. V. Padilla & R. Chavez Chavez (Eds.), *The leaning ivory tower: Latino professors in American universities* (pp. 67–76). Albany, NY: State University of New York Press.

Matias, C. E. (2013). On the" flip" side: A teacher educator of color unveiling the dangerous minds of white teacher candidates. *Teacher Education Quarterly, 40*(2), 53–73.

Mazama, A. (Ed.) (2003). *The Afrocentric paradigm.* Trenton, NJ: Africa World Press, Inc.

Mazrui, A. (1986). *The Africans: A triple heritage.* Lanham, MD: Rowman & Littlefield.

McClellan, P. (2012). Race, gender, and leadership identity: An autoethnography of reconciliation. *International Journal of Qualitative Studies in Education, 25*(1), 89–100. https://doi.org/10.1080/09518398.2011.647720

McIntosh, P. (1988, July–August). White privilege: Unpacking the invisible knapsack. *Peace and Freedom,* 10–12.

Memmi, A. (1965). *The colonizer and the colonized.* New York, NY: Orion Press.

Mills, C. (1997). *The racial contract.* Ithaca, NY: Cornell University Press.

Milner, H. R., IV. (2010). *Start where you are but don't stay there: Understanding diversity, opportunity gaps, and teaching in today's classrooms.* Cambridge, MA: Harvard Education Press.

Milner, H. R., IV. (2015). Black teachers as curriculum texts in urban schools. In M. F. He, B. D. Schultz, & W. H. Schuert (Eds.), *The Sage guide to curriculum in education* (pp. 215–222). Thousand Oaks, CA: Sage.

Mimura, G. M. (2009). *Ghostlife of third cinema: Asian American film and video.* Minneapolis, MN: University of Minnesota Press.

Mirra, N., Garcia, A., & Morrell, E. (2015). *Doing youth participatory action research: Transforming inquiry with researchers, educators, and students.* New York, NY: Routledge.

Mirza, H. S. (1998). Race, gender and IQ: The social consequence of a pseudo-scientific discourse. *Race, Ethnicity and Education, 1*(1), 109–126. https://doi.org/10.1080/1361332980010108

Montagu, A. (1942). *Man's most dangerous myth: The fallacy of race.* New York, NY: Altamira Press.

Myers, B. (2016, February 14). Where are the minority professors? *The Chronicle of Higher Education.* Retrieved from www.chronicle.com/interactives/where-are-the-minority-professor

Myers, V. (n.d.). *How to overcome our biases? Walk boldly toward them.* Retrieved June 11, 2017 from http://vernamyers.com

National Center for Education Statistics. (2017). *Digest of education statistics 2017.* Washington, DC: U.S. Department of Education. Retrieved from https://nces.ed.gov/programs/digest/d17/tables/dt17_315.20.asp

NdCAD (n.d.). Retrieved December 13, 2018 from https://ndcad.org/

Nguyen, N. (2016). *A curriculum of fear: Homeland security in US public schools.* Minneapolis, MN: University of Minnesota Press.

Njeri, I. (1989, September 20). Academic acrimony: Minority professors claim racism plays a role in obtaining tenure. *Los Angeles Times.* Retrieved from www.latimes.com/archives/la-xpm-1989-09-20-vw-328-story.html

Noguera, P. A. (2004). Social capital and the education of immigrant students: Categories and generalizations. *Sociology of Education, 77*(2), 180–183. https://doi.org/10.1177/003804070407700206

Ogbu, J. (2003). *Black American students in an affluent suburb: A study of academic disengagement.* Mahwah, NJ: Erlbaum.

Ogbu, J. (2004). Collective identity and the burden of "acting White" in Black history, community, and education. *The Urban Review, 36*(1), 1–35. https://doi.org/10.1023/B:URRE.0000042734.83194.f6

Oliver, M. (1996). A sociology of disability or a disablist sociology? In L. Barton (Ed.), *Disability and society* (pp. 18–42). London, UK: Longman.

Omi, M., & Winant, H. (1994). *Racial formation in the United States: From the 1960s to the 1990s* (2nd ed.). New York, NY: Routledge.

Padilla, R. V., & Chavez Chavez, R. (1995). *The leaning ivory tower: Latino professors in American universities* (pp. 1–16). Albany, NY: State University of New York Press.

Particelli, B. (2016). Teaching with Dave Chappelle. *Pedagogy, 16*(3), 551–562. https://doi.org/10.1215/15314200-3600909

Patel, L. (2016). Pedagogies of resistance and survivance: Learning as marronage. *Equity & Excellence in Education, 49*(4), 397–401. https:/doi.org/10.1080/10665684.2016.1227585

Perez, L. E. (1993). Opposition and the education of Chicana/os. In C. McCarthy & W. Crichlow (Eds.), *Race, identity, and representation in education* (pp. 268–279). New York, NY: Routledge.

Picower, B. (2012). Using their words: Six elements of social justice curriculum design for the elementary classroom. *International Journal of Multicultural Education, 14*(1), 1–17.

Pierce, C. (1970). Offensive mechanisms. In F. Barbour (Ed.), *In the Black seventies* (pp. 265–282). Boston, MA: Porter Sargent.

Pinar, W. F. (2012). *What is curriculum theory?* (2nd ed). New York, NY: Routledge.

Pittman, C. T. (2010). Race and gender oppression in the classroom: The experiences of women faculty of color with White male students. *Teaching Sociology, 38*(3), 183–196. https://doi.org/10.1177/0092055X10370120

Plummer, D. L. (1996). Black racial identity attitudes and stages of the life span: An exploratory investigation. *Journal of Black Psychology, 22*(2), 169–181. https://doi.org/10.1177/00957984960222003

Rains, F. V. (1995). *Views from within: Women faculty of color in a research university* (Unpublished doctoral dissertation), Indiana University.

Reed-Danahay, D. (1997). *Auto/ethnography: Rewriting the self and the social.* New York, NY: Berg.

Reese, D. (2011). American Indians are not "People of Color." *ASCD Express, 6*(15). Retrieved from www.ascd.org/ascd-express/vol6/615-newvoices.aspx

Rickford, R. (2016). *We are an African people: Independent education, black power, and the radical imagination.* London, UK: Oxford University Press.

Robinson, C. J. (1983). *Black Marxism: The making of the Black radical tradition.* Chapel Hill, NC: University of North Carolina Press.

Rowe, M. (1990). Barriers to equality: The power of subtle discrimination to maintain unequal opportunity. *Employee Responsibilities and Rights Journal, 3*(2), 153–163. https://doi.org/10.1007/BF01388340

Ryan, A. M. (2000). Peer groups as a context for the socialization of adolescents' motivation, engagement, and achievement in school. *Educational Psychologist, 35*(2), 101–111. https://doi.org/10.1207/S15326985EP3502_4

Sadker, D., & Zittleman, K. (2005). Gender bias lives, for both sexes. *The Education Digest, 70*(8), 27–30.

Saltman, K. J. (2016). *Scripted bodies: Corporate power, smart technologies, and the undoing of public education.* New York, NY: Routledge.

Sandoval, C. (1991). US third world feminism: The theory and method of oppositional consciousness in the postmodern world. *Genders, 10*, 1–24. https://doi.org/10.4324/9780203825235

Seto, T. (1995). Multiculturalism is not Halloween. *Horn Book Magazine, 71*(2), 169–174.

Sharpe, C. (2016). *In the wake: On Blackness and being.* Durham, NC: Duke University Press.

Simpson, A. (2007). On ethnographic refusal: Indigeneity, 'voice' and colonial citizenship. *Junctures: The Journal for Thematic Dialogue, 9*, 67–80.

Skiba, R. H., Simmons, A. B., Ritter, S., Gibb, A. C., Rausch, M. K., Cuadrado, J., & Chung, C. (2008). Achieving equity in special education: History, status, and current challenges. *Exceptional Children, 74*(3), 264–288. https://doi.org/10.1177/001440290807400301

Sleeter, C. E. (2017). Critical race theory and the whiteness of teacher education. *Urban Education, 52*(2), 155–169. https://doi.org/10.1177/0042085916668957

Smith, E. R., Calderwood, P. E., Storms, S. B., Lopez, P. G., & Colwell, R. P. (2016). Institutionalizing faculty mentoring within a community of practice model. *To Improve the Academy*, 35(1), 35–71. https://doi.org/10.1002/tia2.20033

Smith, L. (1999). *Decolonizing methodologies: Research and indigenous peoples.* Chicago, IL: Zed Books.

Smith, W. A., Yosso, T., & Solórzano, D. (2006). Challenging racial battle fatigue on historically white campuses: A critical race examination of race-related stress. In C. A. Stanley (Ed.), *Faculty of color: Teaching in predominantly white colleges and universities* (pp. 299–327). Bolton, MA: Anker Publishing.

Sojoyner, D. M. (2016). *First strike: Educational enclosures in Black Los Angeles.* Minneapolis, MN: University of Minnesota Press.

Solórzano, D., Ceja, M., & Yosso, T. (2009). Critical race theory, racial microaggressions, and campus racial climate: The experiences of African American college students. *Journal of Negro Education*, 69(1–2), 60–73.

Soltero, S. W. (2011). *Schoolwide approaches to educating ELLs: Creating linguistically and culturally responsive K-12 schools.* Portsmouth, NH: Heinemann.

Span, C., Robinson, R. V., & Villegas, T. M. (2007). Education, American style: A brief history of race-based school policies and practices in the United States. In R. Joshee & L. Johnson (Eds.), *Multicultural education policies in Canada and the United States* (pp. 146–158). Seattle, WA: University of Washington Press.

Spry, T. (2001). Performing autoethnography: An embodied methodological praxis. *Qualitative Inquiry*, 7(6), 706–732. https://doi.org/10.1177/107780040100700605

Stainback, W., & Stainback, S. (1984). A rationale for the merger of special and regular education. *Exceptional Children*, 51(2), 102–111.

Steele, S. (1990). *The content of our character* (Vol. 38). New York, NY: St. Martin's Press.

Style, E. (1996). *Curriculum as window and mirror. The S.E.E.D. project on inclusive curriculum.* Retrieved from www.wcwonline.org

Sue, D. (2010). *Microaggressions in everyday life: Race, gender, and sexual orientation.* Hoboken, NJ: John Wiley & Sons.

Sue, D. W., Capodilupo, C. M., Torino, G. C., Bucceri, J. M., Holder, A., Nadal, K. L., & Esquilin, M. (2007). Racial microaggressions in everyday life: Implications for clinical practice. *American Psychologist*, 62(4), 271–286. https://doi.org/10.1037/0003-066X.62.4.271

Takaki, R. (1998). *Strangers from a different shore: A history of Asian Americans* (updated and revised). New York, NY: Little Brown & Company (Original work published 1989).

Tatum, B. D. (1997). *"Why are all the black kids sitting together in the cafeteria?": And other conversations about race* (1st ed.). New York, NY: Basic Books.

Thompson, C. (2008). Recruitment, retention, and mentoring faculty of color: The chronicle continues. *New Directions for Higher Education*, 143, 47–54. https://doi.org/10.1002/he.312

Torres-Guzman, M. E. (1995). Surviving the journey. In R. V. Padilla & R. Chavez Chavez (Eds.), *The leaning ivory tower: Latino professors in American universities* (pp. 53–65). Albany, NY: State University of New York Press.

Tuck, E. (2009). Suspending damage: A letter to communities. *Harvard Educational Review*, 79(3), 409–428. https://doi.org/10.17763/haer.79.3.n0016675661t3n15

Tuck, E., & Yang, K. W. (2014a). R-words: Refusing research. In D. Paris & M. Wynn (Eds.), *Humanizing research: Decolonizing qualitative inquiry with youth and communities* (pp. 223–248). Thousand Oaks, CA: Sage.

Tuck, E., & Yang, K. W. (2014b). Unbecoming claims: Pedagogies of refusal in qualitative research. *Qualitative Inquiry, 20*(6), 811–818. https://doi.org/10.1177/1077800414530265

Turner, C. S. V., González, J. C., & Wong, K. (2011). Faculty women of color: The critical nexus of race and gender. *Journal of Diversity in Higher Education, 4*(4), 199–211. https://doi.org/10.1037/a0024630

Turner, C. S. V., González, J. C., & Wood, J. (2008). Faculty of color in academe: What 20 years of literature tells us. *Journal of Diversity in Higher Education, 1*(3), 139–168. https://doi.org/10.1037/a0012837

Turner, C. S. V., & Myers, S. L., Jr. (2000). *Faculty of color in academe: Bittersweet success.* Needham Heights, MA: Allyn & Bacon.

TuSmith, B. (2002). Out on a limb: Race and evaluation of frontline teaching. In B. TuSmith & M. T. Reddy (Eds.), *Race in the college classroom: Pedagogy and politics* (pp. 112–125). New Brunswick, NJ: Rutgers University Press.

University of Houston Division of Student Enrollment and Student Service. (n.d.). *Diversity, equity and inclusion terms.* Retrieved December 10, 2018 from www.uh.edu/cdi/diversity_education/resources/pdf/terms.pdf

US Citizenship and Immigration Services Glossary. (n.d.). Retrieved December 10, 2018 from www.uscis.gov/tools/glossary

Uy, P. (2009). Asian American dropouts: A case study of Chinese and Vietnamese high school students in a New England urban school district. *AAPI Nexus: Policy, Practice and Community, 7*(1), 83–104. http://dx.doi.org/10.17953/appc.7.1.gwx5538478465477

Valenzuela, A. (1999). *Subtractive schooling: U.S.-Mexican youth and the politics of caring.* Albany, NY: State University of New York Press.

Valverde, L. A. (2003). *Leaders of color in higher education: Unrecognized triumphs in harsh institutions.* Walnut Creek, CA: AltaMira Press.

van Manen, M. (1990). *Researching lived experience: Human science for an action sensitive pedagogy.* Albany, NY: State University of New York Press.

Vaught, S. E. (2017). *Compulsory: Education and the dispossession of youth in a prison school.* Minneapolis, MN: University of Minnesota Press.

Walkington, L. (2017). How far have we really come? Black women faculty and graduate students' experiences in higher education. *Humboldt Journal of Social Relations, 1*(39), 51–65.

Webster, Y. O. (1993). *The racialization of America.* New York, NY: Palgrave Macmillan.

Weiler, K. (1988). *Women teaching for change: Gender, class and power.* South Hadley, MA: Bergin & Garvey.

Williams, D. (1996). *Living testimony* [video file]. Retrieved from https://youtu.be/bgb-X40-1_k

Wilson, R. (1989). Women of color in academic administration: Trends, progress, & barriers. *Sex Roles, 21*(1–2), 85–97. https://doi.org/10.1007/BF00289729

Wise, T. (2012). *Dear White America: Letter to a new minority.* San Francisco, CA: City Light Bookstore.

Woods, C. (2002). Life after death. *The Professional Geographer, 54*(1), 62–66. https://doi.org/10.1111/0033-0124.00315

Woodson, C. G. (1990). *The mis-education of the Negro.* Trenton, NJ: Africa World Press (Original work published 1933).

Wynter, S. (1994). No humans involved: An open letter to my colleagues. *Forum N.H.I.: Knowledge for the 21st Century, 1*(1), 42–73.

Yim, H. (2002). Cultural identity and cultural policy in South Korea. *The International Journal of Cultural Policy, 8*(1), 37–48. https://doi.org/10.1080/10286630290032422

Index